Have a Little Faith

THE HISTORY AND PHILOSOPHY OF EDUCATION SERIES

Edited by Randall Curren and Jonathan Zimmerman

Teaching Evolution in a Creation Nation
By Adam Laats and Harvey Siegel

Have a Little Faith

Religion, Democracy, and the American Public School

BENJAMIN JUSTICE
COLIN MACLEOD

The University of Chicago Press   Chicago and London

The History and Philosophy of Education Series is published in cooperation with the Association for Philosophy of Education and the History of Education Society.

The University of Chicago Press, Chicago 60637
The University of Chicago Press, Ltd., London
© 2016 by The University of Chicago
All rights reserved. Published 2016.
Printed in the United States of America

25 24 23 22 21 20 19 18 17 16   1 2 3 4 5

ISBN-13: 978-0-226-40031-0 (cloth)
ISBN-13: 978-0-226-40045-7 (paper)
ISBN-13: 978-0-226-40059-4 (e-book)
DOI: 10.7208/chicago/9780226400594.001.0001

Library of Congress Cataloging-in-Publication Data

Names: Justice, Benjamin, 1971– author. | Macleod, Colin M. (Colin Murray), 1962– author.
Title: Have a little faith: religion, democracy, and the American public school / Benjamin Justice and Colin Macleod.
Other titles: History and philosophy of education.
Description: Chicago: The University of Chicago Press, 2016. | Series: History and philosophy of education series | Includes bibliographical references and index.
Identifiers: LCCN 2016005055 | ISBN 9780226400310 (cloth: alk. paper) | ISBN 9780226400457 (pbk.: alk. paper) | ISBN 9780226400594 (e-book)
Subjects: LCSH: Religion in the public schools—United States—History. | Religious education—United States—History. | Democracy—United States—Religious aspects. | Church and state—United States—History.
Classification: LCC LC111 .J89 2016 | DDC 379.2/8—dc23 LC record available at http://lccn.loc.gov/2016005055

♾ This paper meets the requirements of ANSI/NISO Z39.48-1992 (Permanence of Paper).

Contents

Acknowledgments

In writing this book we have benefited from feedback, advice, and help from many people. Before Randy Curren and Jon Zimmerman, the series editors, proposed that we write a book together, we did not know one another. So we thank Jon and Randy for introducing us and for the invitation to examine the place of religion in American public schools from a historical and philosophical perspective. Jon and Randy have provided us with excellent comments, and their enthusiasm for our work was very encouraging. Through the support of the Spencer Foundation, Jon and Randy also organized workshops that brought together other pairs of historians and philosophers working on themes in American education. We learned a good deal from the other teams, and we very much appreciate the suggestions we received from them at early stages of the project. We also are very grateful to John Adamus, Avigail Eisenberg, Catherine Lugg, Tracey Meares, and Tom Tyler for their helpful comments and encouragement. Our editor, Elizabeth Branch Dyson, with Joann Hoy and the anonymous peer reviewers at University of Chicago Press, made valuable suggestions about the manuscript, and we are grateful for the care and attention they devoted to assessing the book. Finally, thanks to Tristan James, Rachel Kelly, and Jon Weiss for their assistance in preparing the manuscript for publication.

Introduction

In September 2014 the popular radio program *This American Life* featured a story about East Ramapo Central School District in Rockland County, New York, a suburb about an hour north of New York City. East Ramapo district is unusual in that roughly half of the voting population, and two-thirds of the children, are Hasidic Jews. For that radically orthodox religious community, public education is to be avoided at all costs. Complaining about the double burden of having to pay taxes for public schools and tuition for private ones, the Hasidic community took control of the East Ramapo school board and orchestrated a massive defunding of public schools, which served primarily low-income black and Latino students. Simultaneously, the board diverted public funds to support private services for their own children—including paying the tuition costs for students with special needs to attend Jewish schools.[1]

The process was ugly and contentious. Citing phony enrollment data, the board closed and sold off public school buildings at below-market rates, to convert them into Jewish private schools. Meanwhile non-Hasidic students crowded into public schools where extracurricular activities and courses were vanishing. Public school parents and students raised loud and sustained objections to no avail, while the board used deceptive tactics, such as holding executive sessions late into the night and not allowing public comment until the end of meetings. Board-hired attorneys verbally attacked and harassed citizens during and after board meetings. Board members labeled their critics "anti-Semites," and in some instances they may have been right. Parents made similar accusations of racism. The local NAACP and county officials weighed in on behalf of the public school children, but to no avail. *This American Life* offered no closure on the story, and neither did New York education authorities, who were critical of the board but unwilling to act decisively in a state where Orthodox Jews form a powerful bloc.[2]

While ostensibly legal, and procedurally democratic (school boards are, after all, elected bodies), the East Ramapo school board's actions raise many important questions about the relationship between religion and democracy in American public education. What are the limits of majority rule? What are the reasonable claims of religious (and nonreligious) minorities? How much support should governments give religious groups, and how much religion should there be in public schools? What happens when a religious group takes advantage of democratic institutions to engage in antidemocratic behaviors that are hostile to the common good, or that victimize particular racial and ethnic groups? Moreover, is East Ramapo something new? How have Americans dealt with these difficult questions in the past?

This book explores the complex and contentious relationship between religion and democracy in American public schools. We write from an interdisciplinary perspective—Benjamin Justice is a historian, and Colin Macleod is a political philosopher. Despite differences in our academic orientations, we have reached a common conclusion: public schooling can and should be a site for fostering mutual understanding between different faith perspectives, and for the creation of a public with shared values of reasonable compromise and reasoned discourse. In order to do that, we believe, Americans need to rethink the place of religion and democracy in our public schools. We do not reject the view that public education should respect the separation between church and state that plays a central role in contemporary American democracy. Yet we think that public education can serve democracy by helping citizens to reason with one another respectfully and productively, and to understand the complex ways that different faith perspectives (including those that reject religion) inform the lives of citizens. This requires that public education engage with religion without endorsing a sectarian view. The conception of democratic education that we develop builds on and is indebted to the work of many scholars. Nevertheless, we hope our approach breaks new ground not only by synthesizing the perspectives of a historian and a philosopher in a single book, but by articulating a novel, and perhaps provocative, way of seeing public education.

In today's political climate, neither reasonable compromise nor reasoned discourse is a high priority. And while the East Ramapo case is unusual in its details, the inability of public officials to resolve the controversy is indicative of a much larger problem. Typically, prominent school reformers seek two unpromising approaches to public education. The first, favored by liberals, seeks to standardize education using one-size-fits-all models that focus narrowly on job training and college readiness, with little or no focus on political readiness for the duties of citizenship in a religiously diverse society. The second path, favored by conservatives, seeks to dismantle public schools altogether, treating children as consumers, not citizens, and promising parents deregulated choices that threaten to balkanize us religiously and to undermine democratic values. This lack of commitment to compromise and deliberation by liberals and conservatives alike runs against both the historical trajectory of public schooling and viable theories of democracy in education. The casualty is a reasonable space for religion in the education of American youth.

For nearly two hundred years, Americans have supported various forms of public education for political purposes, from improving the lives of youth, to boosting the strength of their own communities, to instilling allegiance to the national republic. Organized religion has played a leading role in that conversation—as a political force, but also as a form of personal and group identity, as a source of personal wisdom and strength, ignorance and weakness. Indeed, one cannot describe American history at all without religion. Even today, Americans are by any measure among the most religiously diverse and committed people in the Western world. The relationship between American religion and American democracy has been central to the development of public education.

The question for us, then, is not whether there can be any relationship between democracy and religion in American public education. *There is and there needs to be.* What we explore is how political battles about the place of religion within public schools challenge us to think critically about how a democracy should respond to religious pluralism. What does democracy require of public education? How has public education historically met those requirements, if at all? In this book we consider how a conception of democratic legitimacy can inform civic education in a way that acknowledges and respects religious diversity, and we trace the challenges Americans have historically faced in creating public schools that are inclusive and politically legitimate. From a democratic perspective, the historical record is mixed but shows that people of faith can overcome narrow sectarian disagreements.

The challenges we see are twofold. First, American religion is diverse. True, most Americans are, and historically have been, Christians. But the wide range of religious doctrines and practices that count as Christian is vast, and belies the idea that most Americans share a fully common faith. Although they constitute a relatively small segment of the population, there are many other non-Christian faiths as well as a significant number of Americans who subscribe to no religion at all. Moreover, America is becoming more religiously diverse. The Pew Research Center reports that between 2007 and 2014 the percentage of Americans identifying themselves as Christian dropped from 78.4 percent to 70.6 percent. Protestants remain the single largest religious group, but no longer constitute a majority, with 46.5 percent of adults identifying themselves as Protestant. Catholics now constitute 20.8 percent of the population, and nearly 23 percent of Americans do not identify with any religion. Jewish, Muslim, and Hindu populations have also grown, although they remain a small percentage of the population.[3]

American religious diversity has often been accompanied by, and indeed has often driven, political disagreement and conflict. The American form of democratic republicanism is animated, at least in principle, by an inspiring vision of peaceful, tolerant, and inclusive democracy that affords, as the Pledge of Allegiance declares, "liberty and justice for all." Finding a place for religion within an inclusive American political sphere, and within an inclusive public education that prepares American youth for that sphere, has never been easy, however.

The second challenge, related to the first, is that not all religions are committed to democratic principles, to compromise, or to the idea of public education. Historically, the American republic has often been beset by violence, intolerance, exclusion, and injustice in the name of religion. Prominent religious authorities have urged their followers to reject democratic practices and embrace antidemocratic politics. Still others attack reason and knowledge, which are building blocks of democratic discourse. In a democratic republic with a deep political commitment to protecting religious belief and to treating all religious groups equally, this aspect of religion has created special challenges for public education specifically, and for American democracy generally.

Lessons of Philosophy and History

What lessons do philosophy and history offer us? Philosophy tells us that for democracy to work, public decisions must be reached in a manner that people can acknowledge to be legitimate. Legitimacy is a special but unusual political value: it can make political outcomes that citizens view, perhaps with good reason, as objectionable, into political outcomes that they view as acceptable, or at least tolerable. An outcome is politically legitimate if even those who disagree with it have sufficient reason to accept it and can be expected to conform with laws or policies duly enacted by a political authority. The general idea of legitimacy is illustrated in the attitude that citizens often take toward the outcome of fair elections. Supporters of a losing candidate in an election may think that the views and platform of the winning candidate are bad, but they can acknowledge that implementation of the policies of the winner is politically acceptable.

Legitimacy is defined both procedurally and substantively: in terms of how decisions are reached and by the quality of those decisions. Legitimate procedures depend on people acknowledging that processes are reasonable and fair, and that the results of democratic processes do not violate fundamental moral principles, including the basic human rights of individuals. Of course, the details of what constitutes reasonable democratic procedure or the nature of basic rights are hotly contested among philosophers, just as they are among the general public. The dialogue that negotiates reasonableness is the loom that weaves the fabric of democratic society. One reason that the East Ramapo school board's actions are so upsetting to many observers is that they fail to meet the demands of political legitimacy. For the social fabric to hold together, all parties must respectfully entertain the views of others and stand ready to make reasonable concessions. Those who oppose any entry of religion in the public sphere must concede that such a procedural move could threaten the legitimacy of democratic oversight of education.

Substantively, a public school curriculum that denies the significance of religious faith to its constituent communities or America generally would also be unreasonable, because it would be grossly inaccurate. On the other hand, people of faith must concede that when their beliefs advocate the exclusion or persecution of others, they violate procedural legitimacy, while those articles of faith that are hostile to generally accepted standards of human reason cannot claim "equal time" with those that are. Public reason is as vital to democracy as fair procedures are. All members of the American public must recognize both the procedural and substantive dimensions of legitimacy and not pick those that merely meet their own self-interests.

What is public reason? It is an ideal that identifies the sorts of considerations to which citizens can appeal in the attempt to justify political proposals to one another. At its base, it requires respect for the equal standing of all citizens and common recognition that reasonable people can disagree about religion and other matters. It also requires acknowledgment of high- and low-quality "facts," as well as habits of mind necessary for their analysis and interpretation. Philosophers disagree among themselves about the details, but there is broad consensus that public reason severely limits the manner in which sectarian religious ideals can be invoked in political justification. Explicit appeals to the putative authority of religious doctrines have no place in a diverse democratic community in which citizens acknowledge and respect the lack of consensus about religious dogma. As we will see, public reason sometimes constrains the manner in which citizens can be faithful to their deepest religious convictions, and that may be a source of frustration to some citizens. Yet this does not entail schools' hostility to religion. If Americans are to find a way forward, they need to accept the costs, as well as the benefits, of democratic education. While the challenges to democratic education posed by religious diversity can never be fully resolved to everyone's satisfaction, we argue that they can be, and sometimes have been, managed in ways that are legitimate.

Despite their flaws, public schools are integral to the legitimacy of American democracy. They help create citizens and are crucial to the social reproduction of democracy. Indeed, part of the special challenge of interpreting legitimacy in the context of education involves considering the distinct claims children have to an education that facilitates their autonomy and enables them to meaningfully exercise important liberties such as freedom of religion and freedom of expression. Schools can be, and often are, vibrant sites of democratic activity that bring citizens from different backgrounds together and challenge them to respect one another and cooperate in the name of the common good. Public schools also impart what might be called public knowledge: knowledge that can be shared and appreciated by all citizens because it is grounded in nonsectarian methods of inquiry and canons of evidence. Public schools cultivate habits of mind, such as reasonableness and openness to unfamiliar ideas and perspectives, that form the basis of public reason. All this provides citizens a baseline of shared reality and ways of broaching disagreement that are necessary for identifying and resolving social problems. In terms of religious diversity, public schools are sites where future citizens can learn to respect diversity of belief and faith practices as a necessary component of democratic living. Of course, religious beliefs can conflict both with each other and with a shared sense of reality. Public education provides the space where these conflicts can rise to the surface and where future citizens can learn reasonable approaches to ameliorating them. By doing so, public schooling can enhance the legitimacy of the democratic state.

Historically unique factors have shaped the emergence of American public education and its relationship to religion. We do not claim that these are the ideal, or only, ways to achieve a healthy democracy. Other democracies have public educational systems that differ significantly from our own with respect to religion. For example, Canada, Germany, and the United Kingdom have long traditions of state support of various kinds of religious education. In Canada, the Constitution Act of 1867 expressly permits state support for denominational schools. In Germany, denominational religion is taught in public schools by teachers trained by religious organizations. In England, where the Church of England is officially established, religious education in state schools has an expressly Christian emphasis. These and other countries have charted their own ways of addressing the place of religion in public education. But the United States is a different country, and a distinctly American combination of social and political factors has led to the system we currently have. Not only has there always been significant religious diversity in the United States; there has also been a strong constitutional tradition of protecting rights to religious liberty and sharply limiting state promotion of particular religious creeds. Add to those traditions the decentralized nature of American school governance, and the American public education system is unique in the world.

Historically, public schools have reflected basic tensions over legitimacy that characterize democratic societies. In a country that has had no official state religion and a strong political revulsion toward favoring one religion over others, public schools in the United States have been the sites of attempts to forge a legitimate place for religion in the public sphere by defining and redefining reasonable processes and substantive outcomes. The nature of these processes and outcomes has reflected changing contexts in time and space: what may have been reasonable procedures and substance in 1814 in New York City no longer made sense in 1914, or 2014; and what happened in New York City may have made little sense elsewhere. The historical question that guides our analysis is not whether the relationship between religion and public education was always reasonable, nor whether it was reasonable by the standards of every member of society. Rather, we seek to understand the process by which decisions about the role of religion in public education often reflected, at least to some degree, a concern to achieve legitimacy in the face of religious pluralism. By today's standards, public education of the past sometimes flouted democratic norms. We should not gloss over that fact, but we should also recognize how people at different times have tried to express democratic ideals as they saw them.

History shows that the struggles to define what is legitimate have not always reflected democratic principles. Secular and religious leaders have often engaged in undemocratic procedural and substantive behaviors with regard to public education, as have teachers and students themselves. On the other hand, history also shows that the aspiration to create fair procedures and outcomes for the place of religion in public education has played a powerful and enduring role in the development of public education. Sometimes decisions that today we recognize as antidemocratic were, in their context, understood by most people to be reasonable. This does not mean that they were in fact democratic or substantively legitimate, or that they should be cause for celebration. White supremacy, female subordination, and other "values" were widely held at various points in time and did not diminish without struggle. These and other examples remind us that critical assessments of past failures to realize democratic values must be nuanced and sensitive to the historical context.

Taken together, a historical and philosophical focus on the central importance of legitimacy offers a fruitful framework for understanding our past and for finding a more productive path for the future. We do not pretend that the approach to democratic values we embrace here is the only credible conception of democracy on offer. Nevertheless, we think that it is attractive and that it provides a valuable perspective from which to reflect on the unique history and future of religion and public education in the United States.

Militancy, Multiculturalism, and Democratic Theory

Historians are no more immune to the biases of their political sensibilities than are philosophers. Nevertheless, we hope that democratic theory provides a more useful framework for understanding the historical development of public education in relation to religion than what has come before. For the first half of the twentieth century, two teams—two ways of seeing the past—dominated the history of religion and public education. On one side, public school advocates wrote institutional histories of American education that downplayed the significance of religion in public school history and scorned (or ignored) the critics of public education, most notably those who were Roman Catholic. The other side, led by promoters of Roman Catholic education who wanted public tax money to support their private schools, wrote triumphant histories of Catholic education that read more like promotional literature than thoughtful scholarship.

Beginning in the 1960s, a new generation of historians challenged both views. They questioned the supposed secular origins of public education and demonstrated the many ways in which early school practices alienated religious minorities. A few historians questioned the alleged unity and triumph of Catholic education, and the history of Catholic schools received—if not a balanced and critical view—at least one that was thoughtful enough to fit in with mainstream historical scholarship. These revisionist histories of both teams, which tried to correct the previous generation, in turn inspired another generation of scholars who questioned the very terms of the debate. What about Catholics who supported public schools, or Protestants who opposed them? Where did smaller groups, like Jews, Jehovah's Witnesses, and atheists fit in? Did national debates reflect local practices? How and why did particular groups—such as Protestant fundamentalists—change their stance on public schools over time?

What emerged was a multicultural view of religion in public schools that framed the issue of public education in terms of inclusion and exclusion, insiders and outsiders. New groups have had their story told for the first time, while historians better grasped the biases of their own profession. The underlying orientation of the multicultural school has been that democracy is a big tent, and majoritarian politics exploits unreasonable fear of "strangers in the land" to keep people out. The arc of the story is that schools have become increasingly inclusive over time, as excluded groups have fought for and won a place at the table. Excluders are unreasonable bigots. The excluded are earnest victims. The operative explanatory concept is inclusion, though multiculturalists have struggled to explain the nature of inclusion and exclusion—a task just begun by yet another wave of scholars.

Lacking a solid theoretical framework for dealing with the substance of religious diversity, however, multicultural histories of religion and public education have a difficult time accounting for changing norms of inclusion and exclusion in ways that avoid hindsight—pooh-poohing our benighted ancestors through the lens of present notions of reasonableness. Unlike racial bigotry, which has been directly linked to the slave economy and global patterns of white supremacy, marginalization of religious groups is more difficult to explain as *mere* bigotry. While certainly the greater inclusion of diverse peoples in the civic ken has indeed been a good thing, reducing exclusion and compromise to bigotry does little to help us understand the development of public education in a historically nuanced way. Some historians have linked religious clashes to class struggle, but such treatments have been limited by the fact that religious diversity and disagreement have spanned socioeconomic classes. Additionally, economic analyses have been unable to adequately describe the often explicitly political dimension of religious struggles in their relationship to democratic values. Others have attempted to group religions into pietistic and liturgical camps, though this does little to explain internecine battles. Have people simply grown more reasonable over time? That seems too simplistic. Instead, ideas about what is reasonable in procedure and substance have themselves evolved, constantly renegotiated in the deep churn of historical change. History has given us the luxury of recognizing and learning from our own previous failures of reasonableness. Perhaps we are no more inherently reasonable than our predecessors, but we may nonetheless enjoy some advantages in recognizing what reasonableness requires. No doubt future generations will recognize our own failures to be reasonable.

The idea of legitimacy within democratic theory adds a missing theoretical dimension to multicultural analyses of religion in public education. We pick up the thread of such analyses here. The story of religion in American public schools is not a shiny triumph of ideals, nor a struggle between noble minorities and unethical majorities, but a complex, ongoing negotiation over how to provide public education that balances competing values and interests in a manner acceptable to all citizens. It has been a process marked by both unreasonable exclusion and moves toward reasonable inclusion in many aspects of education. It has been a process that has occurred at different levels of government—in local school districts, state legislatures, and the Supreme Court. Sometimes this process has been driven by religious beliefs, but more often the heart of the matter has been concern over the shape of the secular society.

Four Themes in the History of Religion and Public Education

Viewing the development of public schooling through the lens of democratic processes leads us to focus on four recurring themes: content, purpose, control, and inclusion. Each theme is critical to the story of religion's place in public education and the character of the struggle to achieve democratic legitimacy around which our narrative is constructed. Moreover, each provides a bridge between the expressly historical parts of the book and those that address contemporary issues.

The historical story we tell goes like this: In terms of religious content, public schools have generally offered, from the beginning, what was perceived to be the lowest-common denominator among accepted religious groups. That denominator has increased or decreased according to changing social norms for religiosity, but in cases where there was no common ground, school officials have generally turned to subtraction to resolve religious controversy. As American public schools have become more diverse and welcoming of diversity, religious content has increasingly disappeared. Widely shared views of the purpose of public education have changed too. Once framed as necessary for making good citizens for the public good, public education today is framed largely as a private good—a way for individuals to outcompete others for increasingly scarce middle-class jobs. In terms of their management, public schools began with a radically democratic form of public oversight, which became increasingly bureaucratic and centralized over time. Presently, public school policy is moving in two opposite directions at once: an intensification of centralized control and standardized curriculum on one hand, and privatization on the other. Finally, public schools have grown increasingly diverse and inclusive, though these gains are currently under threat because of privatization. Thus public education in America has become both more and less democratic over time.

Democratic theory helps us understand this story. Take our first theme. Content concerns the quest for appropriate curricula and activities in a society where religion is both highly valued and highly contested. In contrast with public schooling today, where expressly religious materials and practices officially have no—or at best a marginal—place in the curriculum and school activities, early public schools routinely used Christian texts and prayers to teach basic literacy and to encourage religious piety. The modern understanding of the separation of church and state that now establishes a strict partition between public education and religious doctrine is a relatively recent development in American constitutional history. Despite broad acceptance of the suitability of the use of nonsectarian religious materials in the classroom by early school authorities, however, controversies arose about the precise character, purpose, and content of those materials. Protestant sectarians who buried the hatchet by settling on a generic, Pan-Protestant orientation to the school curriculum sometimes expressed outrage that other Christians—read Catholics—felt excluded. In later times, Catholics joined Protestants in their rejection of Jews' and atheists' claims to protection of *their* rights of conscience. The principle of nonsectarian public education was a cherished concept from the beginning, but who gets to define what *sectarian* means has been a matter of some controversy.

It is understandable that many citizens for whom religion is a powerful source of value wish to have aspects of their faith recognized and reflected in educational materials. Yet few citizens wish to see public schools used in the service of religious ideals or values that they reject. Moreover, particular religious claims that violate widely accepted norms of public reason, including norms of evidence and consensus in science, also raise concerns. For example, for much of the twentieth century, religious fundamentalists managed to keep evolutionary biology out of high school science textbooks, attempting to define public reason in ways consistent with their particular religious beliefs about the origins of life. Cold War concerns over the quality of science education transformed the public debate about reason, placing higher value on scientific methods and expertise than on religious tradition. Religiously fueled content controversies continue today about whether schools should include creationism, under the guise of intelligent design, in the science curriculum, or whether students should be encouraged to view gay and lesbian relationships as healthy expressions of love.

Our second theme concerns how religion might be relevant to the purpose of public education. Defining the purpose of education is, of course, a contentious matter. We attribute a basic democratic purpose to public schools, and generally speaking, this purpose has endured in public discourse for two centuries. But making democratic citizens has not always been the only, or primary, purpose attributed to schooling. Some common school reformers, for example, believed that they were hastening the Second Coming of Christ to America. In a different vein, politicians and social reformers have historically turned to public schools to address the problems caused by the capitalist economy: poverty, unemployment, and changing job-skill requirements. Others have looked to schools to reduce crime, encourage obedience and conformity, or reinforce race, gender, and class privilege. Still others have looked to schools with an opposite agenda: to challenge inequality and oppression. Meanwhile, parents might applaud the high ideals of public schools, but appreciate even more the fact that their children have a safe place to go, free of charge, while they work. Kids have still other concerns.

Shifting discourse about the purpose of public schools has had important implications for the role of religion in them. It has also exposed differing conceptions of the meaning of democracy. In the early days of the American republic, many educators thought instruction in Christian doctrines promoted moral virtue and good citizenship in secular society. Nevertheless, as Americans made the shift to truly public schools open to all children free of charge, the place of religion in those schools became contested both as a matter of principle—sectarian instruction was widely regarded as unfair and antidemocratic—and as a matter of substance, with some leaders expressing anxiety about the democratic credentials of religion itself. A century later, during the Cold War, conservative Roman Catholics and Protestants joined in a successful effort to force American school children to recite "one nation, *under God*" in daily pledges of civic allegiance as a way to check the supposed evils of communism. In this case, as liberals at the time observed, the substantively democratic goal of inoculating children against totalitarian ideologies embraced an anti-democratic procedure of coerced professions of faith. While their criticism was technically correct, the general public found the practice consistent with the goal of public education of creating cultural and political conformity.

In still other instances, religious authorities, while taking advantage of rights of religious freedom afforded by democracy, have expressed hostility to democratic principles. For them, the rule of the people represented a challenge to the ultimate authority of God's law, and public schooling in pursuit of democracy represented a threat to faith. This concern is echoed today by religious fundamentalists who say that the secular orientation of public schools is hostile to traditional religious beliefs and values. Such fundamentalists see the democratic ideal of creating open-minded and tolerant citizens capable of reasoning about and challenging traditional values as corrosive to their own religious traditions and commitments. They often prefer to abandon public schools rather than expose their children to an education that they view as corrupting.

But if public schools have a basic democratic purpose, then flight from public schools may pose a serious problem. Indeed, it becomes questionable whether highly sectarian forms of nonpublic education are compatible with democracy. Of course, attributing a democratic purpose to schools raises many other questions as well. How should public schools navigate between the civil function of creating a common identity and the rights of individuals or local communities to promote their own beliefs? How can citizens keep government size and scope in check to ensure democratic processes while also ensuring that all citizens have the capability to engage in those processes? Can schools teach the critical reasoning skills and ideals of mutual respect without alienating religious folk who believe that education should respect, rather than challenge, conservative values grounded in traditional religions? History does not provide answers to these questions, but does demonstrate their enduring salience in the development of public schooling as we know it.

Questions about the purposes of public education naturally lead to our third theme, political control over public education. This theme has two facets, both of which emerged in nineteenth-century America and endure today: the organization and regulation of schools for the general public, and the organization and regulation of religious and secular private schools.

Fundamental to the design of public schools of the nineteenth century was the emergence of democratic localism: a way of running public schools centered on geographically organized school districts and paid for through a combination of property tax and state and federal aid. The model was well suited to the rural character of the northern United States. Diversity required compromise: democratic governance was the solution. In cases where settlement was homogeneous, localism allowed communities to set their own reasonable standards for the influence of religion on the curriculum of the school. In cases where communities were diverse, the democratic, secular model provided a highly legitimate means of decision making. As they assisted the development of school districts, state legislatures often enacted laws forbidding both sectarian control and sectarian instruction, but often supported the demands of evangelical Protestants who insisted that Bible reading without comment be protected or mandated. At first city systems developed along a different path (religious charity schools), but interdenominational conflict led, in most cases, to the adoption of the rural system: ward-based democratic localism in tension with centralized city governance. After the Civil War, Congress required former Confederate states to guarantee the creation of systems of public education in their constitutions as a price of readmission to the Union. At the local level formerly enslaved African Americans forced white legislatures to make good on the promise.

Not all groups were satisfied with these developments, of course. Lutherans and especially the leadership of the Roman Catholic Church, among others, insisted that public education was an impossible ideal, that children of their faith could not receive a civic education in common with other children. Substantively, they pointed to the ways that the content of public education sometimes violated their religious beliefs, since Protestant majorities could be insensitive or outright hostile to them. On the other hand, the Catholic church was most conspicuous in mounting an explicitly antidemocratic mission of civic separation for Catholics in America—building a separate system of social, civic, and educational institutions, and railing against the principles of individual religious freedom and religious diversity. In response, state after state enacted constitutional provisions against funding religious education as a way to protect American democratic civic ideals that had emerged in a diverse, rural context. At the same time, school textbooks and other materials became increasingly secular to accommodate an even wider view of what constituted a civic education.

In the more recent past, minorities both religious and nonreligious have turned to the courts to carve out sharp restrictions on the presence and promotion of religion in public schools. Yet many dominant religious groups still attempt to use their political power to shape public school policies so as to be hospitable to their own sectarian religious doctrines and hostile to secular doctrines they oppose. Similarly, religious groups have pursued other political avenues, such as supporting voucher programs, which permit state funding of schools under private control with expressly religious objectives. These ways of exercising political power challenge the separation of church and state, which has served as a foundational principle of American democracy.

A second facet of the theme of control concerns the degree to which a democratic state can exercise authority over education that occurs *outside of* the public schools. Freedom of religion currently provides legal protection to religious groups from most forms of state intrusion. Groups with a distaste or suspicion of public education can rely on the protection afforded by freedom of religion to establish their own schools or to homeschool. In these nonpublic settings, religious groups are free to promote sectarian religious doctrines and activities. During the 1920s, a number of states followed the example of Oregon in attempting to outlaw all private and parochial schools in the name of protecting democracy and promoting a common American culture. The Ku Klux Klan was a strong proponent of such legislation. In *Pierce v. Society of Sisters* (1925), the Supreme Court overturned the Oregon law in a 5–4 decision—ruling that the state had overreached its powers by violating the contract rights of private schools and threatening the rights of parents.

Unfortunately, religious schools and homeschooling sometimes foster intolerant beliefs and attitudes that clash with democratic commitments and virtues. Parents freely teach their children that widely held scientific explanations for the natural world, such as evolution, are wrong, and then provide their children with deliberately falsified curriculum materials to support their views. In theory the state has a responsibility not only to secure a suitable democratic education for children enrolled in public schools but to ensure that all children are educated to be functionally democratic citizens. As the state cannot, according to the First Amendment, choose among religious groups to support those that embrace democratic principles, it must choose none of them. (To support them all would mean to encourage antidemocratic education.) But this responsibility must be carefully tempered by the need to limit state power and state intrusion into family life and to uphold the rights of parents freely to pursue their own religious beliefs and pass them on to their children. There has never been an easy solution to this problem.

The fourth theme that runs through the book is inclusion. Public schools today are supposed to be accessible and hospitable to all children, irrespective of their sex, race, class, or religion. Historically, the ideal of universal inclusion has never been fully realized. But the range of what is considered reasonable today is far greater than ever before. In the past (and to lesser extent, even today) American public schools discriminated on the basis of race, sex, and class, as well as religion. Common and later public schools were, by law, open to all faiths, but could be inhospitable or even dangerous to children who belonged to unpopular groups. Mormons and Catholics in the nineteenth century, Jews and Jehovah's Witnesses in the twentieth, and Muslims in the twenty-first century could speak to the challenges they faced from school authorities and communities who considered their beliefs outside the realm of acceptable religious affiliations. Against this ugly background, the move toward an expressly secular conception of public education that is officially tolerant and respectful of diverse religious (and nonreligious) perspectives is a welcome democratic development.

A different dimension of inclusion concerns the status of compulsory components of a democratic curriculum. Cultivating the virtue of toleration may involve exposing children to doctrines and values that are, or are perceived to be, in tension with the religious values of some citizens. A democratic curriculum that insists upon the fundamental equality of men and women or that counsels respect for sexual minorities may be interpreted by fundamentalists as a threat to family values. Religious fundamentalists may thus feel alienated by a democratic curriculum and may opt to exclude their children from public education. Given the vital role that religion plays in American history and life, a democratic education obligates schools to help students learn about religious belief systems different from their own. Inclusion does not mean a gathering into emptiness, but the creation of a space where children may better learn to understand themselves and others through free exchange in an information-rich environment.

Student voices are critical to this exchange. Even if public school teachers and officials do not endorse or favor particular religious views, there are ways in which student-led religious activities in schools can work against inclusion of religious minorities. Religious students may wish to express their religious convictions and practices within the confines of school, and freedom of religion presumably provides some protection of such religious expression by students. Yet too much religious expression by students of a particular faith may alienate students with different beliefs and backgrounds. The difficulty is in determining the reasonable purposes and limits of that expression.

Historically, Americans have failed to achieve any simple or pure solution to the multifaceted problem of religion in public education. Instead, the story has been marked by struggles among competing groups to define the content, purposes, control, and limits of inclusion of public education vis-à-vis religion. There never was a golden age when they got it right. Even when groups have appeared to reach reasonable compromises, those compromises were often achieved among those with power, and excluded those deemed to be outsiders. On the other hand, examples of seriously unreasonable religious practices in schools have generally not lasted long. Subject to the same pressures of competing interests and social transformation, in the contest of democratic decision making in public education, many unreasonable practices have been weeded out. What is most significant about the history of religion in American public education has not been the specific policies that Americans have developed, but the dynamic and messy process of defining what is reasonable, what is legitimate, and what is, after all, the nature of American democracy.

What Follows

In the chapters that follow, we begin our examination of religion and public schools by elaborating on the idea of democracy and its key components. We pay particular attention to the role of religion in a democracy, and the implications of that relationship for public schooling. What is legitimate? What is reasonable? The conception of democratic education we adopt provides a critical vantage point from which to identify and critically analyze both historical themes and contemporary challenges concerning the place of religion in public schools.

We then divide the history of American public education into four periods, each characterized by significant changes to public education and to society. Chapter 2 takes us to the early Republic, when American leaders developed their own theories on the relationship between religion and public education. Chapter 3 examines the development of common and later public schools during the mid- to late-nineteenth century, when Americans in the north shifted to a system of universal, nonsectarian, democratically run public schooling, which then spread nationwide after the Civil War. Chapter 4 analyzes the emergence of a progressive, modern, and national system of public education in the twentieth century through the 1950s, when disagreements over religion and public education became truly national in scope. Chapter 5 looks at the major restructuring of religion in American politics and education from 1960 until the present, including the emergence of charters and vouchers. Along the way we will meet some colorful characters embroiled in various cultural, political, and legal contestations about religion and public education. While it is important to examine people and events with due consideration to historical context, we invite readers to consider the degree to which the actions and attitudes of people manifest sufficient appreciation for the demands of democratic legitimacy.

While each of these historical periods has its unique features, we also observe that several long-term trends have emerged over the last two centuries. The first is political. The United States of America did not begin as a democracy, but slowly evolved into one that was dynamic, contradictory, and complex. The second trend has been demographic. Who Americans are and what they believe has changed continuously, and nowhere have these changes brought more challenges and opportunities than in public schooling. A third long-term trend has been the rise of the public school as the largest and most comprehensive educational institution in American society. For nearly two centuries, public school enrollments, attendance, and completion rates have grown, reaching their current wobbly plateau at the end of the twentieth century. At the same time, public *education* has come to mean public *schooling*, and has grown increasingly centralized, standardized, and bureaucratized, governed by state and even national regulations in ways that were once impossible to imagine.

Aside from these long-term trends, even deeper changes continue to unfold. Revolutions in science and social research, in communication, technology, and commerce, have fundamentally altered the world in which we live. Modern scientific theories have explained natural phenomena in ways that challenge religious authority. Most Americans no longer look to religion to prevent hurricanes and floods, to ward off demons, to cure illness, or to make crops grow. Communication revolutions have brought people of faith into contact with alternate viewpoints, both within the United States and around the globe. The intensification of the global economy has revolutionized the way people make a living and organize power. Debates over the place of religion in American public school education today occur within an entirely different context from what existed when public schools began. But the necessity of public education is no less pressing, and the need for mutual understanding, for the advancement of knowledge, and for a common faith in the common good, has never been more urgent.

The final chapter of this book applies the lessons of history and political philosophy, analyzing three critical areas of religious controversy in public education today: student-led religious observances in extracurricular activities; the tension between the freedom of student expression and need for safe, inclusive environments; and the shift from democratic, public control of schools to loosely regulated charter and voucher programs. In each of these areas, we see reasons for hope and cause for concern. As we have noted, American public schools are more inclusive than they have ever been, when it comes to religious diversity. This has partly reflected the spread of people and culture in the global economy. On the other hand, democracy in schools, such as exists, is both procedurally and substantively endangered—reflecting very real tears in the fabric of American democracy and a widespread decline in commitment to public institutions. The lessons of philosophy and the lessons of history bring us to the same place: resolving religious controversies in public schools must proceed from an informed understanding of the role of public schools as legitimate sites of civic education, where children learn to become reasonable citizens of a religiously pluralistic society.

ONE

Religion and Education: A Democratic Perspective

On May 26, 1797, President John Adams presented the Treaty of Tripoli to the US Senate. Six days later, the senate ratified the treaty unanimously. Article 11 of the treaty stated: "[T]he Government of the United States of America is not, in any sense, founded on the Christian religion." Yet in 1864 the phrase "in God we trust" started to appear on American currency, and in 1954 Congress modified the Pledge of Allegiance to include the phrase "under God." Article VI of the Constitution insists that "no religious test shall ever be required as a qualification to any office or public trust under the United States." Yet American presidents routinely say "so help me God" when taking the official oath of office. Polls suggest that most Americans favor prayer in school, yet the Supreme Court has ruled that school prayer is unconstitutional.

Examples like these prompt the question of whether God or a particular religion should have a place in American democratic institutions. Such matters are controversial, contentious, and potentially divisive. Yet they are important. Against this background, it is perhaps not surprising to learn that religion, democracy, and education are the sites of many heated debates in contemporary political philosophy. Although there is near-universal acceptance of the value and importance of democracy, there are many competing interpretations of core democratic values and the institutional arrangements that they require. Everyone agrees that religion is a powerful and important force in politics, but there is widespread disagreement about the appropriate place of religion within legitimate democratic processes and institutions. Similarly, nearly everyone agrees that a modern democratic state is responsible for providing basic primary and secondary education that is accessible to all children. Yet there is a wide range of views of how schools, whether public or private, should respond to the diverse and often conflicting religious beliefs and practices of citizens both young and old. In this chapter, we will provide a general overview of some of the main assumptions and issues that animate the ideal of democratic education we adopt in this book, as well as the way in which religious diversity poses a challenge for democratic communities.[1]

A comprehensive treatment of all approaches and controversies in this complex and varied field is impossible. Other theorists might pursue different themes or place greater weight on different facets of democratic theory or even offer a radically different conception of education in a religiously diverse democracy. As a point of departure, we identify political considerations and principles of political morality that are widely accepted as important. We then explain how these principles form the basis of an attractive conception of democracy. However, the purpose here is not solely to describe what most democratic theorists agree on. Instead, our preliminary discussion provides the basis for defending a substantive conception of public education in the context of a modern and religiously diverse democratic society.

Democracy, Diversity, and Legitimacy

Much democratic theory begins with a simple observation about diversity. Citizens of modern political communities hold a wide variety of religious, moral, political, and philosophical views. They have allegiances to many different cultural, ethnic, national, and linguistic communities. The interests of citizens, though often complementary, sometimes conflict. Citizens have divergent opinions about what political institutions are desirable, how policies should be adopted, and how political disagreements are appropriately resolved. John Rawls calls this the "fact of reasonable pluralism": "This is the fact of profound and irreconcilable differences in citizens' reasonable comprehensive religious and philosophical conceptions of the world, in their views of the moral and aesthetic values to be sought in human life."[2] It is crucial to emphasize the notion of reasonableness at work here. A reasonable person acknowledges that disagreement about profound matters of faith and values is inevitable, and the standing of citizens in political society is not determined by the doctrines—religious or secular—to which they subscribe. Reasonable people recognize the infeasibility and inappropriateness of trying to impose their belief systems on others, and they see the value of cooperating with others in political community for mutual benefit. So they seek ways of living together that appeal to democratic values that can be accepted by all those similarly committed to establishing and maintaining fair terms of social cooperation. To put this in a specifically American political context, consider the social and ideological diversity reflected in the following list of well-known American political figures: Ronald Reagan, Malcolm X, Bernie Sanders, Ron Paul, Sarah Palin, Hillary Clinton, Martin Luther King Jr., Barney Frank, and Cesar Chavez. We seek a vision of democratic politics that would allow these people to negotiate their differences in a respectful and cooperative fashion.

Against the background of this kind of pluralism, political communities must find a feasible, reasonably stable, and just way of reaching decisions about the laws and public policies that shape the economic, social, and political character of a society. Since views on how to organize society diverge in significant ways, we as citizens need to find a way to settle our political differences that all can accept as fair and reasonable. Fortunately, most people today favor peaceful, democratic means of resolving political disputes. Our understanding of the nature and requirements of democracy has evolved significantly over time. At the most abstract level, however, democracy seeks to address diversity through institutions and procedures that are responsive to the will of the people in a way that delivers political decisions that are *legitimate*.

Legitimacy is a very important but unusual standard. Historically, political philosophers have offered different accounts of legitimacy. But one way or another, most accounts treat legitimacy as supplying governments and political officials with the authority to govern that is grounded not in the mere capacity to wield coercive power over people, but rather in the idea that lawmaking and political decision making is regulated by appropriate values. In effect, legitimacy requires that government activity is suitably justifiable to the people it affects.[3] Our approach draws upon a deliberative conception of democracy in which legitimacy depends on processes of reason giving and reason taking by citizens. Legitimacy depends on the public articulation of reason-based justifications of laws and policies.[4] Laws and policies duly enacted by a political authority are politically legitimate if even those who disagree with them have sufficient reason to accept them and can be expected to conform to them. Legitimate laws need not be perfectly just, and they need not meet with the approval of all or even most citizens. But legitimate laws must sufficiently satisfy defensible political standards such that all citizens can accept the laws and basic institutional arrangements of their society.[5] Decisions on important matters or political institutions that merely reflect or are predicated on the exercise of raw political power or coercion will not seem acceptable to those who disagree with them. Instead, decisions must be made via processes that allow reasons for decisions to be articulated and considered by those who are affected by them. Politically legitimate laws and political institutions claiming authority must, in other words, pass some standards of justification.

The justification integral to democratic legitimacy has procedural and substantive dimensions. The democratic processes (e.g., electoral and legislative systems) through which political decisions are generated must be (reasonably) fair and suitably responsive to the expressed preferences of citizens. The fairness of democratic procedures is in turn predicated on the equal standing of citizens. Citizens have an equal right to participate in democratic activity. Each citizen should have an equal vote and equal rights to political expression, assembly, and protest. Moreover, legal recognition and protection of these rights lie at the heart of a decent constitutional democracy. Historically, of course, it is only relatively recently that political communities styling themselves as democratic have practically acknowledged the fundamentality of equal citizenship and equal political rights to democracy. Throughout most of its history, America denied basic equal political standing to many of its inhabitants, even citizens, and hence failed to satisfy a basic democratic requirement. This fact casts a dark shadow over the legitimacy of much of America's political history. Consider the denial of the vote to women. Suffragettes like Susan B. Anthony and Elizabeth Cady Stanton could not consider their disenfranchisement as legitimate, simply because the majority of men who enjoyed the right to vote opposed universal suffrage.

Fair democratic procedures that offer citizens equal input into political decision making provide a way of generating legitimate decisions. In many cases, the fact that a decision is arrived at through a fair system of voting provides those who have lost the vote enough reason to accept the decision as legitimate, even if they believe it is flawed in important respects. For an important range of issues, the fact that a majority of citizens cast a ballot in favor of a policy in a procedurally fair voting scheme will be crucial to conferring legitimacy on the policy. In such cases, the losers can acknowledge both that they lost a fair vote and that the fact of losing the vote gives them an important reason to view the outcome of the vote as acceptable. They reasonably view it as an outcome that they should abide by at least until such time as the policy is changed through a subsequent vote.

But procedural fairness is not always a sufficient guarantee of legitimacy in a democracy. Legitimate political outcomes must also satisfy *some* substantive criteria of justification. Exactly what such criteria are is difficult to specify precisely. But there are some clear cases. For example, a policy disenfranchising an unpopular ethnic minority would not be politically legitimate even if it had been adopted through a fair referendum in which everyone, including the minority, was able to participate on equal terms. Here the ideal of democracy itself places some limits on the policies that democratic majorities can legitimately enact. Similarly, legitimate political decisions must respect the fundamental rights of persons that are grounded in considerations of basic justice. Just what these rights are is a matter of some theoretical and practical controversy,[6] but gross violations of human rights such as those involved in human chattel slavery clearly violate political legitimacy. This will be true even if a majority approves of measures that violate fundamental rights. A slave cannot reasonably view her status as a slave as justifiable merely on the grounds that a majority of citizens favor slavery. The fact that a majority of white Americans, including celebrated founding fathers such as George Washington and Thomas Jefferson, endorsed slavery gave Frederick Douglass, an escaped slave and tireless abolitionist, no reason to think that America's "peculiar institution" had any legitimacy. Slavery, even if it is politically endorsed by a majority of citizens, is not legitimate. Similarly, a procedurally fair vote to deny basic political rights such as freedom of speech or equality before the law to an ethnic, religious, or racial minority is not sufficient to confer political legitimacy on the denial of the rights. In some ways, America's civil rights movement is predicated on recognition of this facet of legitimacy. The Montgomery, Alabama, city ordinance that authorized racial segregation of city buses had no true democratic authority over Rosa Parks. And in 1955, when she refused to yield her seat on the bus to a white person, she acted with, not against, the spirit of democratic legitimacy.

So politically legitimate democratic outcomes are not simply ones that reflect the will of the majority of citizens as determined through some complex electoral system. The processes through which the will of the people is ascertained must be procedurally fair, and they must be structured so as to ensure that political decisions do not violate the basic rights of citizens. The elaborate form of representative democracy in the United States reflects these twin concerns with process and substance. The American constitutional structure provides an array of electoral systems (local, state, and federal) through which legislators are selected. And when they act responsibly, legislators attend to the interests of all their constituents, not just powerful lobbies, and they seek to promote the common good. The exercise of legislative power is constrained by a scheme of basic citizen rights articulated in the Constitution and interpreted and applied by courts. It is, of course, debatable how well the current American system of checks and balances works in the service of core democratic values. Historically, American political institutions have failed many citizens in many ways. But for our purposes, it is instructive to consider some challenges for democratic theory that arise in light of the place of religion in American democracy.

America is highly religious and overwhelmingly Christian. Yet it has significant non-Christian religious minorities as well as many atheists, agnostics, and people with no particular religious affiliation. Moreover, within the Christian community there is a great deal of doctrinal diversity, and no single Christian faith is shared by a majority of Americans. The depth, breadth, and diversity of American religiosity helps explain the value Americans typically assign to the protection of freedom of religion. Religious citizens have an interest in a political society that is hospitable to pursuit of their different faith-based commitments. Freedom of religion speaks to this interest in at least three ways. First, it protects religions from state interference. Providing that they respect the rights of other citizens, religious citizens are free to worship and engage in religious activities without fear of repression or restriction by the state. Second, freedom of religion allows religious citizens to express their religious convictions publicly and to try to persuade others to adopt their faith. Of course, not all religious groups proselytize to people outside their faith communities, but nearly every religious group seeks to pass religious commitments and traditions on to their children. Freedom of religion is often invoked by parents to defend their right to teach their children specific religious doctrines and to raise their children in specific religious traditions and cultures. Third, freedom of religion allows individuals and groups to insulate themselves from the religious or nonreligious beliefs and practices of other people. Some religious citizens may find the practices or beliefs of other citizens objectionable or offensive. Freedom of religion allows such citizens to limit their exposure to the beliefs and practices of others both by avoiding association with others and by restricting access by outsiders to their own religious community.

Freedom of religion also serves a more general value of facilitating deliberation by citizens about the potential value or pitfalls of different religious and nonreligious doctrines and practices. The free exercise of religion provides information and examples of different faiths and philosophical perspectives. Citizens can critically examine their own commitments by considering the beliefs and practices of others. Deliberation may lead to refinement or deepening of a person's religious commitments or to radical changes in one's religious outlook.

Acknowledging freedom of religion as a basic right clearly has implications for the nature of democratic legitimacy. Legitimate democratic decisions must respect freedom of religion, and this means that there are limits to the laws and policies that may be adopted by democratic legislatures. The establishment clause of the First Amendment forbids governments from adopting or promoting an official state religion even if there is widespread popular support for such a measure. Similarly, legislation that impedes the free exercise of religion is democratically illegitimate even if such legislation is extremely popular. For most readers, all this is probably quite familiar terrain. The real puzzles for political philosophy arise when we try to interpret the nature and boundaries of freedom of religion in relation to other democratic values.

Public Reason and Religion

One particularly difficult issue concerns the manner and degree to which religious considerations have a role in democratic debate, discussion, and argument. We have seen how democratic legitimacy depends on more than mere procedural fairness. Citizens, politicians, and officeholders in a democracy try not only to win raw political support for the policies they favor; they must also make good-faith efforts to provide reasonable public justifications for their policies. Genuine democracy is not merely about counting votes; it involves practices of reason giving and reason taking. As Rawls puts it: "To justify our political judgments to others is to convince them by public reason, that is, by ways of reasoning and inference appropriate to beliefs, grounds and political values it is reasonable for others also to acknowledge."[7] Here we encounter a crucial but complex idea: There are constraints on the considerations that are appropriately presented in democratic discourse. Suitable political reasons aimed at justifying policies and laws must be ones that diverse citizens can all acknowledge as germane to respectful political argument. A theory of public reason aims at identifying and explaining what sorts of considerations are admissible as reasons in legitimate democratic discourse and why some considerations are not admissible.

The precise elements and content of a doctrine of public reason are, to put it mildly, contentious subjects in contemporary political philosophy.

Nonetheless, there is broad agreement about some essential features of a credible doctrine of public reason. For instance, expressly religious considerations that emanate from controversial theological doctrines are often cited as paradigmatic examples of considerations that are not suitable public reasons. To illustrate: An evangelical Christian may sincerely believe in the literal truth of the biblical story of creation and may consequently believe that it is appropriate that creationism, and no competing theory, such as evolution, be included in the science curriculum of public schools. From the theological perspective of such a citizen, the religious reasons for teaching creationism seem strong. However, such reasons will not resonate with citizens with different convictions who do not share the contentious metaphysical premises upon which creationism is predicated. Such citizens cannot view appealing to a contentious theological doctrine as an acceptable basis for the public justification of a public policy. Consequently, theological reasons, even if they are shared by a majority of citizens, cannot serve as appropriate public reasons, because they provide no justification to citizens who hold different views.

This brings out an important point about democratic legitimacy: the justification it depends on is justification to citizens on terms that they can reasonably acknowledge as admissible and appropriate, given recognition of the doctrinal pluralism that characterizes modern democracies. The idea is that, despite their diverse religious, ethical, and philosophical commitments, citizens should try to justify the policies that they favor to one another on terms that all can acknowledge as politically relevant. This does not mean that citizens must themselves have a sophisticated and expressly articulated theory of public reason. But they should recognize that some of their deeply held religious beliefs do not belong in public discourse aimed at securing political legitimacy.

The point is not to filter out only religious considerations. Controversial secular doctrines (e.g., contentious ethical or metaphysical theories that are the subject of lively academic debate) may not count as sources of public reason either. For example, the attempt to justify the exclusion of intelligent design from the curriculum on the grounds that God does not exist (and thus intelligent design must be false) will fail as a public reason. The metaphysical claim about the nonexistence of God is too contentious to count as a suitable public reason. Reasonable theists cannot be expected to accept political arguments premised directly on the falsity of their most profound religious convictions. In practice, the responsibility of providing justifications for political positions is primarily borne by officeholders (e.g., elected representatives, civil servants, members of the judiciary) rather than citizens engaged in democratic activity. Nonetheless, in a democracy regulated by public reason, citizens should recognize and respect the basic idea that public political discourse has constraints and that they cannot expect other citizens to accept religious ideals as sources of public justification.

Public reasons are considerations that all citizens can (or should be able to) acknowledge as relevant to public processes of justification. The idea of public reason is, in effect, to find some common ground for conducting democratic discussion and debate in the face of religious, philosophical, and ethical diversity among citizens. It is probably impossible to articulate the full and precise content of public reason, both because the concept itself is somewhat fluid—some of what counts as a genuine public reason may shift over time and may vary in different contexts—and because its specific content is hotly contested by political philosophers. Nonetheless, we can identify three general facets of public reason that come into play in debates about religion and education.

First, public reason is predicated on acknowledgment and respect of other citizens as "free and equal persons."[8] This mutual-respect condition means that public political arguments should recognize the equal moral importance of all citizens. Acknowledging other citizens as free arguably entails recognizing the basic claim we all have to freely develop and pursue our own conceptions of a good life. Discourse that suggests that some citizens by virtue of their religious convictions, class, race, gender, or sexual orientation have an inferior moral status or may be denied access to benefits by virtue of such characteristics does not conform to norms of public reason. The preposterous idea that African American slaves should count as three-fifths of a person for the purposes of calculating political representation is a particularly egregious historical example of violation of this norm. Similarly, even though we may think that the religious views or beliefs about the good life of our fellow citizens are mistaken, we must refrain from imposing our own conceptions of the good on them. The fact that some citizens think Christianity is a false religion does not ground a public reason for a state policy that aims at discouraging Christian beliefs. The mutual-respect condition requires that citizens address each other as equal participants in the creation and maintenance of social, economic, and political cooperation. One does not have to like or agree with one's fellow citizens, but one must respect their equal status and convey this respect in political discourse.

Second, public reason is informed by appreciation of pluralism that undergirds toleration of diversity. Although citizens disagree, sometimes strongly, about the ultimate merits of different conceptions of the good, they should recognize two important aspects of democratic life. First, diversity in the conceptions of the good is an inevitable fact of democratic life. Second, there is no publicly accessible or politically feasible basis on which to evaluate, at least for the purposes of justifying public policy, the comparative merits of many different reasonable conceptions of the good. The Christian and the atheist will disagree about the truth or plausibility of their respective systems of belief, but both should recognize that efforts to settle this kind of disagreement should not occur at the political level. These are matters about which people can and do reasonably disagree. No resolution of the disagreement can occur on terms that all parties can view as acceptable for the purposes of setting public policy. Political argument aimed at securing justification of policies to affected parties should be tempered by toleration of diversity. The devout Catholic may sincerely believe that homosexual sex is wrong, but such a controversial judgment cannot be appealed to in support of legislation banning consensual same-sex relations between adults. Instead, the Catholic must recognize that it is appropriate to tolerate the freely chosen practices of others.[9] Similarly, the atheist cannot object to school prayer by casting aspersions on what he regards as superstitious practices of the religiously devout.[10]

Third, public reason should be nonsectarian. The considerations admissible to public political argument should be ones that can be accepted as relevant to political argument by people who hold diverse religious and philosophical views. A helpful way of capturing this idea is through John Rawls's notion that there is an "overlapping consensus" between diverse comprehensive religious, moral, and philosophical views.[11] Free and equal people committed to finding fair terms on which to organize society so as to achieve mutual benefit will find that they share a rich set of political values that they can employ in processes of political justification. For example, people disagree about religion, but they agree about the importance of freedom of religion; they disagree about what sorts of lives are ultimately best, but they agree that access to various generic resources (e.g., health care, education, and income) is important; and so on. Of course, the degree and extent of this overlapping consensus is probably not so extensive as to furnish an uncontroversial basis for conducting all political argument. But for our purposes, the broad consensus that public policy should not be shaped by sectarian religious doctrine is very important.

Orienting democratic discourse toward a set of sharable nonsectarian ideals does not eliminate political disagreement. Even if citizens broadly agree about how to identify acceptable nonsectarian considerations, they will disagree about the relative weight of such considerations, how they are best interpreted, and how to assess a wide variety of claims from science and social science.

Public Reason and Education: Toward an Ideal of Democratic Education

Political philosophers disagree about the precise content, scope, and ambition of public reason. Those who are optimistic about public reason think that the set of public reasons that all citizens can accept will be robust enough to "give a reasonable answer to all, or nearly all, questions involving constitutional essentials and matters of basic justice."[12] More pessimistic theorists hold that the set of reasons that all can accept is not sufficiently rich to resolve many fundamental political issues. Such theorists tend to be skeptical about the importance of public reason at all.[13] The position on public reason we adopt is somewhere between the poles of extreme optimism and pessimism. Without thinking that public reason can neatly resolve all contentious matters, we suggest that many important issues about religion and public education can be usefully situated against the background of reasonable religious pluralism and can be constructively addressed, if not definitively resolved, via a modest conception of public reason. We do not expect all major political disagreements to be resolved via a set of reasons that all citizens accept. Our more modest suggestion is that in the domain of public education, citizens can and should acknowledge that they cannot justify educational policies to their fellow citizens by invoking controversial theological doctrines. Instead, they can orient democratic deliberation about the appropriate character of public education around broad but shared interests that people have in creating and maintaining a vibrant, tolerant, and inclusive democracy. This approach does not eliminate disagreement or magically resolve controversies, but it does allow us to recognize the common ground we occupy as citizens, which is the essence of legitimacy.

In a democracy, the people are ultimately responsible for determining the structure, purpose, and character of educational institutions. However, we can now see that democratically legitimate public educational institutions are not simply ones that are politically supported by the majority of citizens. Instead, legitimate educational institutions must also satisfy the basic justificatory standards of public reason. They must, in other words, respect the equality of all citizens (and the humanity of noncitizens) and display toleration toward diverse reasonable beliefs and practices, and they must not be grounded in controversial sectarian doctrines. Unfortunately, the interests that citizens have in exercising control over educational matters, especially those that touch directly or indirectly on religious matters dear to their hearts, are not always harmonious. This means that it can be difficult to determine how public schools can achieve democratic legitimacy. Can there be a model of democratic education that is acceptable to all? In order to frame the challenge more precisely, we need to look more closely at the complex set of interests that different citizens have with respect to public education and religion.

Educational Interests and Religion: Children, Parents, and the Democratic Public

Primary and secondary schools serve, and thus are democratically accountable to, different stakeholders—children, parents, and the general public—each with a complex constellation of distinct interests. First and foremost are the interests of children. We can assume that all children have a fundamental interest in becoming literate and numerate. They also have a stake in acquiring reasoning skills and knowledge in a variety of core academic subjects. It is uncontroversial that decent public schools must supply good education along these lines. Of course, much controversy exists about the precise content of a curriculum that pursues these objectives. Similarly, there are many important disagreements about the pedagogical strategies that are most effective in realizing these objectives.

For our purposes, however, young children occupy a special place in democratic theory because, unlike adult citizens, they lack a determinate conception of the good and, by virtue of their lack of knowledge and their immature cognitive and moral capacities, they do not enjoy the authority to make decisions about their own education.[14] It is through education, both formal and informal, that children acquire a conception of the good and develop a determinate sense of themselves as distinct persons. Education also facilitates the acquisition of reasoning skills and moral capacities that permit children to become responsible agents who are entitled to direct their own lives and who can be held accountable, morally and legally, for their conduct. Children may be born into families and communities that have distinct religious beliefs and practices, but children are not born with any religious convictions. Instead, children's (initial) religious beliefs and identity (or lack thereof) will be strongly influenced by the content and character of their education and upbringing. (In a similar vein, children are not born as secular atheists, and a child born to parents who are atheists is not thereby an atheist by default.)

We make this rather obvious point in order to guard against the assumption that children have religious interests that are simply parallel to those of religious adults. Religious adults have an interest in leading lives that display fidelity to their understanding of their faith. They have an interest in deciding for themselves how to manifest adherence to their faith. They may wish to publicly express their beliefs or openly engage in worship, or they may prefer to conduct their religious lives more privately. Some will want to proselytize, while others will seek to insulate themselves from contact with people outside their faith community. Some will want to understand and appreciate the deeply held beliefs of other citizens, while others will be relatively indifferent to the religious (or nonreligious) views of others. The point is that adults are presumed to have the capacities and authority to articulate and manage their own religious beliefs and practices.

Children, by contrast, initially have no fixed religious identity, and the authority to give shape to a religious identity lies with other citizens. Of course, as children mature, they become more able to articulate and manage their own religious convictions. As this happens, they acquire stronger interests in expressing those convictions, which parallel those of adults. So at some point, schools need to determine what kind of religious expression by students is appropriate in various educational settings.

How does the education of children relate to their meaningful exercise of religious liberty when they are adults? Here we can distinguish two facets of religious liberty. First, citizens have an interest in implementing their settled religious convictions. This involves determining what fidelity to one's faith requires and having the capacities needed to act upon and sustain one's religious commitments. Second, citizens have an interest in deliberating about what religious convictions they should adopt. This involves thoughtful reflection on the value of their existing commitments, contemplation of other views, and the capacity to revise their views in light of deliberation.

A bad education can frustrate development of the moral capacities integral to meaningful religious liberty. For instance, a child who is successfully indoctrinated by her parents into a particular faith may be incapable of deliberating about the merits of other religious or nonreligious views. As Eamonn Callan warns, parental despotism can lead to servile children whose capacities to consider alternatives to the view imposed by parents are severely circumscribed. The servile child "remains subordinate to my will because the choices I made in molding her character effectively pre-empt serious thought at any future date about the alternatives to my judgment."[15] To the degree that this happens, the child or the adult she becomes does not exercise full authority over her religious identity. Instead, the authority to set one's own ends has been exercised by others. Similarly, children's interest in religious liberty is poorly served by an education that does not develop and nourish the capacity to make and sustain serious commitments. An education that prepares children for religious liberty should provide an understanding of diverse religious perspectives, including the serious commitments they may entail, and provide opportunities for reasoned contemplation of them.

In effect, children have an interest in an autonomy-facilitating education—one that equips them with the reasoning skills, moral capacities, dispositions, and knowledge to reflectively form, revise (if necessary), and implement their own conception of the good life, whether religious or not. Various considerations are relevant to justifying the importance of autonomy facilitation, and two are worth emphasizing. First, our judgments about the good life are fallible. We may come to realize that a way of life prized by our parents does not suit us and that a different conception of the good is more appropriate for us. Because autonomy enables thoughtful reflection on our commitments, it contributes to the possibility of people leading good lives that are animated by values and convictions that they can freely endorse. Second, autonomy facilitation contributes to a form of democratic citizenship in which citizens can appreciate and respect the diverse values and commitments on display in a pluralistic political community. Citizens capable of thoughtful reflection on their own lives are able to think imaginatively about the commitments of people from whom they differ profoundly. They can be open to debate and discussion in a way that is conducive to the processes of reason giving and reason taking at the heart of legitimacy.[16]

The special relationship between parents and children complicates matters considerably, because parents have a strong stake in influencing the religious identity of their children. Moreover, parents are often thought to have a great deal of authority in such matters. Many religious parents seek to exercise their own religious liberty by providing an education for their children that ensures (or at least attempts to ensure) their children's allegiance to the faith of the parents. This makes such parents sympathetic to features of schooling that can contribute to children's adherence to their religious views. Some Christian parents favor school prayer and Bible readings with an expressly Christian orientation precisely because such activities encourage adherence by their children to Christianity. By the same token, some religious parents seek to insulate their children from possible challenges or alternatives to the faith commitments they favor. As a result, religious parents are sometimes hostile to features of schooling that facilitate consideration and deliberation about religious or nonreligious views that the parents reject. Conservative Christians sometimes seek to shield their children from material in the school curriculum that offers perspectives on sexuality, faith, science, or morality that differs from and possibly challenges traditional teaching on such topics.

Although parents sometimes forget this, it is crucial to recognize that in matters of religion and much else, children are not mere extensions of their parents. They are separate persons who have an interest in forming their own beliefs and commitments about faith. Of course, children are also very dependent on their parents in various ways and are strongly susceptible to parental influence, which parents are often anxious to exercise. And therein lies a tension. Parents' interest in exercising their own religious liberty can, paradoxically, conflict with the liberty of their children. Parents may be motivated to use their political power in democratic processes to create an educational environment that is hospitable to their own religious commitments. Similarly, parents value schools that complement or at are least compatible with family and community practices (e.g., days of worship, holidays, special celebrations, forms of dress, etc.) that have religious or cultural significance. Yet parental authority to shape the religious identity of children needs to be limited by the right of children to an education conducive to the development of autonomy. Recognition of this right means that parents should acknowledge that exposure to and consideration of diverse views in school is a legitimate part of a democratic education. Even when the majority of parents share a common faith, public education should not be oriented to the transmission or encouragement of religion, no matter how popular. Of course, political efforts to secure a modest place for the Christian God in public schools have been and remain popular in some jurisdictions. But even these efforts generate problems. People of faith have widely divergent views about how faith commitments should be expressed. So it is difficult, even within the Christian community, to find ecumenical forms of worship in schools that all can accept.

Finally, schools play a crucial role in the creation and maintenance of democratic institutions and processes that serve the public interest. In addition to teaching basic literacy and numeracy, schools help "create citizens." Civic education should provide children with an understanding of democratic processes and the rights and responsibilities of citizenship. As with an autonomy-facilitating education, a democratic education develops capacities for thoughtful deliberation and cultivates dispositions that are suitable to contemporary democracy. It is reasonable, for instance, that education convey the importance of citizen participation in democracy and foster a commitment to abiding *legitimate* laws.[17] Similarly, against the background of religious pluralism, children need to learn about and come to appreciate the core values of the equal standing of citizens and toleration for diverse conceptions of the good held by others. Somewhat more ambitiously, democratic education should be oriented toward developing an understanding of public reason and the importance of justification, rather than mere majority power, to democratic legitimacy. Of course, public schools themselves should also manifest the democratic values they espouse. So they must be open to all children, irrespective of their religious affiliation, and should respond to diversity among students in an inclusive and respectful fashion.

Interpreting the Ideal of Democratic Education: Challenges and Controversies

The democratic ideal of inclusive, tolerant public schools in which children from diverse religious backgrounds can learn and interact together on an equal and respectful basis is surely an attractive one. But a fully democratic education can be difficult to achieve for a variety of practical and theoretical reasons. Politically, it is clear that not all citizens approach in good faith the task of devising educational policies that satisfy the demands of public reason. For instance, political efforts aimed at securing a place for Christian prayer in public schools are not a thing of the past, and there is little reason to believe that politically active Christian fundamentalists will be moved by considerations of public reason to temper their demands. Throughout most of its history, American education has fallen well short of fulfilling even modest democratic objectives and has flouted even modest standards of public reason.[18] Publicly endorsed educational policies have been expressly racist, sexist, and homophobic. Moreover, public schools have not been tolerant of non-Christian faiths and have often been used, sometimes subtly and sometimes overtly, in the active promotion of sectarian Christian faiths. Of course, these failures must also be placed in a historical context in which many citizens and local communities have struggled to interpret and give better recognition to the animating principles of American democracy. The importance of freedom of religion gets early recognition in American constitutional history and had a salutary effect on the accommodation of religious pluralism in the context of education.

But beyond these difficult political challenges, there are many theoretical puzzles concerning the interpretation and application of norms of public reason to education. Indeed, some political controversies are reflective of good-faith disagreements about the interpretation of public reason. In the remainder of this chapter, we will present four general challenges to a theory of democratic education that are posed by recognition of and sensitivity to religious diversity and the different interests of children, parents, and the public.

The Scope of Democratic Authority over Education

A democratic state has educational responsibilities to all school-age children in its jurisdiction and not only those whose parents elect to send them to public schools. So to some important degree, a democratic state must identify educational objectives and principles that apply to all schools whether public or private, or religious or nonreligious. Thus the state must ensure that *all* primary and secondary schools provide an education that adequately covers the "basics"—for example, reading, writing, mathematics, history, science, and literature. Similarly, to the degree that homeschooling arrangements are permitted by the state, it is reasonable that the state ensure that core educational objectives are met by parents who choose to homeschool. The idea that democratic authority over education extends in this way to nonpublic forms of education is relatively uncontroversial among theorists.

It is less clear, however, what authority a democratic state has to regulate facets of religious education in nonpublic settings. Whereas public schools must not expressly teach religious doctrines or foster participation of students in religious practices, the very purpose of various forms of nonpublic education is to provide children an education that is expressly devoted to the promotion of specific faiths. Religious parents often seek an education that fosters a lasting commitment to a faith and that requires children to participate in distinctive religious practices. Respect for the kind of religious pluralism that characterizes contemporary American democracy permits parents to provide religious education of various kinds for their children outside the public school system. This means that the democratic state will have limited authority to influence the kind of religious instruction that children receive in religious schools. Thus it is not appropriate for the state to make detailed judgments about what the defining tenets of a given religion are in order to mandate a specific religious curriculum. For the most part, such decisions are appropriately left to parents, religious authorities, and educators within a particular religious community. Indeed, some might hold that the state has no authority whatsoever to influence the content and character of religious education that children receive in nonpublic educational settings.

Nonetheless, the right that children have to an autonomy-facilitating education and the importance of educating children for democratic citizenship suggest that the state may have some authority to regulate the manner in which private religious education is provided. First, recognition of children's right to the development of autonomy suggests that private religious education may not consist in indoctrination that denies children the opportunity to reflectively contemplate different religious and non-religious views and traditions. Even within religious schools, it is reasonable to hope that religious instruction be provided in a way that provides children with skills and opportunities to understand and contemplate a variety of religious and nonreligious views. At some point, this will ideally include affording children information and balanced perspectives about potentially controversial matters, such as human sexuality and gender roles, even if such views conflict with views in a given religious tradition.

Second, religious education needs to be compatible with preparing children to be citizens who are equipped to participate in democratic processes and who appreciate and respect the rights of other citizens. The democratic state need not respect the efforts of religious groups to cultivate attitudes that display disrespect for others on the basis of race, religion, sex, ethnicity, or sexual orientation. There is room for the state to insist that even private religious schools teach a curriculum that acknowledges the equal standing and basic rights of all citizens and that fosters toleration of the diversity in the broader democratic community. Similarly, the state can insist that children in religious schools receive a civic education that not only teaches them about basic constitutional matters and democratic processes but also facilitates their participation in democratic processes as free and equal citizens. From this perspective, private religious education that fosters sexist, racist, or homophobic attitudes is objectionable and does not fall outside the purview of democratic authority. The precise manner in which the democratic state should monitor and regulate the education that children receive in private schools is a delicate political matter. Our point is not to craft educational policy in this potentially controversial domain. Rather, we simply wish to observe that a democratic state can and should discourage religious education that cultivates bigotry and intolerance.[19]

Doctrinal Tensions

The precise boundaries of parental authority with respect to religious education are often controversial because some religious parents view elements of the curriculum of public schools as hostile to or corrosive to the religious convictions they wish to instill in their children. For instance, some conservative Christians who believe in the literal truth of the biblical story of creation view the teaching of the scientifically established theory of evolution as a direct and illegitimate challenge to important facets of their faith. So it is not surprising that some religious groups have sought to remove evolution from the standard public school curriculum or have tried to secure a place within the curriculum for alternatives to evolutionary theory, such as intelligent design, that are congenial to their theological convictions and can be portrayed as scientific. Similarly, many conservative religious groups who hold patriarchal ideals of the family or who view homosexuality as deeply sinful object to educational materials that expressly or implicitly endorse gender equality as a social and political ideal or that provide information about and encourage respect for gay and lesbian sexuality. From the perspective of such religious conservatives, exposing children to such liberal secular views in public education is offensive and wrongly encumbers the rights of religious parents to shape their children's religious identity. Religious parents may wish either to ensure that their doctrines are at least presented as credible alternatives to the secular teachings favored by the state, or they may demand that their children be insulated from exposure to views they find objectionable (e.g., by exemption from parts of the standard school curriculum).

An ideal of democratic education that takes seriously religious diversity must find a way to negotiate the doctrinal conflicts between the secular and the divine about the appropriate content of the core curriculum. However, finding a curriculum that all reasonable citizens can accept is rendered (practically and theoretically) difficult because some religious doctrines reject or come very close to rejecting the basic ideals of the equal standing of citizens, irrespective of race, sex, ethnicity, or sexual orientation, on which the ideal of public reason is predicated. Stated bluntly, some (relatively popular) religious doctrines are unreasonable when evaluated from the perspective of public reason.

Cultivating Religious Toleration

Toleration is a central democratic virtue, but as many theorists have observed, it is a puzzling and even paradoxical virtue: a tolerant person manifests a kind of respectful acceptance of practices or doctrines that she believes are, along some significant dimension, seriously objectionable. The atheist may believe that religion is false and pernicious, but if she is tolerant, she will acknowledge that other reasonable members of the community disagree with her, and will allow both that people of faith are entitled to respect and that it is acceptable for them to voice and give expression to their beliefs. Similarly, she will allow her children to consider religion and the arguments that people of faith make for their view. Toleration involves a willingness to eschew the use of coercive political power to impose one's values on others or to discourage others from adopting values that one views as objectionable or mistaken.

Yet toleration has limits. A democratic community may vigorously promote the adoption of democratic values by its citizens and may prohibit conduct that violates the rights of citizens or conveys contempt for the equal dignity of people in the political community. Toleration is an elusive virtue precisely because the boundary between what is and is not tolerable is often contested by citizens.

As we will see in later chapters, the place of religion in education has historically been the site of many disputes about the requirements of toleration. In the nineteenth century, Protestant religious majorities had, by contemporary standards, a fairly narrow view of the domain of toleration in education. For them, there was little question as to whether schools should have a role in shaping the religious identity of students by promoting a broadly Protestant conception of Christian faith. Protestants were themselves diverse and sought to find ecumenical ways of expressing a common Christian faith in the face of significant doctrinal diversity. So there was recognition of the need to grapple with religious diversity. Of course, many Catholics did not find the Protestant vision of ecumenical religious education congenial to their religious views, and they objected vigorously to educational practices (e.g., the use of the Lord's Prayer in school) that were disrespectful of a Catholic conception of the Christian faith. But while Catholics contested the Protestant understanding of religious toleration, neither they nor the Protestants often saw much reason to extend toleration to non-Christian religions or other minorities. The commitment to a much broader and inclusive conception of toleration in American education is a hard-fought and relatively recent phenomenon.

Today there is general recognition that schools should respect and welcome students with very diverse religious backgrounds. In our view, democratic schools should be sites of religious toleration in two respects. First, they should manifest respect for the diverse religious convictions of students. In part this involves creating an educational environment in which school officials and teachers studiously refrain from advocating or criticizing religious ideals. Since intolerance is often predicated upon and exacerbated by ignorance, the cultivation of toleration requires education about religion. A democratic curriculum should include accurate and balanced education about the commitments, history, and cultural practices of different faith communities. Second, schools have a role to play in cultivating toleration in students and ensuring that relations among students are characterized by toleration. The thought here is that toleration regulates not only relations between school officials and students but also relations among students.

But here we encounter a puzzle: How can toleration be practiced and cultivated when students hold (or are sympathetic to) religious views that preach intolerance? For example, many religious conservatives consider homosexuality sinful and express contempt for gay people. They often believe that discrimination on the basis of sexual orientation is appropriate. Allowing hateful attitudes and beliefs to go unchallenged in schools is harmful to gay students and is antithetical to the ideal of mutual respect at the heart of toleration. Yet when intolerant views are grounded in religious convictions, confronting them seems to require teachers and school authorities to pass judgment on religious doctrines in a way that is in tension with the idea that public schools should scrupulously avoid evaluating the merits of the views of different faiths. Adherents to conservative religious doctrines will view challenges to their views about sexuality as offensive and disrespectful. How can schools help cultivate the democratic virtue of religious toleration while manifesting that virtue to those who are committed to intolerant religious doctrines? Should parents have the authority to exclude their children from parts of the curriculum that foster toleration but that are perceived as hostile to their faith?

Student Religious Observance and Expression

On a democratic conception of education, schools not only prepare students for democratic citizenship; they are also sites for the exercise of citizenship. As such it is unsurprising that many students wish to exercise their rights of free speech and religion to explore and give expression to their own religious convictions. They may wish to engage in private worship during part of the school day, or they may wish to proselytize or to mark and celebrate important religious holidays. Giving students the opportunity to profess their religious convictions in public schools can contribute to a hospitable and inclusive educational environment for children of different faiths. It can also facilitate debate and discussion between students that fosters mutual understanding and respect about different faith traditions and the cultural practices associated with them. All this fits with, and indeed is a natural extension of, the mission of autonomy facilitation we have attributed to schools.

Allowing some room within the public school setting for student-led religious activity is not necessarily inconsistent with nonsectarianism. However, when, as is often the case, a particular religious viewpoint is dominant within a school, allowing students wide latitude to express their religious convictions can threaten the inclusiveness of schools. Cultural and religious majorities often fail to appreciate the extent and nature of their dominance and are sometimes insensitive to the ways minorities are marginalized or alienated by a social environment that reflects the cultural and religious mores of the majority. Erecting a tree and adorning a school with Christmas decorations may seem—to a culturally Christian majority—like a wholly innocent and innocuous cultural celebration. When such activities effectively convey the message that a school has an expressly Christian orientation, however, serious issues of inclusion can arise. Even more serious challenges to inclusion arise if religious students wish to aggressively promote controversial facets of their faith. Some such manifestations of faith demean other faiths or express contempt for sexual minorities. Do the free-speech rights of students protect these kinds of religious expression, or do the requirements of mutual respect and inclusion limit the religious liberty of students in schools?

We do not think that the democratic conception of education we have presented provides straightforward solutions to the foregoing issues or other controversies. Rather, we advance the conception as an invitation to examine the place of religion in education from a democratic perspective in which legitimacy involving mutual justification is taken seriously. We invite readers to consider how a view of public reason animated by the fundamental equality of people should grapple with education in the face of religious pluralism. We have identified some considerations that we believe should inform that project. But these considerations are themselves advanced in the spirit of public reason. We hope that acknowledging the different and distinct interests of children, parents, and the public contributes to the ongoing democratic conversation about religion and education. Our point is not to end the conversation but rather to encourage reflection on what approach to public education can be justified to all reasonable citizens in the face of pluralism.

Reading History Democratically: Looking Back and Looking Forward

In the following chapters, we turn to closer examination of the history of religion within American public schools. Readers may be struck by the distance between the egalitarian conception of democratic education articulated in this chapter and the educational practices of the past. Even judged by crude conceptions of democracy, American political institutions were not initially fully democratic.[20] Moreover, the idea that legitimacy in the domain of education might depend on the willingness of citizens to regulate their political demands through a genuinely inclusive ideal of public reason would be alien to most Americans at most periods in American history. Even today, political discourse is not fully animated by a shared commitment to public reason. Similarly, the suggestion that *all* children—boys and girls of all colors, ethnicity, and religious background—have a right to an education that facilitates autonomy, cultivates civic virtue, and fosters an expansive conception of toleration would not resonate with many generations of Americans.

Much of the history we recount involves highly partisan, and sometimes bitter, political battles between rival groups with little interest in resolving disputes in a fully democratic and respectful fashion. The manner in which modern public schools emerged as fundamental institutions of the American republic does not simply reflect the triumphant realization of democratic principle. On the contrary, the complex and varied place of religion within public schools owes much to the forces of political expediency and compromise.

Nonetheless, at various points in this history we detect sensitivity to democratic values by political actors and some recognition of the need to create educational policies that address religious pluralism in a reasonable and politically legitimate way. During the early Republic, American leaders articulated a strong belief in the responsibility of government for providing mass education to enhance public reason—by inculcating intelligence, virtue, and useful knowledge, and by reducing sectarian bigotry. As Americans developed public schools during the nineteenth century, they created an institution that was highly decentralized and procedurally democratic. Yet despite their relatively high legitimacy for the majority, these schools often reflected undemocratic majoritarianism that mediated diversity in part through informal and formal, voluntary and involuntary segregation across racial, ethnic, and religious lines. They failed to produce a democratic pedagogy for the classroom, gradually resolving religious controversy by removing it from the formal curriculum, substituting symbols of Protestant (or later, Christian) hegemony. In more recent history, even as the assumption that public schools can include generic affirmations of God has fallen in the face of Supreme Court decisions, market-based school reform has opened the door for publicly funded religious schooling. On the other hand, rigorous science curricula in biology and geology, once suppressed by powerful religious interest groups, now flourish across the country.

The idea that the authority of parents over children in religious matters might have limits grounded in the rights of children remains contested today as well. But even here we see indications of acceptance that a democratic education need not accommodate the wishes of religious parents to insulate their children from putatively corrupting influences. By the late twentieth century the idea that children have their own distinctive rights in matters of religion and education became a firmly established principle of American jurisprudence.

Thus while the history of the relationship between religion and democracy in American public education is not a simple story of progress, we do see grounds for optimism that a democratic education is possible in our religiously diverse society. As our title suggests, there always has been strong faith in public education, and some room for religious faith within it. Americans' understanding of the appropriate place of religion in education has responded significantly to the changing diversity of American religious identity. We have some faith that public education can continue to move toward democracy.

TWO

The Founding Fathers, Religion, and Education

Even before a shot was fired, Massachusetts patriot and future president John Adams was talking about a revolution—in education. In one of the first documents of the American Revolution, *A Dissertation on the Canon and the Feudal Law* (1765), Adams accused the British of using the Stamp Act to undermine the education of Americans as a way to enslave them. New Englanders, he argued, had built a system of nearly universal education through town schooling and a free press to protect themselves from the two greatest historical sources of tyranny: feudalism and high-church Christianity—the unhealthy union of church and state epitomized by, but not exclusive to, Roman Catholicism.[1] By the time British and colonial militias were fighting openly, Adams was certain that whatever government resulted from the revolution, it would require a new level of investment in public education. "Laws for the liberal education of youth, especially of the lower class of people, are so extremely wise and useful, that to a humane and generous mind, no expence [*sic*] for this purpose would be thought extravagant," he wrote in April 1776.[2] Adams was exaggerating, but his arguments captured one of the key themes of the American Revolution and constitutional period: an educated citizenry was vital to the success of a republican form of government. Finding the right place for religion within that education, and within the republic itself, was a chief concern of educational theorists.

Americans love to look back to the ideas and actions of

men like Adams in order to understand the original meanings of American laws and institutions. Of course, Adams and his fellow revolutionaries could not foresee today's world and its problems any more than they could agree on how to solve problems of their own time. Nevertheless, there is value in hearing what these men thought about the role of religion in mass education, both because of the importance that so many people today place on their words, and because their ideas help us understand our past on its own terms.

Many of the men popularly referred to as the founding fathers expressed a deep interest in universal education at public expense for the public good. They saw a virtuous, educated populace and enlightened leaders as fundamental to the survival of the American republic. Their ideas about *universal*, of course, usually did not include African Americans, indigenous nations, or women, and thus fell well short of meeting the demands of full democratic legitimacy. These groups had to fight hard to win equal places at the table of American public education. Part of what made these educational ideas revolutionary was their emphasis on political, rather than religious, purposes. We can detect here an early, albeit imperfect, expression of the democratic purpose of education: preparing people for a form of democratic citizenship. In order to understand the significance of this momentous shift, we need to step back and look at the context.

The plans of the founders were shaped, in part at least, by the legacies of the British colonial education of which they were all products. In late-eighteenth-century America there was no such thing as public school in the modern sense. Different regions of the United States had developed distinctive educational traditions, institutions, and ideologies. In New England, the legacy of Puritans' insistence that every person be able to read the Bible, that intellectually pure leaders be trained in America, and that individual congregations run their own affairs, resulted in laws requiring individual parents, apprentice masters, and whole towns to take responsibility for the elementary education of all children. Towns of a minimum size were required to provide schools to teach a basic education, while larger towns had to provide advanced education in Latin grammar schools to prepare boys for college. While not well enforced and sometimes ignored, these regulations reflected a widespread belief that the education of any one child was a community responsibility—a kind of public good. Colonial governments in Massachusetts and Connecticut did not tolerate much religious diversity, and not until the revolutionary period did a significant number of towns allow girls to attend elementary schools.[3] Nevertheless, the underlying traditions of communal responsibility and schooling for salvation led colonial New Englanders to be among the most literate people in the world.[4]

Southern states, by contrast, inherited a colonial tradition of resistance against public regulation or support of education. These patterns reinforced social-class differences. Planters hired tutors and sent their children to England for higher learning. The few middle-class parents in population centers might patronize a private "venture" school or one of a handful of endowed academies. In the countryside, parents might organize an "old field school" on vacant land, or attend a missionary school. Nevertheless, formal education was not available to the typical family, outside of what parents could provide personally. Anglican parish ministers did not usually see educating children as their regular responsibility, nor did legislatures require towns or counties to support community schools. As enslaved people rebelled against the plantation system, southern colonies, and then states, began to regulate who could *not* get an education. The result of these traditions left southerners well behind northerners in terms of literacy and formal schooling, and resulted in a widespread belief that educational and religious matters should be kept in the private sphere; keeping them that way was an expression of liberty.

The Middle Atlantic states mixed the New England and southern traditions to some degree, but also inherited their own patterns of education. The great diversity of religion, language, and nationality of the region led many communities to support their own schools as a form of cultural preservation. Some groups, especially former Anglicans, saw education as a family matter. Presbyterians, Baptists, Catholics, and Jews would support a community school if they had a large enough population. Quakers opened the doors of their schools to all comers—girls as well as boys, Indians and African Americans as well as Anglos.

Given the great diversity of educational institutions and opportunities, the actual content of a basic education at the time of the revolution was surprisingly uniform, at least among English speakers. Children learned to read from primers or hornbooks (a piece of wood with a handle and writing on it, covered with a transparent, plastic-like layer made from animal horn) that included the alphabet, simple letter combinations, alphabet rhymes, and the Lord's Prayer. From there they would work through spellers and perhaps grammars, using catechisms, psalms, and other readings, both sacred and secular.[5]

Children commonly used the Bible for reading practice, it being the only book that many families owned. Noah Webster later recalled, "[I] had, in [my] early years, no other education than that which a common school offered, when rarely a book was used in the schools, except a spelling book, a Psalter, testament or Bible."[6] For many Protestants, especially in New England, reading the Bible was the primary reason for literacy, because it was required for salvation. For others, the ability to read the catechism and sing in church were of greater importance.

A basic education served secular ends as well. The ability to read, write, and do math enabled a person to communicate, transact business, acquire knowledge, enjoy a growing body of entertaining literature, and participate in the intellectual life of the colony. Reading, 'riting, and 'rithmetic, the joke went, were the three R's of a common education. Advanced education by tutors, in private academies, in Latin grammar schools, and in colleges prepared young men for positions in business, politics, professions, and the clergy. With very few exceptions, schooling and advanced education were closed to girls until the early nineteenth century.[7]

Native Americans and enslaved African Americans lived on the margins of European-American colonial society. Native American societies traditionally educated their children without institutions. Instead they relied on formal and informal interactions among extended family and community members, ceremonies, and oral tradition. Religious belief did not have the same hierarchical or political significance that it did among Europeans, and so was not a contested aspect of education. A small percentage of Native Americans embraced Christianity, but usually integrated that belief into their existing cultural systems. African Americans later sought formal education whenever possible, especially as the Plantation South withheld it as an expression of dominance. Free African Americans could acquire an education in middle and northeastern colonies, though they might face local white resistance. By the end of the eighteenth century, moreover, some African Americans had developed a form of Christianity focused on political education and liberation theology.

Religion and the Revolution

Taken in a global context, the American Revolution was a shockingly secular event. The Declaration of Independence, which carefully spells out the reasons for the American Revolution, says nothing about Christian principles or creeds, while the idea that a "Creator" had endowed all people with natural political rights contradicted the doctrines of the Roman Catholic Church. When the revolutionaries sat down and formed a lasting government in 1789, they wrote and ratified a constitution that makes no mention of religious principles (Article VI forbids religious tests), while the Bill of Rights mentions religion only in the negative—as something the federal government can neither establish nor regulate. When the federal and state governments redrew their official seals after the revolution, they used icons from the ancient, pagan world more often than they used symbols from the Bible.[8]

The secular orientation of the revolution reflected a broader reality. Church membership was very low by today's standards, and American religion tended to follow politics, not lead it. No more than 20 percent of American adults were church members in 1790, for example. That number did not reach 50 percent until the early twentieth century, peaking at 65 percent in the 1950s. As historian Gordon Wood observes, the disintegration of traditional forms of church organization and membership in the period did not mean that many Americans had no religious beliefs. They could be both strongly anticlerical and strongly faithful. Certainly organized religion played an important role in how many Americans understood the events of their day, as did belief in magic and supernatural forces. Preachers on both sides of the revolution used the pulpit as an opportunity to fuse religion and revolution or counterrevolution. Nevertheless, the main ideas that guided the revolution, and the claims that it made, reflected Enlightenment political theories, not Christian principles.[9]

In addition to Enlightenment influence, American leaders developed their unique system of secular government because of two mutually reinforcing factors. On one hand, during the colonial period, religious and state authority was relatively weak. On the other hand, the colonies hosted such a vast diversity of groups and individuals that no single, unifying religious creed was possible. The First Amendment prevented the federal government from establishing a national religion, but did not prohibit states from doing so. At the time of the revolution, the Anglican Church was the established church of southern states, while New England states (except Rhode Island) had a form of multiple establishment, whereby a town's minister (usually a member of the Congregational Church) was elected democratically. The Middle Atlantic states of Delaware, New Jersey, Pennsylvania, and (most of) New York, as well as Rhode Island, had no establishment at all. By the end of the revolutionary and constitution-making period, southern states had abandoned establishment. The practice survived only in New England, where it was finally abandoned by the last holdout, Massachusetts, in 1833.[10]

If one were to make the argument that the United States was a Christian nation based on cultural grounds—that most European Americans were Christian and so America was a Christian nation—here again, we are imposing a contemporary idea of a Christian nation upon the past. The vast majority of European Americans in the United States were culturally, if not officially, Protestant. At the local and state level, Protestant majorities worried about whether Catholics could be trusted as full American citizens, and the Roman Catholic Church's traditional hostility toward Protestants and the Enlightenment did not do American Catholics any favors. Most Protestant writers, looking at the long history of church and state in Europe, associated the Catholic Church with political repression, just as John Adams did. We could say the United States was a nation founded through compromise among Protestants, guided by Enlightenment principles, resulting in a secular form of government. Claiming more is wishful thinking.

So from the outset of the republic, we see a form of reasonable pluralism forming the backdrop for democratic politics. The compromises between religious groups that permitted a secular form of government to emerge reflected a nascent concern with democratic legitimacy. Since not all groups were given equal voice in the crafting of compromise, the political dialogue was not fully inclusive and hence not fully democratic. Nonetheless, many diverse religious groups found it possible and even attractive to endorse a polity without a sectarian religious character.

The Founders' Ideas about Religion and Public Education

While these debates over religion in federal and state constitutions were not directly about education, they point to the ways in which people understood the place of religion within the American political sphere. The relationship generally reflected a belief—articulated by John Locke and echoed in the writings of Madison and Jefferson, among others—that there were separate public and private spheres, with religious practices and beliefs properly cabined in the latter.[11] Thus religion appeared in cultural forms through the symbolic actions of leaders (swearing oaths on Bibles, for example, or declaring days of prayer and fasting), but not in the design or purposes of government. Governments, on the other hand, often encouraged the religiosity of the people at the local level in the process of settlement. Setting aside land to support a local church was, in Massachusetts, Connecticut, and New Hampshire, a key feature of settlement patterns and state law. Such policies looked to religious ideas as providing public cohesion. Over the course of the nineteenth century, common schools would follow that same pattern—seeking to promote secular ends, using religion to the degree that was politically viable in a diverse society.

The founding fathers disagreed among themselves on the precise role of religion in public education. Some wondered whether the promotion of political goals—a stable society, a virtuous citizenry—might require the assistance of religion. Others saw religion as too divisive, too anti-republican, or too unintelligent. But what they all agreed on was that the civic purposes of education were more important than the religious ones and, as a result, that the latter should serve the former. Moreover, nearly every major writer on the question of mass public education saw government control, nonsectarian moral instruction, and education for enhancing public reason as central features. The devil was in the details.

For John Adams, the New England district school should be a model for the nation, though it should be expanded to reach more people, especially the poor. Adams had a deep faith in the Christian God, espousing an enlightened Christianity that, especially later in life, bordered on deism. He believed that education in "Literature and Morals" could make good citizens by sharpening their intellects and restraining their passions.[12] And he believed fully in the humanist tradition: that it was up to people to make the best of the world around them, including their government. Education should enable men to build their society according to reason. Belief in true religion could help, but when it came to government, God did not play favorites.[13]

Of course, Adams had a long list of what did not qualify as true religion. He feared the Anglican and Roman Catholic churches and saw their teachings as synonymous with superstition and political tyranny. Nor was he a friend of later movements in evangelical Protestantism, religious enthusiasm, and the growth of missionary societies. He found belief in the literal truth of the Bible to be ignorant and dangerous. "Wisdom, and knowledge, as well as virtue, diffused generally among the body of the people," he wrote into the Massachusetts State Constitution, were "necessary for the preservation of their rights and liberties."[14] In modern terms, he had a limited conception of reasonable pluralism.

Connecticut patriot Noah Webster also advocated a New England–style system of district schools for the new nation. In the 1780s, Webster demanded the equal distribution of property, the strict separation of church and state (stemming from a deep suspicion of the clergy), complete religious toleration, and the abolition of slavery. Webster shared with Adams a belief in a Christian God but skepticism toward organized religion.[15] During the 1780s and 1790s, the revolutionary Webster published numerous essays and newspaper articles advocating education for all American children—even, to some extent, girls.[16] The purpose of universal education shifted over time in his writing, but in 1788 he said it was the "diffusion of knowledge."[17] The federal government, he hoped, would organize a system of district schools, overseen by lay trustees, staffed with competent schoolmasters. These schools should teach children to love their country, to speak and write in a common form of English, to share a common history, and to read a common canon of popular literature.

Webster's most significant contribution, however, was publishing school materials. Thanks to his aggressive marketing, innovative pedagogy, and nationalistic tone, Webster's spelling book became the best-selling book in the nineteenth century, next to the Bible, and became the standard work of its kind in most American schools. He wrote other books as well, including revisions of the ubiquitous *New England Primer*, the first ABC book most American children encountered in the colonial and early national periods.[18] Webster advocated teaching morals to children, and he strongly supported raising children with religious beliefs. But he downplayed the role for religious instruction in public schools. Webster's speller, for example, stood out in its lack of explicit references to God. Webster's *Reader* offered children a collection of secular works as an alternative to sacred ones. Even his revised *New England Primer*, designed for young Abcdarians, replaced religious references with fun, familiar ones. For example, traditional editions began with

A. In Adams Fall
   We sinned all.
B. Thy Life to Mend
   This *Book* Attend. [including a drawing of a Bible]

Webster's version read:

A. Was an Apple-pie made by the cook.
B. Was a Boy that was fond of his book.[19]

Webster explained that frequent references to God cheapened religion and taught children (and teachers) to treat their faith casually. He also opposed the practice of reading the Bible regularly in schools. Instead, Webster viewed moral instruction, based on broadly Protestant moral values, with very occasional use of the Bible for specific reasons, as the ideal for a common education.[20]

Philadelphia physician, patriot, and essayist Benjamin Rush offered a different approach. Among founding fathers, Rush proved to be the strongest advocate for religious education within a universal, tax-supported system. A native of the most multicultural and religiously diverse colony,

Rush wanted to give public money directly to each religious sect to run its own charity schools for the poor—even to offer instruction in languages other than English. (These schools would be inspected by lay trustees.) Rush wanted, simultaneously, a school curriculum based on the model of ancient Sparta, where all children learned to have a common civic identity. Rush argued that schools should teach children to be "republican machines," who loved their country more than they loved their own families. "Let our pupil be taught that he does not belong to himself, but that he is public property," he wrote. Whether citizens should love the specific religious group that educated them more than their country he did not say.[21] But he viewed religion as a higher power than Enlightenment science, and he feared the secular orientation of the revolution. Rush believed that a "moral faculty," installed by God and nurtured by religion, was the source of man's goodness and the foundation of civilized society.

Contrary to most revolutionary thinkers, who saw religious sectarianism as a source of bigotry, Rush wrote, "I believe [sectarianism] prevents [bigotry] by removing young men from those opportunities of controversy which a variety of sects mixed together are apt to create." More importantly, religion was "necessary to correct the effects of learning," he reasoned. "Without religion I believe learning does real mischief to the morals and principles of mankind."[22] Naturally Rush disagreed with Webster about limiting Bible reading in public schools.[23] And true to his conservative outlook, Rush preferred to limit the education of the masses to the basics, lest they ask questions that undermined the stability of society.[24]

Virginians James Madison and Thomas Jefferson saw Rush's nightmare as their guiding principle. Let men rise in learning as far as they could, they urged, guided by talent and reason, uninhibited by religious superstition or authoritarianism. Both men were products of Virginia's plantation society, where many people considered religion and education to be private matters, and where the state legislature pioneered disestablishment and religious toleration—even for non-Christians. Both men cherished limited government and individual liberty. But by the same token, both argued that the people must have sufficient virtue to govern themselves. They advocated widely accessible, publicly supported primary education along the lines of the New England model, but without the religious orientation.

Jefferson devised a plan. Like Adams, he saw the connection between education and revolution early, proposing in 1778 a "Bill for the More General Diffusion of Knowledge" to the Virginia legislature. In this plan, each county would divide into "hundreds," or districts, which would support a tuition-free school open to all free children, girls as well as boys. (For its time, this was a remarkably inclusive plan but not fully universal. It could not be justified to those excluded and hence was not fully legitimate.) The curriculum would include the three R's and history. From these primary schools, the top boys would be selected to go on to academies on scholarship. The top academy boys would go to college for free. In this way, a natural aristocracy, based on merit, would rise to take leadership roles in society.

Jefferson's plan made no place for religion. Nevertheless, he hoped to instill basic morality in all students:

Instead therefore of putting the Bible and Testament into the hands of the children, at an age when their judgments are not sufficiently matured for religious enquiries, their memories may here be stored with the most useful facts from Grecian, Roman, European and American history. The first elements of morality too may be instilled into their minds; such as, when further developed as their judgments advance in strength, may teach them how to work out their own greatest happiness.[25]

For Jefferson, religious education represented a threat more than an opportunity.

Jefferson's opinion reflected his lifelong crusade against religious superstition and orthodoxy, and his belief that freedom of religion was the "most inalienable and sacred of all human rights."[26] Jefferson believed in the god of nature, the deist god, and spent a considerable part of his intellectual energies applying rational analysis to Christianity. He rejected the divinity of Christ and miracles, and criticized the idea that Christians must follow one specific set of rules. "Millions of innocent men, women and children, since the introduction of Christianity, have been burnt, tortured, fined, imprisoned," he wrote. "What has been the effect of coercion? To make one half the world fools, and the other half hypocrites."[27] For Jefferson, reason and evidence, not emotional enthusiasm and belief in magic, could lead man to a true understanding of God.

James Madison, who followed Jefferson into two terms in the White House, did not write nearly as much as Jefferson about the subjects of education and religion. But Madison was a lifelong supporter of Jefferson's efforts in Virginia and advocated state and federal involvement in education. In 1822 he advised the lieutenant governor of Kentucky on the creation of a system of common schools, including a detailed curriculum that had no reference to religion. In 1823 he advised Harvard's Edward Everett against creating college professorships for ministers of specific religious sects. While there was no problem establishing religion in a university per se, he wrote, allowing one meant allowing them all, lest there be a

"Sectarian Monopoly." A one-size-fits-all solution would not work either, because even something as simple as finding a prayer that all students can say in common would fail, because "many sects reject all set forms of Worship." In other words, there is not sufficient common ground to satisfy everyone.[28] Robert Coram, a rising star in Delaware politics, imagined a plan similar (if even more explicitly secular) to that of the Virginians before his untimely death in 1795.[29]

The problem of devising the ideal system of public education for the new republic was not lost on the American Philosophical Society, either. As the nation's premier learned society (founded by Benjamin Franklin and patronized by America's and western Europe's leading thinkers), it offered a cash prize of $100 for the best essay on a system of public education suited to the "genius" of the new nation. The seven entries the society received reflected the broader intellectual consensus on the relationship between religion and public education. Of the seven, not a single one assigned religious groups a role in the management of public education, and five implicitly rejected the idea by creating district systems under secular, public control. Two explained why. Religious groups, they argued, encouraged bigotry and superstition, both of which undermined public reason. Similarly, no author proposed a curriculum that included the tenets of a particular religion or use of the Bible. Five of the seven proposed a nonsectarian system of moral instruction, such as a "Catechism or Treatise on universal morality," or periodic visiting lectures by "moral-politic missionaries from the colleges." Some used the word "religion" in their descriptions of moral instruction; others did not.[30]

The Limitations and Legacy of the Founders' Ideas

Despite their differences, none of these early republican writers limited their educational plans to schooling. Formal education, in their day, was a scarce commodity in many regions of the United States; furthermore, school was hardly the ideal place for learning. The writer who was most influential for their generation, John Locke, had argued that home, not school, was the best place to shape a child's mind. Part of the revolutionary aspect of the founders' plans for education was that they claimed a place for schooling as the universal educational institution, and as integral to the project of democracy.

In the short run, however, Americans did not revolutionize their education—at least, not in the ways that the founders hoped. Webster, Rush, the Virginians, and the essayists of the American Philosophical Society contest did not live to see their elaborate plans for public education succeed. Historians generally explain these failures in practical terms: supplying mass public education was prohibitively expensive, while there was not much demand for expansion of schooling for political purposes in an agrarian society that cherished low taxes and disliked government. Not until the market revolution and universal white male suffrage transformed American society did a consensus emerge on the desirability of mass public education.

In addition, a theoretical flaw in these plans explains their lack of popular appeal and highlights their limitations as models for democratic education. American educational writings from the 1780s and 1790s reflect an understanding of political legitimacy rooted almost entirely in substance. What made public education legitimate was the degree to which its design, content, and outcomes comported with republican theory. Uniformity was crucial. All students should study the same curriculum, which perfectly contained their competing needs within an ideal political conception. The bureaucratic design of schools, too, balanced the local, the state, and the national not because local voices or variation mattered per se, but because local officials were necessary for the finance and administration of the uniform system. Religious officials, on the other hand, were inappropriate custodians of republican education because of their prejudices.

Just as they did when designing federal and state constitutions, late-eighteenth-century educational theorists applied a Newtonian view of the universe (which for many extended to a deist view of faith) to educational design. Government and education were scientific matters, to be perfected as a clockmaker might make a fine watch. In a slave republic where most people could not vote, the people's interests were to be represented by enlightened men of property. In such a system the people needed a basic formal education, and they needed a political process to some extent to run and fund the local schools. The founding generation understood the ways in which governmental frameworks could enhance the legitimacy of government, honoring the social contract between the government and the governed.

But in educational practice the founders did not grasp the school as a place where diversity was a valued asset. Common people did not need a strong voice in contributing to the content of educational systems that were designed for them by their intellectual betters. The purpose of public schooling was to disseminate the most useful knowledge and skills, not to construct communal meaning on site. In other words, the founding fathers offered no pedagogical conception of democratic education. Benjamin Rush alone conceived of religious diversity as having a positive role in republican education, though he could not work out theories or mechanisms for connecting it to the homogenizing purposes he also valued.

In practice the founding generation did not have to deal with the problem of democratic education in the context of religious diversity. That would happen in a later generation, when democracy, religious enthusiasm, and the market revolution broke upon American society and politics with full force. Nevertheless, the founders left two significant legacies for future generations. The first were federal and state constitutional frameworks that protected religious minorities and separated the spheres of church and state sufficiently to allow for diverse citizens to claim full civil status. Combined with early republican statutory law, these constitutions declared that the encouragement of an educated public was a central concern of the state.[31]

The founders also left a rich body of theoretical writing that laid out arguments for understanding the relationship between the separation of church and state and the purposes of public education. They expressed an awareness of the need to grapple with religious diversity in the context of education, along with the possibility of orienting education to the cultivation of civic virtue. They recognized that public education should be accessible to people of all faiths, even if they did so imperfectly. And strikingly, they articulated the manner in which religious sectarianism could be politically corrosive, alongside a recognition that banishment of all traces of religion from education is fraught with difficulties. Religion had a place in their conceptions of public education, but the appropriate character of that place was the subject of reasoned contestation. This kind of discourse about religion, education, and democracy was not, of course, expressly animated by a doctrine of public reason and the objective of devising a democratic education acceptable to all. Yet the debates and discussion of the founding generation gave at least partial expression to the idea that political legitimacy in the domain of education depends on the reason giving and reason taking among people with dramatically different views about religion.

THREE

Religion and the Origins of Public Education

In 1875 an English visitor named Francis Adams published a study of America's "free school system." Like many foreign observers, Adams was struck by the contrast between the mature structures and institutions of European society and the scrappy chaos of America—a nation he described as still being in its infancy. Within the general disorder, however, Adams saw one institution emerging as the central organizing feature of American civic life. "That which impresses us most in regard to America is the grasp which the schools have upon the sympathy and intelligence of the people," he wrote. Indeed, Americans viewed their public schools with pride often reserved for monuments and other tourist attractions.

[The public schools] of the cities are the lions of America. The intelligent foreigner, and also, as it would appear from some recent criticisms, the unintelligent foreigner who visits the States, into whatever town he goes, is taken to the schools as the first objects of interest. Amongst public questions education occupies the foremost place, and of all topics it is that upon which the American speaker is most ready and most willing to enlarge.[1]

This popularity he attributed to two features we would today associate with democratic legitimacy: "government by the people, and ownership by the people." While he conceded that not all Americans were equally proud of their schools, nevertheless he observed that "it is also certain that their

existence immensely stimulates public interest and diffuses a sense of responsibility through the entire community."[2]

In fact, Adams was stepping into the developmental arc of American educational history not in its infancy, but in its adolescence. Over the course
of the nineteenth century, the United States grew from a sparsely popu-
lated, sparely governed federation of former British colonies to a modern,
multicultural, industrial nation-state. As they did all over the Western
world, public schools emerged in this process as the key social institution
to support the many demands of this new kind of state—providing social
stability, nationalism, workforce training, and babysitting, to name a few
functions.[3] The tension between religious pluralism and democracy stood
at the center of this formative process, raising difficult questions. Why
have schools at public expense in public buildings (as opposed to private
expense in churches), and what ends should such schools serve? Could
all people educate their children in common despite their religious differences, or should every group have their own publicly financed schools?
What kind of content, if any, was appropriate for all children to learn? In
an era of unprecedented political democracy for white men, the answers
to these questions laid the foundation for the unique system the United
States has today.

American public education emerged in two phases. The first phase,
known as the common school movement, saw the rise of publicly supported, democratically controlled, nonsectarian schools to which all
(white) children in a given community could go, either at a reduced cost
or, eventually, for free. These schools emerged in state after state outside
of most of the South and became, by the eve of the Civil War, a ubiquitous feature of northern small-town American life and a reform model for
city systems. Political leaders framed the purposes of these institutions in
terms of making virtuous, industrious, and intelligent citizens. The second
phase of development, from the Civil War to the end of the century, saw
these schools spread to the entire nation and to all populations within it,
becoming a national and comprehensive network of locally controlled institutions enrolling 70 percent of all children aged five to seventeen, with
nonpublic schools enrolling only 8 percent.[4] The word "public" replaced
the word "common" to reflect their more national, and nationalist, scope.
As the market revolution spread unevenly across the country during this
period, the publicly stated reasons for supporting public schools became
increasingly complex: alongside the emphasis on virtuous and reasoned
political behavior came more explicit references to the development of a
more skilled workforce, more patriotic immigrants, and the promotion of
personal economic opportunity through academic merit (for whites) and

political submission and physical and psychological acclimation to racial caste (for blacks).[5]

Common Schools

Common schools were a highly popular response to rapidly changing times. In the half century after the ratification of the US Constitution, Americans experienced three more revolutions—in politics, economics, and religion. The political revolution stretched from the 1790s to around 1840, as individual states reduced and then dropped requirements that voters own a certain amount of property, or that they be taxpayers, in order to vote.[6] It was part of a trend on both sides of the Atlantic, whereby colonies revolted and advocates of republican and democratic forms of government challenged feudal traditions of church and state. By the late 1830s, the United States as a whole had achieved nearly universal white male suffrage, which renewed the founding generation's anxieties about the education level of the citizenry. Paradoxically, while they increased suffrage, state legislatures tightened restrictions on free African Americans and women in the political sphere, and tried (where it applied) to remove Native Americans altogether.

The same loosening of authority that pushed white Americans to seize control of their government enabled an explosion in religious enthusiasm, expansion, and experimentation known as the Second Great Awakening. This movement rejected traditional, stern Calvinistic Protestantism in favor of a more positive Christianity. Leading Protestant ministers organized revivals and emphasized God's grace, self-improvement, and social activism. Charismatic preachers conducted vast outdoor meetings, some lasting for days and numbering thousands of participants, where audience members shouted, had fits and convulsions, or fell into trances. Across the country new religions and utopian societies sprouted like mushrooms, enjoying a freedom of religious expression and organization unrivaled in Europe. Better adapted to the decentralized and democratic dynamics of a changing American society, Methodists and Baptists overtook Congregationalists, Presbyterians, and Episcopalians as America's largest denominations. Overall, church membership grew to approximately 30–40 percent of adults by the 1840s, and would continue to rise.[7]

Protestant revivalism and white (imperfect) democracy encouraged social reform and, for many Americans, linked American identity to religion as never before. Although Protestant denominations sometimes disagreed bitterly, and some state governments favored some groups over others, most Protestants found occasion to work together for the public good. Evangelical Protestants organized Sunday schools, charity schools, orphan asylums, temperance leagues, poorhouses, prisons, and missionary societies. And they were a driving force behind the movement for free, common schooling.

The perceived *need* for social reform reflected a third revolution, in economic behavior. The market revolution of the early nineteenth century had no one single cause or effect, but was characterized by increasingly powerful cycles of boom and bust; the growth of large cities and small towns; more efficient, impersonal, and extensive trade and transportation networks; the development of manufacturing; a shift away from barter toward cash, from work at home to wage labor elsewhere; and a constant movement of people. (In frontier towns, for example, less than half the population of a given year would still live there a decade later.)[8] Cities attracted levels of poverty and crime formerly unknown, and not well understood.

Within the emotional and social ferment of the early nineteenth century, demand for universal schooling increased. Americans outside of the South (and even some in it) developed a consensus that a common education for all whites—not only commonly accessible, but *in common*—was necessary for the common good, and that public support on some level should be extended to encourage the education of all citizens.[9] Common schools could provide the social capital lost in the shift to the fast-paced market economy, building a broad-based system of common knowledge and moral standards.[10] Common schools also provided a sorting mechanism whereby school achievement, understood as merit, could certify students for future positions in the middle class.[11] Workingmen's organizations generally favored free public elementary education for all children, emphasizing the shame that parents and children felt in accepting charity schooling. "Our main objective is to secure the benefits of education for those who would otherwise be destitute, and to place them mentally on a level with the most favored in the world's gifts," a Pennsylvania group explained in 1830. "As poverty is a not a crime, neither is wealth a virtue."[12]

At the start of the common school movement, Americans did not have the same sharp distinctions between public and private education that they do today. Subscription schools, church-run schools, charity-society schools, academies, seminaries, and colleges, few of them strictly public or private, enjoyed government support and a quasi-public status throughout the country. The Sunday school movement, for example, arrived from England during the 1780s and 1790s in Virginia and South Carolina, and quickly spread nationwide. These schools provided weekly, day-long secular instruction in the three R's under the auspices of churches. Likewise, cities saw the rise of church-run poor schools, mono- and pan-denominational charity schools, and schools run by mission societies— all of which performed a public function of educating children and often enjoyed a share of public funding.

Nevertheless, with the spread of the market revolution, suffrage, and religious revivalism, Americans increasingly chose to organize responsibility for financing and regulating elementary schooling away from the church and private spheres to the local, public one. Private subscription schools for children were not reliably available through economic cycles of boom and bust. Outside of long-settled areas, churches could not keep pace with westward settlement and evangelical enthusiasm, never mind provide education for the mass of Americans. Communities chose to organize school districts, build public school buildings, and hire teachers in common. Over time, states encouraged and then joined this effort, increasingly supporting and regulating the process. Whether they were the old New England district schools now under secular control, or private subscription schools that elected to join a public system of finance and oversight, or common schools from the get-go, nearly all such schools shared a basic blueprint—one well suited to the age of American democracy. They were administered by locally elected committees or trustees, supported at least in part through local property tax combined with some form of state funding. Early in the century they charged tuition, or were free only until state funds ran out.[13]

From the late 1830s through the 1850s, the movement picked up steam, inspiring the improvement of existing district schools and the creation of new ones across the North and Midwest, and even into parts of the South (especially North Carolina). Movement leaders hoped to spread and expand the district school model by making it universally available, longer in duration, and higher in quality.

These reformers were often evangelical Protestants, though the movement included others, including some Catholics. Common school crusaders sought, and usually won, legislation making district schools free of tuition, open to all (white) students, more strictly regulated by the state, and more strictly nonsectarian in their curriculum. The transition from a private or charity model to a district school to common school happened unevenly but inexorably, serving as the simplest way to ensure consistent, universal education at low cost in a rural nation with varying degrees of religious diversity.

The purposes of these schools were many and complex. They kept children out of the house and out of trouble. They taught skills that were useful in the increasingly impersonal and industrial marketplace—delayed gratification, obedience to strangers, patience with mundane tasks, even punctuality. They inculcated republican political values and patriotism, and offered children access to cosmopolitan culture in a local setting. Most of all, according to their promoters, these schools taught children to be good people. In the first half of the nineteenth century, that meant religion, but in the most general sense. The success of the common school movement can be attributed in part to the ability of school leaders and textbook authors to develop a civic ethos that claimed to be religious but nonsectarian, acknowledging God's authority but favoring no particular religious body.

The most famous spokesman for common schools, Horace Mann, fused the economic, social, political, and religious anxieties of the age into a coherent faith in the power of free public schools for personal and social transformation. Improving them, he argued, was the greatest reform work of the age. Common schools were to be the engine that enabled republican democracy to function properly. "And until all this work of improvement is done," he warned in 1842, "until [the] indifference of the wealthy and the educated towards the masses shall cease . . . there can be no security for any class or description of men, nor for any interest, human or divine." Indeed, Mann warned with characteristic hyperbole, the founding fathers themselves were watching school reform work from beyond the grave. Should the common schools fail, the country would fall into such degenerate chaos that even if George Washington himself "should arise, and from the battlements of the capitol, should utter a warning voice, the mad populace would hurl him from the Tarpeian."[14]

By today's standards, the pedagogy of these schools was crude. Common school promoters hailed the democratic power of bringing children of all classes and faiths together into one classroom. But while providing a school common to all children in a district was certainly a step toward building a democratic community, the pedagogy of these schools was not designed to foster mutual understanding or a process for determining public reasonableness. Children sat in rows, on benches or at desks, quietly read from textbooks (if they could read), and intellectually ingested information by rote. When the time came, the teacher would call them to the front of the room to recite answers to questions written in the book. Children learned to read from basic primers, or hornbooks, and to write on handheld slates. Children of all ages learned together (from different textbooks), and the teacher's job was to hear recitations, keep order, and keep children on task. School terms were short, attendance sporadic, and the quality of the untrained teaching force ranged from decent to abysmal. By the 1830s, district schools were usually coeducational, and the teacher, especially in the Northeast, was increasingly female.

What these schools did provide for American democracy, however, was to train a literate, numerate white populace exposed to a common literary culture. Textbooks determined most of the curriculum. By the common school era, textbooks replaced the Bible as a main tool for learning the first R, reading. Webster's *Blue Back Speller* was the best-selling book of its kind, while books called "readers" assembled a wide and eclectic variety of texts—excerpts from classic and contemporary authors in fiction, poetry, political writing, and pithy sayings. Teachers could choose what children read, though taken in the whole, the authors' selections promoted American nationalism with a strongly Protestant, occasionally explicitly anti-Catholic, viewpoint. Due to a number of factors—the need to reach the largest possible markets, the desire to avoid controversy, and the shift to widespread belief in nonsectarian Protestant republicanism—textbooks did not usually advance a particular religious denomination among Protestants, and over the course of the nineteenth century would become increasingly neutral toward all faiths, including Catholics (and by the end of the century, not religious at all). Nevertheless, common school promoters such as Horace Mann argued that some religious truths were shared by all faiths and that these could be taught and celebrated in an ecumenical, civic spirit. Mann's greatest foes were outspoken orthodox Protestant ministers and traditionalist schoolmasters, although he also counted many of the same among his allies.[15] For non-Protestants, or for those Protestants who objected to this nonsectarian mission, what they saw as a Unitarian heresy, the Pan-Protestant approach could be biased indeed.[16]

Aside from the religious tone of textbooks, explicitly religious education within common schools occurred in three ways, each on the edges of the school day, but all of emotional significance to many parents and children: reading brief portions of the Bible as a whole-school, reverential activity; reciting a prayer in unison or hearing a teacher-led prayer; and singing religious songs. All three types of exercises became controversial when schooling became a formally "public" enterprise supported by tax and open by law to all faiths.

We do not have good statistics for national trends until much later periods. Initially in New York and Massachusetts, the move to officially common schools led to a sharp decrease in Bible use. From 1830 to 1840, the number of towns in New York State reporting that their districts used the Bible plummeted—from a high of 28 percent of all towns in 1829 to a low of 10 percent in 1839. Historians debate whether these statistics indicate a decrease in *any* use of the Bible (as opposed to Bible use as a textbook), but either way, the Bible's place within the curriculum decreased rapidly because of the individual decisions at the local level.[17] Horace Mann noted a similar decline in Massachusetts during that same period, before he took the helm of Massachusetts common schools in 1837.[18] Bible use as a textbook decreased at least in part because of the profusion of actual textbooks, which were more pedagogically appropriate and less controversial (at least among Protestants). We do not have data on school prayer or on singing for the early nineteenth century, though anecdotal evidence suggests the former was more common than the latter, and neither was as common as using the Bible. Religion also took on special meaning in school when local groups used the school building after hours and on weekends for religious purposes—a common practice in communities where the school building was the only meeting space.

Many leaders promoted the common school as God's work, saw America as a kind of Protestant utopia, and advocated what they saw as a generous religious compromise suited to Protestants, Catholics, and Jews alike: using their Bible in a nonsectarian way, by reading a portion of it without note or comment. What they did not realize, or chose to ignore, was that their Bible was a Protestant Bible, and that for others—such as Jews and nonbelievers—the Bible could be a symbol of majoritarian oppression. For the small but growing Roman Catholic population, Catholic Church leaders insisted that the note and comment from an ordained priest were the whole point of Bible reading. On the other hand, we should not assume that symbolic exercises at the start of the school day necessarily made a deep impression or that all parents cared. Enthusiasts reported that Bible reading without comment was popular, and some states began to require it by law. But just how widespread the Bible-reading reform was we cannot know until national surveys conducted decades later.[19]

In practice, common schools answered to the needs of the local community while they conferred a generalizable form of capital: a common school education. Some communities were fairly homogeneous in terms of culture and religion. In cities and in the country, people often settled in groups. A common school in a German settlement might use German-language instruction; a Presbyterian village might make their minister a trustee; a Roman Catholic neighborhood might have nuns or priests teach the class, or in rare cases hold school within a church building. In Massachusetts some Calvinist ministers resisted the trend toward nonsectarian teaching in their district schools, while other district leaders removed Bible reading altogether. Using a textbook, such as McGuffey's *Eclectic Reader*, a sensitive teacher might instruct children to skip offensive or controversial passages. An insensitive one, on the other hand, might embarrass a child by forcing the issue. Common schools had plenty of both. And of course, we should also remember that the majority of Americans belonged to no church, and/or were culturally Protestant, Catholic, or otherwise without necessarily endorsing the agenda of religious leaders. Over time states developed laws determining what crossed the line between what was reasonably "common" belief and what was "sectarian." Usually these focused on the question of whether the activity included commentary and interpretation on the part of the teacher and, less frequently, whether it was coercive.

As a result of their organizational features and universalistic purposes, common schools enjoyed high political legitimacy in the eyes of the majority. But this legitimacy to the majority of participants made it all the more difficult for them to understand the ways in which these schools could be illegitimate for others. Relying on self-segregated ethnoreligious communities to diffuse some of this tension still begged the question of how individual schools could be sites of democracy building in the face of pluralism. While the common school had a variety of detractors, challenges by the Roman Catholic Church in particular forced a public debate over what the reasonable place for religion should be in a republican education.

The Catholic Challenge and Nativist Response

During the 1840s and 1850s, over a million Catholics immigrated to the United States to escape famine in Ireland and political and religious upheaval in continental Europe. There had been Catholics in North America before there were Protestants, of course, and even within the thirteen colonies there was a tiny Catholic population, especially in Maryland and in cosmopolitan urban centers like Philadelphia and New York. For centuries, rivalries and warfare between Protestant British colonies and the Catholic empires of Spain and France played a major role in the political history of colonial America. As a result, many Americans harbored deep suspicions about the political allegiance of Catholics to the United States, not to mention grievances dating back to European religious wars of the sixteenth century.

By the early nineteenth century, the Roman Catholic Church remained the world's largest, richest, and most powerful organization. Politically, the church fought hard against the Enlightenment, increasingly opposed republican reforms that were taking place in Europe, and opposed the most basic principles of the American Revolution and the US Constitution: free speech, freedom of religion, and the separation of church and state. Where the church did have direct political power in Europe, in the Papal States, popes ruled absolutely, and legally recognized only two religions: Roman Catholicism and Judaism. The Catholic Church segregated Jews into ghettos by law. Not surprisingly, Americans who cherished the country's unique traditions of democracy were deeply offended by the politics of the Roman Catholic Church and alarmed at its rising presence in America. Combined with xenophobia and worries over immigrants taking jobs, this fear became so irrational and frenzied that it led to riots and attacks on Catholics and Catholic institutions.

For their part, newly arrived American Catholics had to negotiate the tension between their faith and the freedoms and opportunities of life in these former British colonies. Most were neither rich nor powerful—quite the reverse—and their national church traditions, personal beliefs, politics, and attitudes toward common schooling were complex and diverse. The antidemocratic stance of the church hierarchy was by no means an article of faith (nor was it much different from some Protestant groups' beliefs), and well into the twentieth century, lay Catholics—and even members of the American clergy—would forge their own distinct American identities. There were, and are, many meanings to Catholicism.

Initially, Catholic Church leaders in America had mixed opinions about common schooling, if they thought much about it at all. There were two related issues at stake: the content of the curriculum and who controlled the schools. Clearly Catholic religious officials wanted all Catholic children to receive a proper Catholic education (though not necessarily at school), and objected to aggressively anti-Catholic curricula. Nevertheless, clergy seemed quietly split on whether a generic Christian approach to a common school curriculum was acceptable, with the older, more liberal generation of clergy and European radicals more open to cooperation with emerging schools. The issue of control, however, was more complex. Across Europe and the United States, an ultramontane revival within the church during the 1840s and 1850s insisted that Catholics reject cooperation with emerging democratic public institutions, and fight for state support of separate Catholic ones. This revival also encouraged mysticism and rumors of magical events—just the opposite of the Protestant political ethos that emphasized democracy and reason. The American church was by no means monolithic, however. In some cases, local clergy approved the creation of special Catholic schools within a publicly run system, with Catholic teachers and religious exercises informally approved by local Catholic Church leaders. Some tolerated minimal religious exercises and a moralistic curriculum, hoping that Catholic children could get their religious instruction outside of school. Others opposed the idea of a common education entirely, if it meant allowing Catholic children to sit in school with non-Catholics, have non-Catholic teachers, and learn a non-Catholic curriculum, all under the supervision of a democratically elected school board. Church leaders wanted to control the spiritual and intellectual lives of Catholic children, lest they learn to question the church's authority, or marry outside the faith.[20]

If church doctrine pulled the American hierarchy toward creating a separate Catholic system of schools, the rise of organized American Protestant opposition gave it a push. The growth of Roman Catholicism in America, especially in cities, aroused the same political and religious passions that boiled in Europe. During the 1840s, nativist Protestants organized their own political party, remembered today by their nickname, the Know-Nothings, and swept into national politics during the 1850s only to fade into obscurity by the Civil War. In northern cities, Protestants and Catholics fought in the streets over what it meant to be American. Not only did nativists seek to block Catholics at the polls and drive them from their neighborhoods, but they opposed any cooperation between public institutions and Catholic ones, fearing that Catholic leaders took orders from a foreign power: the pope. The common school system and the King James Bible became powerful symbols for nativists, who insisted that reading the Bible, without note or comment, was an affirmation of American democratic principles—acknowledging God's special relationship with America without pushing a particular religious creed on anyone. They did not see any irony in this, even if Catholics at the time did, and readers today do too.

Cities were the location of the most spectacular struggles between Catholics and Protestants. (Rural religious controversies were usually among Protestants. Jews usually avoided controversy and rural areas.) We should not overstate the significance of cities in the development of common schooling; city schools were the exception in a country where fewer than one in five people lived in places with populations of 2,500 or more as late as 1860.[21] Nevertheless, these controversies captured the attention of national media at the time and framed a discussion that would endure for a century.

During the common school era, many cities switched from systems of charity schools for the poor to common public systems free of charge and open to all children. This switch raised difficult questions about the place of religion in schools. New York and Philadelphia provide two critical examples.

Beginning in the early nineteenth century, New York City developed a system of charity schools for the poor, handled by the private nonsectarian Public School Society, composed of a diverse group of the city's elite. These schools used a monitorial system developed by Joseph Lancaster—a popular model that crammed large numbers of children into rows by ability, each one monitored by a head child. The curriculum was simple, utilitarian, and exceptionally dependent on the textbook. While the Public School Society attempted to work with churches to provide supplemental religious instruction, some groups challenged the arrangement. Baptists protested the private group's right to monopolize the public funds, and sought money for their own school. John Hughes, the Roman Catholic bishop of New York, blasted the content of the textbooks, which contained passages contradicting his church's view of history, as well as ones insulting the very group the Public School Society sought to serve—Irish Catholics. The militant Hughes refused society offers to clean up the curriculum, arguing that there could be no "common" curriculum for all Americans. Any education without God was dangerous. Any education with God was inherently sectarian. It was unjust to deny Catholics the opportunity to educate their children in a manner acceptable to their conscience.[22]

Eventually the New York State legislature resolved the dispute by revising the curriculum and turning to the statewide common school model. The city could now form public school districts within a larger centralized system. Catholic neighborhoods could elect Catholic trustees and hire Catholic teachers, even though they would be officially nonsectarian public schools. Citywide regulations required teacher-led Bible reading without note or comment, with no particular version of the Bible required.[23]

In the City of Brotherly Love, religion and public education snarled together in violence. Most of Philadelphia's Catholic children went to public school when the city converted its charity schools to a public system in 1834. Although the schools were open to all children (not just the poor) and theoretically free from sectarian orientation or control, school law required the teacher to read a portion of scripture at the start of the school day. The law did not specify a version of the Bible nor did it require teachers to comment, which they generally did not. Neither the bishop of Philadelphia nor other Catholics complained about the Bible-reading requirement. When they raised concerns about some teachers using textbooks offensive to Catholics, the school board issued a series of resolutions affirming that the public schools of Philadelphia were for students of all faiths, and must not promote any one in particular.[24]

The trouble began in 1838, when the Pennsylvania legislature passed a law requiring public school teachers to use the Bible as a reader (though without note or comment), moving the Bible from a briefly noted symbol at the start of the day to a substantive part of the curriculum. Catholic children could now be required to read a Protestant Bible in public—not as a form of critical scholarly investigation, but as what was clearly an attempt to coerce their participation in Pan-Protestant religious belief. This form of coercion violated the fundamental American political principle of separation of church and state, and robbed the common school of much of its legitimacy as a neutral civic space. Some Catholics protested the law with increasing vigor. In 1842 a Catholic teacher was fired for refusing to read. Reluctant children were kept after school, and one was whipped.[25] Some school districts added fuel to the fire by requiring the singing of religious hymns at the end of the day, which also offended church officials, who forbade their flock from celebrating God together with non-Catholics.

Nativist Protestant politicians and many of the city's Protestant clergy seized on the controversy as an opportunity to rally Protestants against "foreign papists." Ironically, even as they used the common school coercively, nativists tarred Philadelphia Catholics with the anti-republican politics of their church leadership in Rome and accused them of plotting the overthrow of common school—and, by extension, even the United States itself! Nativists organized rallies in Catholic neighborhoods. By May 1844 hot words escalated into bloodshed when a series of riots broke out between Catholics and Protestants, leaving twenty dead, a hundred wounded, and Catholic homes, buildings, and even two churches burned to the ground.[26]

In the unique context of Philadelphia, social change, political demagoguery, and ancient religious tensions all led to an exaggerated sense of the significance of the Bible in common schools—that it was something worth killing or dying for. Outside of Philadelphia, the press generally condemned the nativists for their actions, asking how Protestant mob violence was any better than papist tyranny.[27] As a result of the riots, the Catholic Church in Philadelphia backed down from its demands for relief from hymns and Bible reading without comment, but it also resolved to build its own separate system of schools.[28]

The common school model marked the meeting between popular culture and local context: a democratic, nonsectarian institution meant to meet the needs of a religiously diverse, vastly rural, Protestant population.

The system had high legitimacy for many Americans—a curriculum that was increasingly acceptable to diverse faiths; a mode of governance that relied on local democracy, and a broadly stated and widely accepted view that the purpose of the school was to make more moral, capable citizens by teaching universal religious principles. But without protections for minorities within neighborhood schools, lacking sufficiently neutral curriculum materials and a pedagogy that supported the multiplicity of civic identities, these schools were limited in their achievement of a reasonable answer to the problem of public education in the key democratic principle of reasonableness.

Appeals to public reason did not resolve dramatic conflicts about the place of religion in common schools. Nevertheless, the conflicts themselves do illustrate how the legitimacy and stability of democratic institutions can be jeopardized by inattention to a standard of mutual justification by majorities *and* minorities. In relatively small and homogeneous cultural settings, citizens found it relatively easy to hit upon compromises about the role of religious texts, themes, and rituals in schools. But as Americans began to address these matters in larger and more religiously diverse political contexts, the challenge of identifying an approach to religion in schools that all could accept proved more difficult and more elusive. Part of the problem was the unwillingness of a powerful majority to acknowledge the reasonable objections of a religious minority to the imposition of a majority view of religion. Exacerbating this problem was the stance of the minority in rejecting any state claim of encouraging democratic pluralism through provision of common education. The effort to find nonsectarian expressions of Christian ideals that would be palatable to all students and their families can be seen as partial recognition of the ideal that privileging one faith perspective in public schools is problematic. It would take a later generation of Americans, however, to appreciate that religious minorities and nonreligious people might have reasonable objections to even generic official expressions of Christianity in public schools.

Underlying the messy and sometimes ruthless politics of the era lurks the fundamental question of what a principled democratic response to the educational aspirations of religious minorities involves. At this point in history, most Americans were far from recognizing the distinct interests children have in understanding and deliberating about religious matters in an autonomous fashion.[29] So the parameters of the antebellum public debate about what legitimacy in education requires were limited. But allowing that a democracy must consider the interests of unpopular religious minorities helped pave the way for fuller and more adequate democratic deliberation in the coming decades.

Religion and Education in Post–Civil War America

At a town meeting in November 1865, the inhabitants of Medford, Massachusetts, voted in support of an unusual resolution: to petition Congress to secure "the free education of all the children of the United States." And they really meant *all*: "without regard to locality, condition, sex, or color." They tapped a local minister, Rev. Charles Brooks, to aid the town selectmen in drafting the document, and it was presented to Congress in December by Representative Nathaniel Banks, a former general of the Union Army.

As the petitioners observed, their town of Medford stood almost in the shadow of the Bunker Hill Memorial,[30] a stone obelisk marking the first major battle of the American Revolution. The monument was quite similar to the more massive, if unrealized, erection to the first president of the Unites States that stood, incomplete and underfunded, in the center of the Capitol Mall. As heirs to the American revolutionary tradition, the Medford memorialists called for Congress to take a revolutionary step by creating a new, national system of public education. "We are thoroughly convinced that a new educational era is opening before our country, in which free schools and public education must be relied upon as the . . . means for securing to the republic its fullest power, prosperity, and renown." A national system, from primary schools through a national university, capped by a federal bureau of education, would be, they gushed, a "monument for your country and for yourselves that will be higher and more durable than that on Bunker Hill," and, presumably, General Washington's granite stump.[31]

The petition was both perspicacious and representative of the paradoxes of democratic republican ideology in American public schooling after the Civil War. It called for the creation of a federal bureau of education and the spread of public schooling to every nook and cranny of the continental United States, both of which came to pass by the end of the century, though not without struggle, and not always to glorious ends. The petition called for public education for freed slaves in the condescending language of paternalism. It called for the United States to fulfill its destiny as the leading nation among the republics of the Americas. "The Anglo-Saxon blood on this side of the globe must lead the other races," they declared. And most interestingly, the petitioners understood the work of public education as "Christian" work, even as they looked for ways to counter the ill effects of religion on civic life. The trouble, they explained, was European immigrants: "Some of them have opinions and principles adverse to our established institutions, especially on the subject of ecclesiastical rights and sway." These immigrants did not recognize the unique American traditions of separation of church and state, which attendance in public schools, the Medford petitioners hoped, would correct.[32]

The proposal certainly did contain ideas first seen in the educational writings of the founding fathers (see chapter 2), and fused the old values of the common school era and the new nationalism occasioned by the Civil War. The effects of the war were profound. From 1861 to 1865, the war claimed approximately one million casualties, including the death of over 600,000 soldiers—8 percent of all white males aged thirteen to forty-three.[33] No aspect of daily life remained untouched, from small towns to large cities. The South was devastated; slavery ended; state and federal governments grew in size and power; the industrial economy picked up pace; new transportation and communications networks knitted the country together. Whether or not the Civil War was animated by democratic principles, it did eliminate the most grotesque obstacle to the democratic legitimacy of the American republic. It would take another century of political struggle to secure the basic democratic rights for African American citizens that are prerequisites for full legitimacy, but the abolition of slavery necessitated reconsideration of the nature of democratic citizenship and the educational measures needed to foster it.

Religion took on new meaning, too. Church membership continued to rise as people turned to religion for consolation and meaning. During the war, soldiers held revivals, built churches, and organized Bible-study groups. Preachers on both sides of the conflict argued that God was on their side. When God appeared to pick the Union, Northern Protestant nationalists claimed victory for their vision of America as God's nation. Despite his bitter dislike for abolitionists, John Hughes backed the Union cause, urging New York Catholics to enlist, which some did, and demanding in return that Protestants recognize them as full citizens. Many Jews did the same. In popular culture, religion took on a new, special relationship with patriotism. Capturing the spirit of the age, Congress inscribed "in God we trust" on US currency.[34] At the same time, though, the state continued to take the place of the church as the organizing principle of daily life. In public discourse, nationalism displaced religious belief as the primary form of allegiance.

Once again, public education emerged as the new, symbolic battlefield where Americans would fight for what it meant to be a citizen. For Northern Protestant school reformers like the petitioners from Medford, the Civil War highlighted what the founding fathers had warned of: a republic without a well-educated citizenry would fail. The very *idea* of public school took on a life of its own. Northern writers blamed the Civil War on the South's lack of public schools. In cities especially, a protracted economic depression in the 1870s brought greater levels of poverty and crime than had ever been seen—social problems also associated with lack of education. Race riots and antiwar protests during the war in Catholic and immigrant-heavy Northern cities left native Protestants more convinced than ever that public schools were necessary to save the republic. And then, of course, the war freed four million slaves in desperate need of formal education.

Political parties and church leaders traded in fear, using public discourse to further party interest instead of seeking reasonable solutions. The Republican Party (strongly Protestant) used the idea of endangered public schools as a bloody shirt to rally voters, conjuring the pope as the bogeyman. The Democratic Party (strongly Catholic in the North) whipped up anti-black fear and hatred, attempting to unify Southern whites and Northern immigrants against the radical, big-government agenda of the Republicans.[35] Church leaders exploited the public school for their ends too, with Protestants and Catholics sparring over the question of religion in public school. Extreme Protestants encouraged schools to show no compromise with families who objected to religious exercises. Extreme Catholic bishops threatened to withhold sacraments from children whose parents chose public schools. Meanwhile, to the dismay of many liberal Catholics and the alarm of many Protestants, the Vatican grew increasingly hostile to religious freedom and democracy, issuing the brazenly intolerant *Syllabus of Errors* in 1864, and declaring the infallibility of the pope in 1870. Church leaders resolved to build a separate world for American Catholics—social clubs, schools, political organizations—to prevent them from being corrupted by Protestant ideas.[36]

The federal government took a new interest in education as a national project. In 1867 Congress created the office of the US commissioner of education to collect and report school statistics. The Constitution never granted the government power to run schools. What it did grant, however, was congressional power to grant statehood to territories that had republican forms of government. Congress now insisted that a republic must, by definition, include nonsectarian, free public schools. Likewise, Congress insisted that former Confederate states create systems of public schools in order to be readmitted to the Union. In the meantime, the federal government took responsibility for educating freed people, though in ways wholly inadequate to their thirst for education. Today, the existence of most statewide public school systems in the American South can be attributed to the Union's requirements and the activism of African Americans at the local level.[37] From 1865 to 1900 schooling expanded to all regions of the United States and to all groups. Overall enrollments grew steadily to reach 78 percent of all children aged five to seventeen by 1900, with over 90 percent of these in public schools.[38]

In 1876 Republicans proposed a constitutional amendment preventing public funding of sectarian schools, ostensibly in order to protect the republic, but really to embarrass the Catholic Church for its hostility to public schooling. The amendment failed. At the state level, however, voters approved a series of similar amendments preventing public funding of sectarian schools. Proponents argued that public schooling inspired nationalism and unity within a diverse nation, and sectarian hatred among faiths (the Catholic Church, soon joined by Mormons, being the most-cited examples) could tear the nation apart again.[39]

As the public school moved to the center of American politics, states passed numerous reforms seeking to improve it. Localism increasingly became viewed as a problem, not an asset, of democratic control. States required higher teacher-licensure standards, passed compulsory education laws, extended school years and school days, propped up building codes, and centralized and consolidated school districts and school boards. Towns and cities built larger, graded schools and added selective high schools.[40]

The place of religion in public schools was precarious and complex. Textbook publishers responded to the complaints of religious minorities, and textbooks became largely free of explicit religious bias or reference.[41] In that sense, there was no fourth R for religion in the curriculum of public schools by the end of the nineteenth century. Knowledge became increasingly secular. Religious organizations seeking to abolish public schooling failed; religious organizations seeking to use public schools to teach specific religious beliefs also failed. All this signaled a wide, implicit—though not complete—consensus that the successful pursuit of educational objectives did not depend on a curriculum infused with religious doctrines or special religious reasons. Common standards of evidence and canons of reasoning seemed both possible and widely acceptable. Of course, with the vast majority of children leaving the system before high school, conflicts between religious beliefs and scientific evidence and theory were not yet widespread.

Those seeking a robust place for majoritarian religion in schools won symbolic victories. One survey in 1898 found that eight states required a brief reading from the Bible without comment at the start of the school day. All states, however, reported that such Bible reading, and to a lesser extent reciting the Lord's Prayer, were common practices at the start of the day in many of their public schools. City school systems commonly required such exercises when their state legislatures did not. While it was never universal, symbolic Bible reading in public schools probably became typical in the decades after the Civil War.[42] By today's standards it is problematic that teachers and school officials orchestrated these activities. Yet the rather modest place the activities occupied in the school day should be borne in mind when considering the degree to which these practices diminished the overall legitimacy of public education at the time.

During the common school period before the war, state courts in Massachusetts and Maine had upheld the principle of nonsectarian religious exercises, supporting school officials' right to require students to read portions of the King James Bible despite Catholic objections. Courts justified these decisions on secular grounds, however, arguing that such exercises were religiously neutral and secular in purpose: promoting the common good through the moral and intellectual development of children.[43] In New York the practice was upheld, but compelling students to participate was not.[44]

After the Civil War, however, state courts found it more difficult to defend supposedly nonsectarian religious instruction, beginning with a Cincinnati case in 1869, when the city school board outlawed Bible reading in public schools, citing Catholic concerns. The case gained national attention and occasioned a wide-ranging national debate over the relationship between church and state. In 1873 the Ohio Supreme Court upheld the board's decision unanimously. Legal historian Steven K. Green observes that this decision marked a lasting change in how future courts would consider the issue: the Bible was no longer seen as necessary to the purposes of education; indeed, its presence in the school would now be judged in terms of whether it undermined those purposes. Courts would continue to rule for and against Bible reading, but the question became whether *any* use of the Bible was compatible with the secular purposes of public education.[45]

Despite all the heated rhetoric *about* schools, however, in practice the deep-seated tradition of democratic localism led to a rich variety of local practices *within* them. State governments were too small to monitor or enforce many requirements. The average size of a state department of education was two people: a commissioner and his secretary. Compulsory school laws, increasingly popular in this period, were dead letters. Localism thrived even in cities. Across the United States, Protestants, Catholics, Jews, nonbelievers, and others worked at the local level to reach a variety of compromises over religious practices in the schools. One study of three thousand legal appeals and seven thousand letters to the state superintendent of New York State, for example, found that religious exercises were at the bottom of the list of things that people worried most about with their local schools. Homogeneous school districting helped diffuse conflict. So, too, did a democratic governance process that most people accepted as legitimate.[46]

Compromise came in many forms, though it rarely threatened the basic organizational and pedagogical arrangements of public schools. Bible reading without note or comment was, of course, itself a form of compromise among Protestants, although it also represented a coherent civic viewpoint that saw America as God's country. A district-level compromise found among Protestant sects, or between Protestants and Catholics, might include hiring teachers of different faiths in alternate years. More common compromises included allowing the Douay (Catholic) Bible in lieu of the King James Version, finding religious readings common to all Judeo-Christian religions, or, obviously, leaving religious exercises out of school altogether. Catholic authorities walked a fine line in these efforts. On one hand, admitting that compromise was possible undermined the church's resolve to abolish public schools in favor of vouchers for religious schools. On the other hand, with the majority of Catholics enrolled in public schools, clergy had an interest in seeing the promotion of Christian religion.

Yet another approach, known as the Poughkeepsie or Faribault-Stillwater plan, tinkered with the issue of who controlled schools. The explosion of city populations after the Civil War overwhelmed public school systems to the point where they could often not accommodate all the children who wanted to go to school. School districts scrambled to rent space for classrooms, which churches (usually empty during the school day) were uniquely suited to provide. In Faribault and Stillwater, Minnesota, and Poughkeepsie, New York, as well as numerous cities and towns across the country, public school officials rented space in Catholic churches. The school board then agreed to hire nuns or priests as regular school teachers for a nonsectarian, regular public school education during the school day. Children could come early and remain late for extracurricular Catholic religious instruction. The schedule from Poughkeepsie looked like this:

8.45—Morning prayers.
9 to 12—Regular secular course as in other schools.
12—Short prayer; then recess.
1 P.M.—Religious instruction.
1.30—Regular secular course.
4—Closing religious exercises.[47]

Critics of Poughkeepsie-like plans argued that religious instruction after school could not be so easily separated from the issue of control. In nearby Elmira, for example, the church invited children from surrounding districts to come to their "public" school, violating the neighborhood principle of public schooling. When the school board insisted on limiting enrollment to children who lived in the district, the church abruptly canceled their contract, leaving the city's schools in chaos. As a result, the school board concluded it could not trust private groups to provide reliable educational services for the city. In Pittsburgh, on the other hand, the bishop canceled a similar plan when Catholic children themselves refused to show up for extra instruction. In other districts, quiet arrangements between church and state sprang up across the nation, from New Mexico to Georgia, Iowa to New Hampshire.[48]

Tax policy too became an area of contention where compromises blurred the strict separation between public and private schooling. Historian Robert Gross has shown that Catholic schools successfully resisted a movement in the urban North to tax private schools as a way to enrich tax-strapped public school districts. Paradoxically, church officials argued that their schools were "public" institutions because they educated so many local children and were subject to (basic) state regulation. Their claims were true: in northern cities with large Catholic populations in this period, the church educated about a third, and sometimes almost half, of all children. In compromising, public officials were motivated by pecuniary considerations: the cost of all those children being dumped on the school district if the Catholic school closed would have far outweighed the value of the lost tax revenue. No doubt the political clout of Catholic voters didn't hurt the compromise process, either.[49]

The relationship between who ran the schools and what was taught in them raised new questions about what we would today call the hidden curriculum. Did programs like that of Poughkeepsie subtly pressure children to believe in a particular religion? In the Utah Territory, Mormon church communities struggled with public school officials over who had the right to teach, serve as trustees, and set school policy. In Poughkeepsie, suspicious public school inspectors looked for religious symbols on the walls, on furniture, and even on the bodies of teachers. Headscarves caused headaches for officials in Suspension Bridge, a small town just north of Niagara Falls, where the board of education contracted with Saint Raphael's Parochial School in 1885. As part of the agreement, nuns working for the parochial school continued on as public school teachers, still wearing their habits and addressed as "Sister," not "Miss." In this case the state superintendent overrode the arrangement, insisting that public school teachers dress in secular clothes and be addressed in secular terms as agents of the state.

Religious holidays posed another challenge. With the majority setting the school schedule district by district (or city by city), religious minorities were often expected to show up to school every scheduled day, whether they were teachers or students. In Brooklyn, Jewish parents did not once protest Bible reading at the start of the school day, but they requested (and received) permission for students to be absent on their holidays without penalty.[50]

Symbolic religious exercises in schooling could be used for affirmation of minority power, as well as of majorities. During Reconstruction, freed slaves overwhelmed inadequate public and private efforts to provide mass education. Denied education under slavery, freed people made incredible personal sacrifices to learn the three R's. One of their chief reasons, they reported, was to read the Bible for themselves.[51] Symbolic religious exercises affirmed the powerful role of the black church in African American life.

During the 1880s and 1890s, Native Americans on the Great Plains embraced religious revival in their resistance to white imperialism. The Ghost Dance briefly rose as a popular ceremony of resistance and affirmation, but led to violence and a massacre at Wounded Knee, South Dakota, where federal troops slaughtered nearly two hundred Oglala Sioux men, women, and children. In publicly funded boarding schools for Native Americans, Bible reading continued to be a weapon in the arsenal of cultural annihilation, just as it had been for centuries. Christian teachers and missionaries used religious exercises of their particular faith in hopes of "saving" or "uplifting" Indian children, which in reality meant inoculating them against their home religion, culture, and language. Some Native American peoples accepted Christianity on their own terms and for their own purposes; others resisted.[52] Overall, the state's treatment of indigenous people fell far short of even modest standards of democratic legitimacy. Indigenous people were not acknowledged as political equals, and efforts to use schools to Christianize native children were deeply disrespectful to the indigenous cultural and spiritual traditions. Although European settlers gained an appreciation of the need to negotiate religious pluralism within their own ranks, they failed to include native peoples within the domain of reasonable pluralism.

Nineteenth-century America hosted the most diverse collection of religions, old and new, in the Western world. In practice, public battles over religious exercises were about identity and control, and not about instruction in religion, which had disappeared by the end of the century. The remarkable political transformations of the post–Civil War era eroded the intense localism of the common school era, but nevertheless moved the country toward greater democratic legitimacy in the content of schooling. A fuller, yet still incomplete, understanding of democratic equality emerged, and Americans increasingly accepted the need to negotiate their religious differences in the context of schools that they shared. They often sought and sometimes achieved fairly reasonable compromises. The idea that a democratic state must take the leading role in providing public education firmly took root and set the stage for broader and more systematic political debates and deliberation about the appropriate character of a public and democratic education. As we have seen, the emerging system of fully public schools still retained a significant place for Christian rituals, but the idea that schools could have a more complete secular orientation gained traction in the American political imagination.

FOUR

Religion and Public Education in the Era of Progress

In a series of lectures at the University of Virginia in 1928, journalist Walter Lippmann asked his audience to imagine a dialogue on Mount Olympus between the university's founder, Thomas Jefferson, and the recently deceased star prosecutor in the Scopes monkey trial, populist hero William Jennings Bryan. This hilarious, heavenly dialogue was moderated by none other than the Greek philosopher Socrates. Ever the troublemaker, the imaginary Socrates forced both men to concede paradoxes in their "fundamental principles"—Jefferson's defense of reason, on one hand, and Bryan's defense of Christian popular rule, on the other. In one instance, Socrates asks Bryan,

Socrates: Did you say you believe in the separation of church and state?
Bryan: I did. It is a fundamental principle.
Socrates: Is it the right of a majority to rule a fundamental principle?
Bryan: It is.
Socrates: Is freedom of thought a fundamental principle, Mr. Jefferson?
Jefferson: It is.
Socrates: Well, how would you gentlemen compose your fundamental principles, if a majority, exercising its fundamental right to rule, ordained that Buddhism should be taught in the public schools?
Bryan: I'd move to a Christian country.

Jefferson: I'd exercise the sacred right of revolution. What would you do, Socrates?
Socrates: I'd re-examine my fundamental principles.[1]

Setting the great champion of reason against the great champion of popular democracy allowed Lippmann to explore what he saw as a key educational issue of his time: the transition from traditional nineteenth-century democratic life to twentieth-century modernity. With the rise of modern scientific knowledge and the increasing diversity of American communities, he argued, the relationship between "faith and reason and authority" raised difficult questions for the modern public school teacher. "He is the servant of a community which is in part fundamentalist in its mode of thought and in part modernist," Lippmann explained. "His intellectual duty is to modernism, that is to say, to the belief that human reason has the last word. But politically, economically, legally, he is subject to the orders of those who may believe that the preservation of the ancient fundamentalism either in religion or in nationalism is the first duty of man." While nineteenth-century schools had avoided these controversies through their democratic local governance and emphasis on the three R's and basic moral instruction, Lippmann argued, the growth of modern scientific knowledge in the twentieth century was forcing the issue in new ways.[2]

Lippmann was partially right: the tension between popular belief and expert knowledge widened in the twentieth century, as modern scholarship in science, history, and other fields busily demolished traditional beliefs. But the story was much more complex than that. Indeed, the first half of the twentieth century saw religion fade as the primary issue in school reform (which focused foremost on responses to industrial capitalism and immigration), but it lingered as a powerful expression of identity politics. With the public system firmly in place, religious enthusiasts rarely challenged the existence of public education, but instead focused on how to use the public school to their own advantage. The old struggle for symbolic exercises continued at the local and state levels, of course, as did compromises over control; but new themes emerged too. Concern over the political beliefs of immigrants and radical challenges to capitalism led to nationwide efforts to use state law to require religious and patriotic exercises in public schools, a cause that tended to bring liberal and conservative Protestants together. On other issues they split, as did Catholics and Jews. Christian fundamentalists, alarmed by the threats of modern science, pushed anti-evolution legislation, monkeyed with biology textbooks, and launched well-coordinated attacks against academic and scientific expertise. Religious liberals sought to use the school as a clearinghouse for religious instruction in all faiths, using schools as feeders for special in- and after-school religious education programs. Still other groups, including much of the American Jewish leadership, opposed any religious encroachment on public education, seeing it as a force for intolerance.

In a democracy, as Lippmann's Olympic dialogues asserted, public reason had to find a way to be attentive to the rights of unpopular groups. During the first half of the twentieth century, state and federal courts took on a greater role in school policy; adjudication of disputes provided one way to safeguard minority rights. But legal debates about the interpretation of rights were themselves highly political and often revealed competing visions of the goals and values of a democratic community. Prominent federal cases showed how dissent from religion itself might be legitimate, and that traditional theological teachings (e.g., about creation) that once were comfortably accepted in schools could be challenged by secular science. While nineteenth-century debates about religion in public education had focused primarily on establishment questions—how much and what kind of religion could legitimately be taught by a public school—the twentieth century saw the rise of the individual rights–focused political discourse with which we are so familiar today. The emergence of such discourse reflected recognition of the idea that educational legitimacy cannot be secured fully by majoritarian legislative processes alone.[3]

Context

Whether inside or outside of courts, struggles over religion in schools reflected the broader context of the period. American politics of the early twentieth century elevated ethnic and religious tribalism to new highs, and lows. Many Americans, especially Protestants, felt under siege as their political and cultural dominance faded, and they sought a variety of ways to stamp their own "100 percent American" view of culture and politics on the newcomers. The country passed the Eighteenth Amendment, banning the manufacture, sale, and transportation of alcohol. Starting in 1917 and continuing through the 1920s, Congress enacted a series of racist laws limiting immigration by groups deemed less fit for American society. Outside of the law (but exerting pressure on it) the Second Ku Klux Klan emerged as a popular right-wing Protestant social movement and sometime terrorist organization—attacking immigrants, Catholics, Jews, union members, and above all, Americans of African descent. At its peak in the mid-1920s, the Klan boasted five million members across all sec-tions of the United States, roughly 15 percent of eligible men.[4] On other issues, such as the economy, Americans formed different alliances: Catholic and even some Jewish groups joined conservative Protestants in persecuting Communists and atheists, for example. Enforced belief in God, they believed without irony, protected children from the lure of totalitarian government.

In popular discourse, the purpose of public schooling changed. Leading school reformers focused on two clusters of secular problems. The first, and less successful, sought to make the school more child friendly, pedagogically evocative, and democratic. Inspired by the writings of John Dewey,[5] these pedagogical progressives hoped to transform public school classrooms into laboratories of democracy, where children learned to think critically about social problems, to deliberate, and to more fully realize a democratic social ethos. These reforms enjoyed mixed success outside of primary schools, resulting in small modifications to curriculum and teaching, but no fundamental changes to traditional modes of either.

The more successful cluster of reforms applied the latest theories of factory management, known as Taylorism, to make schools more efficient at educating children for their future place in the American economy. Reformers consolidated small school districts, and built big, compartmentalized school buildings. They took the school "out of politics" by limiting community involvement, curtailing ward-based control in cities, and shrinking school boards. At the same time, massive immigration from new places—eastern and southern Europe in particular—prompted reformers to focus on "Americanization," helping children and their families learn English and understand distinctively American democratic political and cultural traditions. Few reformers outside of the African American community challenged the taken-for-granted segregation of black children, or the scandalously second-rate educational opportunities offered to them.

The big winner of this period was the public high school. Enrollment exploded, doubling every ten years, from 110,000 public high school students in 1880 to 4.4 million in 1930.[6] Going to high school went from being something for the select few to something typical. School districts built large, comprehensive high schools, which became multipurpose institutions where students could learn from experts about the latest advances in knowledge, from vocational and technical skills to foreign languages, physical education, nutrition, and advanced academic fields. Using intelligence tests, schools began steering children into specific academic tracks deemed appropriate for their future lives. During the first half of the twentieth century, public schools oriented their curriculum toward improving the workforce and patriotism.[7]

Patriotic Education and Religious Identity

The new emphasis on patriotic education offered a whole new set of challenges for the place of religion in public education. Before the 1890s, the typical public school did not fly a flag. But flag displays and patriotic exercises swept across the United States in the 1890s and early 1900s, and flag salutes quickly followed. Patriotic civic organizations like the YMCA offered classes for immigrants; cities and towns began regular public displays of national affection. The private sector pitched in, too. Starting in 1914, Ford Motor Company required foreign workers to attend its citizenship programs or be fired. Other companies followed. The American Bar Association lobbied state legislatures to teach the Constitution and patriotic American history. The First World War, and the red scare that followed, intensified the patriotic zeal of school leaders and state legislators, and strengthened their resolve that state law should regulate what got taught in public schools.[8]

Immigrant responses were complex and often culturally specific. Foreign-language immigrant newspapers generally accepted American patriotism and encouraged learning English, but rejected other forms of assimilation that threatened traditional culture. While Americanization efforts strike us as draconian today, in their day most "Americanizers" offered a far more inclusive vision of American citizenship (open to white people of any ethnicity) than the vicious ethnic nationalism arising in fascist European countries, or even in right-wing American politics. Of course, few of these programs challenged white supremacy in America.[9]

In public schools, flag ceremonies varied in their references, or lack of references, to God. What would become the most famous exercise, written by Christian Socialist Edward Bellamy in 1892, read: "I pledge allegiance to my flag and the republic for which it stands—one nation indivisible—with liberty and justice for all." *Youth's Companion* magazine published Bellamy's pledge as part of a recommended program for schools celebrating the three hundredth anniversary of Columbus's voyage to America. In addition to the pledge, the *Youth's Companion* recommended a whole program for the day, including singing, the reading of an ode, and some "Acknowledgement of God," which it left up to locals.[10] A popular New York City pledge used daily in the 1890s clearly targeted immigrants in the language of pan-religious nationalism: "We give our heads and our hearts to God and our country: one country, one language, one Flag."[11]

Although some promoters insisted that patriotic exercises must be voluntary, states soon began requiring them. From 1890 to the eve of World

War I, twenty-nine states passed laws requiring public schools to fly flags.[12] Mandatory flag salutes and pledges followed suit, with the hearty support of conservative civic groups. Still smarting from the Civil War, southern states resisted the movement at first or, in the case of Georgia, required children to salute the *state* flag.[13] The surge of enforced patriotism in American society during and after World War I led to stricter requirements and harsher penalties for noncompliance.[14]

Mandatory patriotic exercises created problems similar to the mandatory religious ones in the nineteenth century. Challenges arose across the country for multiple reasons. Some left-wing families objected to the government's support of wealthy capitalists over workers; others saw the flag as a symbol of militarism; still others claimed loyalty to other nation-states. Objectors received little sympathy from public school officials, who coerced children into standing and saluting—sometimes forcibly—or expelled them when they refused. When a Bellingham, Washington, father pulled his son out of public school rather than have him forced to pledge, local officials jailed the man, stripped him of custody, and put the boy in a state-run children's home. Although other states did not go quite so far, state courts consistently upheld mandatory flag pledging—a perfectly reasonable requirement, they argued, in exchange for a free public education. American public schools were, in essence, American government schools, and allegiance could be coerced.[15]

Religious objections to patriotic exercises posed a difficult problem for the federal Constitution, however. Did the act of pledging violate the long-cherished American right to free practice of religion? While mainstream religions had no problem with flag pledging per se, a few outliers did. The most prominent of these, Jehovah's Witnesses, believed that God forbade them to salute any earthly object; violation of this precept would cost them their souls. While there were only an estimated 70,000 Witnesses in America by a 1943 count, they were well organized and deeply dedicated.[16] Their aggressive proselytizing, rejection of modernity and civil society, dogmatic and authoritarian structure, and hostility to other religions (especially Roman Catholicism) made them extremely unpopular with local authorities even without their conscientious objection to saluting the flag.[17] In Europe, Hitler was so annoyed by German Jehovah's Witnesses' resistance to the Nazi state that he banned the movement and eventually shipped members to concentration camps.

While teachers and school officials often found ways to quietly accommodate Witness children, state laws forced the issue, and state courts doggedly enforced it. Right-wing patriotic groups such as the American Legion, the Daughters of the American Revolution, and the Ku Klux Klan egged them on.[18] By the time the issue reached the US Supreme Court in 1940, eighteen states had laws requiring teaching about the flag, which sometimes included mandatory saluting; six required new teachers to take oaths that they would teach children to respect the flag; three more states officially encouraged flag saluting. Required or not, however, flag saluting had become common practice.[19]

So did Witness resistance. As confrontations escalated, the Supreme Court agreed to hear a case. In *Minersville* [West Virginia] *School District v. Gobitis* (1940), the Court ruled 8-1 that public schools could indeed require all children to salute the flag. Led by Felix Frankfurter, himself a Jewish immigrant, the court declared that the greater good—the interest of all Americans—was served by compulsory flag pledges. Frankfurter felt America needed to prepare for war, and now was not the time to indulge dissent. The price of national cohesion was, he argued, that some religious groups had to compromise their convictions. Framed in the negative, the court seemed to suggest that Witnesses' conscientious objections threatened America.

The decision was a disaster. Across the United States, self-proclaimed patriotic Americans used the court's declaration as a license to kill—a situation made worse by the hyper-patriotic response of America's entry into the Second World War. In hundreds of documented incidents in every region of the United States, but especially in Texas and Oklahoma, vigilante thugs, often members of the American Legion and encouraged by the organization, harassed, attacked, and tortured Witnesses in a fashion similar to Nazi-inspired mobs running riot in Europe. Local police and government officials often lent a hand. Attackers in Kennebunk, Maine, burned down a Witness church. A Nebraska mob castrated a man. Police in Odessa, Texas, detained a group of seventy Witnesses, interrogated them overnight on their refusal to salute the flag, and released them the following morning to a stoning by a gathered mob. Fearing that Witnesses were a subversive "fifth column," ignorant rioters often accused Witnesses as being "Nazis," sometimes painting their property and persons with swastikas. School officials grew increasingly intolerant of Witness children as well, expelling them by the thousands over their refusal to salute the flag.[20]

Within two years the Supreme Court revisited the issue in *West Virginia State Board of Education v. Barnette* and overturned its *Gobitis* decision. The resounding 6–3 majority decision, issued on Flag Day, 1943, highlighted the irony of forcing people to pledge themselves to a free government, and explicitly contrasted American democracy with the historical examples of ancient Rome persecuting Christians, Roman Catholic inquisitions, and the contemporary governments of the Axis powers. "Those who begin coercive elimination of dissent," Justice Jackson wrote ominously, "soon find themselves exterminating dissenters. Compulsory unification of opinion achieves only the unanimity of the graveyard." Indeed, he concluded famously, "if there is any fixed star in our constitutional constellation, it is that no official, high or petty, can prescribe what shall be orthodox in politics, nationalism, religion, or other matters of opinion or force citizens to confess by word or act their faith therein." Public schools could not force students to pledge their allegiance to a particular belief.[21]

Undaunted by the court's decision, enthusiasts continued their crusade to infuse government and public life with religion—an effort supported by the patriotism of the 1940s and Cold War politics of the 1950s. Once again, these efforts yielded symbolic victories. In pop culture and in politics, references to God rose, as did associations between belief in God and support of American democracy.[22] In 1954 Congress added "under God" to the Pledge of Allegiance.

What impact did the pledge have? Studies at the time found the predictable result: few children understood the meaning of the words they listlessly repeated each morning, and many did not even know the correct words. But then, the purpose of the pledge was not to instill deep understanding of democratic principles, or religion, but to form an emotional attachment to the symbols of government and religion.[23] In other words, to pledge taught unthinking obedience, not democratic values. It did not foster an ethos of critical citizenship that encouraged reasoned deliberation on political matters. It was an empty vessel, a shallow exercise in the cultivation of civic virtue. Or as the mumbling of many a schoolchild suggests, the pledge taught a tragicomic civic obscurity—that America was "one nation, invisible."

Finding the Limits of Public Control

Both the *Gobitis* and *Barnette* decisions reflected a new, twentieth-century reality: the federal Supreme Court had begun to rule on state educational law. The pivotal case that set the precedent came twenty years earlier, from Oregon, and concerned a new twist on an old question: who should control education, and how?

Having failed to stop the creation of secular, democratically controlled, Protestant flavored public schools, the Roman Catholic Church in America expanded its alternative system. In 1895 and 1899, Pope Leo XIII again warned American Catholics against being seduced by the dangers of American democracy. A Roman Catholic establishment was the ideal form of government for a Catholic, he declared. As much as possible, Catholics—especially Catholic children—should separate themselves from other Americans.[24] By 1920 Catholic schools enrolled 1.8 million children, accounting for over 90 percent of private school enrollment.[25] Catholic school leaders positioned their schools as a patriotic alternative to the secular public school, as special places where students could preserve their religious and cultural traditions while learning obedience to secular American law.

While the Catholic Church continued its effort to limit state authority in education (successfully helping to block the formation of a federal department of education, for example), Pan-Protestant groups continued their efforts to curb the influence of the Catholic Church.[26] In 1922 the Oregon Ku Klux Klan and Scottish Rite Freemasons rallied voters to make the boldest move yet: a state initiative requiring *all* children to attend public schools, eliminating private ones. The law required parents to be fined and jailed for noncompliance. Even Benjamin Rush's eighteenth-century plan to make children into "republican machines" (see chapter 2) did not go so far. Advocates outside of Oregon hoped the law would spread to their states as well.[27]

The law passed with a comfortable majority, including the support of many professional educators. But it alarmed other groups, especially those who traditionally preferred private schooling or feared a one-size-fits-all education for their children: Lutherans, Catholics, Jews, private school families, and business leaders who would pay more in taxes when public school enrollments increased.

Challenges made their way to the Supreme Court, which struck down the law in its 1925 decision *Pierce v. Society of Sisters*. In its decision, the court ruled that the Fourteenth Amendment to the federal Constitution afforded citizens and corporations of all states the protections of due process. The Oregon law unreasonably denied private schools the right to do business. The court made two further observations, however: the State of Oregon overstepped its bounds by unduly limiting parents' rights to direct their children's education. At the same time the court declared that it was reasonable for the state to regulate what and how teachers taught.[28] From now on, the high court could review state education laws. *Pierce* made *Gobitis*, *Barnette*, and every federal education decision since then possible. Constitutional civil rights—especially the First Amendment—applied to all Americans.[29]

Fundamentalist Attacks against Science in the Curriculum

In its 1943 *Barnette* decision, the Supreme Court had protected the right of private citizens to object to state-mandated professions of belief. But flag salutes were small potatoes compared to a much deeper change in education—one that had little to do with schools per se, and much to do with a fundamental human question: what is knowledge? If the purpose of schooling was to spread knowledge, who had the power to determine what counted and what did not?

During the nineteenth century, few children had remained in school long enough to get more than a basic education in the three R's. Public and private high schools catered to a very small percentage of the population. While it was by no means easy to develop a curriculum "common" to all religious viewpoints, objectively speaking the common school content did not challenge the fundamental assumptions of most mainstream religions: God had created man in his image; miraculous Bible stories could actually have happened; faith-based religion could coexist comfortably with what most experts considered to be "truth."

By the early decades of the twentieth century, however, human knowledge presented an unprecedented challenge to traditional religion. Evolutionary theory explained the origin of human beings without a garden of Eden. Einstein's theory of general relativity shattered the simple regularity of Isaac Newton's physics—the clockwork universe the founding fathers found so comforting. Historians critically reassessed the Bible's authenticity and accuracy. America's most prestigious universities made the switch to the German research model, divorcing themselves from religious orthodoxy. In the face of modern scientific inquiry, nothing, it seemed, was sacred. Framed in terms of public reason, the developments in scientific inquiry brought sharply into view the question of whether even generic Christian beliefs could justifiably retain a place in public education. Because new discoveries revealed a gap between what could be established through objective scientific inquiry and traditional articles of religious faith, it became intellectually harder to allow that religious reasons had a legitimate role to play in public education acceptable to all students. But resistance to this point by some religious groups was often fierce. The justificatory requirements of legitimacy do not always sit well with those who are constrained by them.

The creation of transferrable knowledge and skills—social and human capital—had been at the heart of the public school mission since the early nineteenth century, and had driven Americans to build a system of common schools from the bottom up. As the public school shifted from a place for making the masses into good people to a place for providing advanced learning to make the masses expert and efficient, however, school content brought more science to more people. While this shift was not absolute—early common school leaders certainly wanted to teach children accurate information, and progressive leaders wanted children to learn to be obedient and respectful to authority—the change in emphasis was clear. Moreover, the progressive-era curriculum could now teach children subjects and ideas unimaginable in the one-room common school. The explosion of high schooling magnified this shift. For some religions, the shift constituted a clear and present danger.

During the first half of the twentieth century, conservative evangelical Protestants continued their fight to control American public education. Like Catholic leaders, these Protestants rejected the notion that schooling could, or should, be neutral toward all religious faiths. Unlike Catholic Church leaders, however, these Protestants supported public schooling, an institution they helped build and over which they enjoyed some political power. Pressuring legislatures and local school boards to require Bible reading and prayer had been a popular and somewhat successful symbolic crusade since the nineteenth century.[30] By the early twentieth century, however, Protestant fundamentalists mounted a coordinated national campaign. They took their cues from the Women's Christian Temperance Union (WCTU), a nineteenth-century reform organization that pioneered a radical approach to social reform: requiring all public schools to teach the same specific content. Building a national network of local chapters, the WCTU had pressured state governments to require anti-alcohol education in public schools—a clear departure from the days of democratic, local control over cultural symbols and practices.[31]

With the genie out of the bottle, advocates for religious observances in public schools used the WCTU model to mobilize an all-out assault on local variation in religious practices. As a result, from 1913 to 1930 twelve states enacted Bible-reading laws.[32] Whether local or statewide, these requirements continued the nineteenth-century tradition of keeping the reading free from commentary and interpretation, and rested on a constellation of political, cultural, and religious claims: reading the Bible empowered students to resist tyranny by going straight to the source; reading the Bible reinforced the moral foundations of American culture; and some proponents argued, reading the Bible attracted the favor of God and could have magical benefits.[33] Some African American secular intellectuals took the opportunity to assail the links between biblical literalism and racism, casting their lot with science. Most African American preachers, on the other hand, declared for a fundamentalist defense of scripture.[34]

Mandatory Bible reading and school prayer did not address the underlying threat of new knowledge, however, which fundamentalists found deeply disturbing. Crusaders mounted a two-pronged attack. First, they cracked the whip of censorship. In a sweeping national effort, fundamentalists at the local level pressured school boards and state legislatures to boycott textbooks and ban teaching that included anything that "called into question" or "disrespected" the Bible. Darwin's theory of evolution topped the list, but the attempted fundamentalist purges targeted any heresy, including atheism, agnosticism, or any idea deemed "vulgar, obscene, or indecent" according to fundamentalist standards.[35] The effort gained lasting notoriety in 1925 through the so-called Scopes monkey trial in Dayton, Ohio, in which everyman evangelical hero William Jennings Bryan squared off against the brilliant agnostic Clarence Darrow over a Tennessee anti-evolution statute. Bryan carried the day in Dayton, but lost in the court of mainstream American media.[36] Overall, fundamentalists introduced new anti-evolution bills in thirty-seven state legislatures during the 1920s. They passed in three: Mississippi (1926), Arkansas (1928), and Texas (1929).[37]

Not content with playing defense against scientific research, however, fundamentalists launched a second attack against its source. They spoke out against the immorality of academic freedom and modern thought in higher education, pressured college and university administrators to profess their religious beliefs and affirm the literal truth of Bible stories. As historian Adam Laats has shown, these efforts failed at the modernist and research-oriented institutions, but succeeded where there was sufficient popular support or where conservative Protestant denominational control was strong. In addition fundamentalists created their own, intellectually pure institutions, forming the Dallas Theological Seminary in 1924, and Bryan College and Bob Jones College in 1926, among others. By the 1930s their efforts had driven a deep wedge between colleges and universities dedicated to their traditional nineteenth-century missions of preserving religious faith and modern ones concerned with producing and imparting knowledge. The extremes to which some fundamentalists went also drove a wedge into the movement itself, alienating moderates who did not see an inherent contradiction between conservative Protestant faith and reason.[38]

While their assault on the scientific revolution in universities failed, fundamentalists succeeded in their attack on evolution in public schools. Thanks to their efforts, most American schoolchildren were denied access to education about human evolution until well into the 1960s. By then, Cold War competition with the Soviet Union and concern over America's lack of decent science education prompted a rediscovery of the fundamental place of evolutionary theory in biological sciences.[39] Fundamentalists' victories were subtractive, however. They proved far less successful at adding their religious views to public school curricula, rarely gaining ground beyond brief, intellectually empty exercises at the start of the school day or culturally inclusive Christian holiday celebrations—both of which pleased pluralistic-minded Protestant liberals more than conservatives.

From a multicultural history standpoint, it's clear that fundamentalists struggled against what they perceived to be threats to their own cherished beliefs, and to their larger understanding of what America should be. In that sense, they were no different from the many groups who once sought to define what "common" meant in the common school, or the bounds of "the public" in the public school. And in public discourse, they were not always as backward-minded as the media portrayed them. Leading fundamentalists, including Bryan, conceded that older children might, in the right conditions, be taught about the flawed theory of evolution alongside the actual true account of Adam and Eve. But despite these public statements of leaders, fundamentalists mounted successful efforts to disparage, distort, and deny evidence and reasoned inquiry, to intimidate textbook companies, to harass professors and pressure school boards and legislatures into censoring inconvenient truths. With characteristic irony, social critic Walter Lippmann jabbed at the often anti-Catholic movement's antidemocratic tendencies, deriding the reformers as "American Inquisitors."[40]

Weekday Religious Instruction

While conservative Christians attacked modern science and cultural pluralism, liberal Protestants found an alternative way to promote God in the schools: altering the weekly schedule to allow for off-site (and sometimes on-site) religious instruction. This "released time" movement evolved out of continuing efforts that, like the Poughkeepsie plan, sought to accommodate religious groups' claims to a voice in public education. Popular programs in New York, Utah, and especially Gary, Indiana, during the 1910s led the way. During the 1920s the idea spread to hundreds of cities and towns, accelerating to thousands during the 1940s and 1950s.[41]

Liberal and moderate Protestants led the movement, or attempted to, through the International Council of Religious Education (ICRE). Their goals were explicitly Protestant. But unlike their fundamentalist counterparts, the ICRE embraced religious pluralism. They urged local religious authorities, including Catholics and Jews, to cooperate with each other, even as they hoped to win the hearts and minds of the "unchurched" children for Christ. For Protestant liberals, the acknowledgment that all groups had equal claim to civic identity (an important aspect of democracy) could be found in that bedrock of Christian ethics, the golden rule. That other groups might not tolerate the liberal Protestants was not the point—at least not while the liberals enjoyed political power.

While not explicitly rejecting science, the ICRE preached a soft antimodernism, teaching children a "Christian interpretation of life and the universe; the ability to see in it God's purpose and plan." Or as a director wrote more bluntly decades later, "The greater emphasis upon the social and physical sciences in public education has tended—except where these scientific facts are given a religious interpretation—toward an increasingly secular and humanistic view of life." ICRE promoters saw no contradiction between these goals and the mission of public schools— indeed, they viewed weekday religious instruction as rounding out the progressive vision of education for life.[42]

Initially other Christian groups adopted a wait-and-see approach. Within two decades, Catholic and Lutheran leaders, historically hostile to public schools and religious instruction within them, warmed to the idea of weekday religious instruction. Mormons embraced it enthusiastically, as did African American educators, most of whom taught in segregated schools. On the other hand, Jewish leaders usually opposed such programs, as did freethinkers, atheists, and others—especially when programs were just thinly disguised efforts to Christianize public school students.[43]

In high schools, religious instruction fell easily within the organizational structure of the school: classes in Bible study and religious history could provide advanced knowledge of religion without, in theory, promoting belief in its supernatural aspects. Elementary schools were more challenging. For these, weekday religious education programs fell into three general types. In the first, least common, and most logistically challenging type, individual religious bodies coordinated with public schools to require children to attend weekly off-campus religious instruction in that faith. Liberals frowned on this "denominational" method, primarily (they argued) because it tended to sow division among children. Religious conservatives, on the other hand, favored its autonomy and doctrinal purity. In the second type, religious bodies coordinated their individual efforts, negotiating together with the school board, sharing resources, training instructors, and organizing cooperative events and interfaith visits, while retaining their individual curricular programs. The third, most popular type, according to the ICRE, involved an ecumenical approach in which consortia of religious bodies created a common curriculum for all children. Such programs were the cheapest and easiest to coordinate, since they did not depend on getting children to a particular church at a particular time. They also maximized economies of scale, allowing all to share the same materials and personnel, and to require higher standards of teaching and learning.

We can never know what took place in each of the various programs, their quality, or their effect, though these probably varied tremendously—especially within the denominational model. Programs typically met for forty-five to sixty minutes per week, on a Wednesday, with grade levels cycling out of the school throughout the day. A sample grade 4–6 curriculum included

one whole year [on] early Hebrew life through the Joseph stories; the next year they spend on the Moses stories. In the first year [pupils] sought with their teachers to understand fully the wonderings of early man about the mysteries all about him, about the sounds in the forests, the wonder of the wind, the vastness of the heavens, and the majesty of the Maker of it all. They dramatized nomadic life as it appeared to them, sitting in front of tents they had made . . . Other activities included visits to Jewish synagogues and return visits of Rabbis with groups of Jewish children to interpret modern Jewish customs.[44]

ICRE examples emulated the type of hands-on, active learning espoused by progressive educators, and tried to connect to the existing public school curriculum. A 1940 handbook recommended discussion, storytelling and drama, music, handicrafts, prayer and worship practices, and community service.[45]

In 1933 the US Bureau of Education endorsed weekday religious education as being consistent with, though separate from, the public school's mission to "guide the pupil's thinking in social and ethical situations as well as in subject matter." The bureau released a report surveying all American towns and cities having 2,500 people or more, receiving back 50–75 percent of surveys (the response rate rising with city size). Eleven percent of all respondents reported having programs. Seven percent reported having once had them but discontinuing them. Eighty-two percent reported no such program ever. The main obstacle to such programs, respondents wrote, was logistical.[46] The financial pressures of the Great Depression did not help.

The religious patriotic fervor that swept the United States in the late 1940s and 1950s fueled a surge in weekday religious programs. Religious groups found creative ways to overcome logistical problems. The Church of Jesus Christ of Latter-day Saints, for example, created over a hundred religious education centers next to public schools. Other groups used nearby homes, rented spaces, or even rolled in "mobile classrooms."[47] Former foes withdrew their objections or joined the bandwagon.

While they seemed to advocate tolerance for religious pluralism, weekday religious programs often exerted pressure on children and their families to conform to particular religious beliefs, and left religions that objected to the program out in the cold. Even the liberal ICRE (swallowed by the even more liberal National Council of Churches in 1950) conceded that reaching the "unchurched" would best be achieved by making participation in religious education programs the default, requiring parents to actively opt out (as opposed to making parents do the work of opting in). Children who did opt out were not always offered stigma-free, equally attractive alternatives. Opponents to the practices charged that regardless of their off-campus status, religious programs that relied on public schools for their promotion violated the long-established policy of nonsectarian public education.

Historically, the Supreme Court avoided such struggles. But at the same time that weekday religious education swept across American public education, constitutional law evolved in a new direction. The fact that the Supreme Court *would* hear religious education cases was, historically speaking, a major change. The First Amendment defines the relationship between the federal government and religion: "Congress shall make no law respecting an establishment of religion, or prohibiting the free exercise thereof; or abridging the freedom of speech, or of the press; or the right of the people peaceably to assemble, and to petition the Government for a redress of grievances." In terms of religion and public education, the amendment has two main components. The first, the establishment clause, denies the federal government the authority to establish an official American religion. The second component of the amendment, the free exercise clause, prevents Congress from interfering with a person's religious belief or behavior. The First Amendment says nothing about state law, however, and historically the federal government did not interfere with state-level religious issues. In fact, for decades after the ratification of the First Amendment in 1789, a few New England states required local towns to democratically choose an official church to support with tax money.

But the court's ruling in *Pierce v. Society of Sisters* (1925), that the Four-

teenth Amendment guaranteed federal protection from state-level violations of due process, proved to be the proverbial camel's nose under the
tent. By 1947 the court ruled in *Everson v. Board of Education* (a case concerning tax-supported transportation to parochial schools) that the First
Amendment prohibition of religious establishment applied to state and
local school laws, giving the federal court the jurisdiction to decide on
local and state religious education issues.

After a series of state-level legal challenges to weekday religious instruction, the Supreme Court heard two cases on the subject. In *McCollum v.
Board of Education* (1948), the court considered the case of Vashti McCollum, an atheist mother whose son attended Champaign, Illinois, public
schools. The Champaign "voluntary" religious education program, organized by local Protestant, Catholic, and Jewish groups, met in public
school classrooms during regular school hours and was supervised by
public school administrators. McCollum made three complaints: that
some religious groups had advantages over others, that in practice it was
coercive for children (especially since attending public schools was itself
compulsory), and that by coordinating and supporting the program in
these ways, the Champaign public schools were establishing religion and
violating individual children's First Amendment rights. Several prominent national organizations of Baptists, Jews, Seventh-Day Adventists,
and Unitarians supported McCollum's suit, as did the court in an 8–1
decision.[48]

But the court did not make it clear whether it was the spirit of the program or its details that were objectionable. When a similar suit tested a
New York City weekday religious program, the court ruled 6–3 in *Zorach v.
Clauson* (1952) that an off-campus program, also during the regular school
day and done in cooperation with school officials, was constitutionally
permissible. The dissenting judges saw the underlying spirit as being the
same as in *McCollum*, with the location of the program being the only
difference. On the other hand, that one detail was critical to the majority.
Expressing the Cold War preoccupation with belief in God (and throwing
the McCollum family under the proverbial bus), Douglas wrote famously,
"We are a religious people whose institutions presuppose a Supreme Being." Public schools' aiding private citizens in making their own religious
decisions was no more a violation of the First Amendment than a police
officer's helping people cross the street on their way to church. Indeed,
Douglas wrote, prohibiting a program like New York's would be "hostile"
to religion.[49]

While numbers declined modestly in the face of the 1948 *McCollum*
case, they exploded after *Zorach*. By 1959 an estimated four million public

school children (at least) participated in weekday religious education programs, 27 percent of public school enrollment grades 4–8 that year.[50] The liberal orientation of released-time programs made them far more successful than previous attempts to bring religion into public schools, because they validated the notion of religious pluralism and did not touch the secular core of daily instruction.

Yet this liberal orientation proved to be a liability when the civil rights movement erupted into the mainstream during the late 1950s and 1960s. Rather than undermine the authority of the Supreme Court's work in civil rights, liberal religionists supported a stricter separation of church and state in the school.[51] Within a few years, new court decisions and a new politics of education would cause the movement to decline, while a new press for high-quality science education in the wake of the Soviet Union's launch of the Sputnik satellite would undo the achievements of the Protestant fundamentalists in censoring science textbooks. The same forces of modernity that drove the God-fearing Cold War consensus during the first half of the century would shortly rip that consensus apart.

The growing role of the high court in resolving controversies brought more sustained attention to constitutional principles, which enriched democratic deliberation, even as judicial activism and political centralization diminished democratic localism. The court did not guarantee legitimacy in all aspects of educational policy: as we have seen, court rulings were (and are) not always fully reasonable. Nevertheless, the emergence of the court as a major player in educational matters created greater space for considering new questions about legitimacy in education. Democratic deliberation now had to grapple with the rights of students conceived as citizens in their own right. The democratic objections to using public education to favor a faith perspective—even in relatively mild and ineffectual ways—could be more forcefully articulated. The subsequent era would see even greater recourse to courts and a vast expansion in rights discourse as integral to democratic deliberation. What remained unresolved (and largely untried), however, was whether schools and even classrooms themselves could become non-coercive spaces for learning about religion in ways consonant with democratic values—laboratories of religiously pluralist democracy.

FIVE

Religion and Public Education since 1960

The story of religion and the public school since 1960 is actually a series of stories: the civil rights revolution and subsequent conservative counterrevolution, a profound restructuring of American religion, the ever-expanding role of the Supreme Court as an arbitrator of local school practices, and the rise of a new politics of American education. The two major results of these stories have been paradoxical: a greatly reduced range of permissible compromises in the curriculum and daily practices of public schools and a deterioration of the managerial separation between church and state schooling. Both are important and complex when viewed from the vantage of democratic legitimacy and the meaning of public reason.

Three brief vignettes of people at the center of disputes about religion and public education highlight the complexity of religion in a religiously diverse society. Madalyn Murray O'Hair, a strident atheist who founded the organization American Atheists, vigorously defended the civil liberties of nonbelievers and aggressively promoted atheism with the zeal of an evangelical proselytizer until her murder in 1995. Jonas Yoder was a devout member of the Old Order Amish who valued the conservative cultural and religious traditions of the tight-knit rural Wisconsin community to which he belonged. Vicki Frost was a born-again Christian from Tennessee with deep antipathy to secular humanism. Frost feared that secular humanism posed a serious threat to the spiritual and moral integrity of American society and, in concert with Christian lobby groups, was determined to stem humanism's corrosive influence. O'Hair, Yoder, and Frost were all parents with strong views about what public schools should be teaching their children. In a manner characteristic of the political climate of the era, all three parents would eventually ask the courts to address their concerns about religion and education. We will return to their stories soon.

There are many ways that democratic communities can reasonably negotiate the challenges posed to public education by religious pluralism. Public reason does not preclude local compromises. But fully legitimate democratic compromise must be grounded in mutual respect between citizens. When this respect is absent, central authority is necessary to assert the reasonable rights claims of minorities.

We do not deny that a diminished form of democratic governance can obtain in the absence of mutual respect. Even bitter enemies can sometimes negotiate agreements that serve their interests, and they can abide by the rule of law. But the tendency of those with power to press for deals that are unfair is greatly exacerbated when they do not respect those with whom they disagree. So it is doubtful that compromises forged against the background of enmity will be stable or just.

Educational politics after 1960 frequently departed from the ideal of mutual respect. At the same time, however, the efforts of groups seeking recognition of their status as fully equal citizens greatly enhanced American political discourse about rights and democracy. As a result, previously underappreciated facets of legitimacy entered national debate. Judges, lawmakers, and school leaders articulated the implications of the separation of church and state for public education with greater force and precision. And for the first time, it became politically possible to raise questions about whether concern for the autonomy of children limited the authority of parents to tightly control the religious identity of their children.[1]

The most significant story in American public education since 1960 has been the rights revolution. The struggle for civil rights has been an ongoing feature of American life for centuries, of course. Led by the African American civil rights movement, this struggle broke into the educational mainstream during the 1950s with the landmark *Brown v. Board of Education* (1954) decision, which declared racial segregation in public education unconstitutional. For the next thirty years, the movement battled white supremacy and legal apartheid at the heart of American life, and soon civil rights activism spread to other forms of legal oppression—against Latinos, Native Americans, women, the disabled, and others. As the quilters of the social fabric, child by child, community by community, public schools became the prime focus of the movement, and the federal courts became the movement's primary instrument.

State and local governments, as well as private citizens, mounted a massive resistance. At first most southern school boards ignored or actively resisted the movement and the court's substantive declaration that segregation based on race was not constitutional. When the judicial and executive branches of the federal government forced the issue, some states closed all public schools rather than mix white children with black ones. Others closed black schools and sent all children to white ones. Private Christian academies for white children sprang up across the South. School-voucher programs offered parents a "choice" of their school that was rarely a choice at all. By the 1970s, desegregation plans in the South and North bussed children across county, or city, to change the racial composition of schools. When whites fled their urban ethnic enclaves for the safety of the suburbs, however, the Supreme Court ruled that mandatory desegregation efforts could not follow them. Beyond bodies in seats, the movement targeted racist curriculum materials and tracking policies, insisted on child welfare programs to keep children healthy and fed, and emphasized the importance of hiring teachers and administrators of color even as, ironically, they were being fired in record numbers when officials closed black schools and sent black children to white-controlled ones.[2]

As the institution in government most willing and able to acknowledge and address the outrageous injustices done to Americans of African descent, the federal judiciary took an unprecedented role in regulating public education. The ensuing "rights revolution" attempted to dismantle many of the most obvious antidemocratic American tendencies. Its legacy was mixed, however, as legal decisions and court orders are the bluntest instruments of social surgery. Many Americans experienced the effects of the movement as an unreasonable intrusion into their community affairs, and saw the courts as being antidemocratic themselves—busting community schools and violating traditional customs.

The second major story in education has been, to a large degree, a backlash against the first. Beginning in the 1950s and gaining prominence in the 1980s, conservative critics resisted the intrusion of federal authority into local schools. By the 1970s, they argued that public school quality was in decline, schools were chaotic, and American children could not compete with those of other countries. Leading reformers advocated business models of accountability, deregulation, and privatization. Nationally, the Republican Party mobilized voters through racial and religious hot-button issues—including school prayer—that cut across traditional denominational boundaries. Meanwhile, standards of living and wages stagnated for many American workers, which, combined with Watergate and an unpopular war in Vietnam, led to decreased confidence in government, including public schools. (Interestingly, Americans' approval of their own local public schools remained high, while their approval of schools generally declined.)[3]

By the 1990s, prominent reformers targeted the very notion of public education. State governments adopted charter school legislation in the name of promoting innovation, but often as a way to enable public funding of religious schools. Coalitions of inner-city African Americans, anti-public libertarian reformers, and conservative Catholics, among others, demanded vouchers (redeemable at public or private schools) as the solution to low quality schooling. The No Child Left Behind Act (2001) attached the rhetoric of equality from the civil rights era to sweeping school reforms based on high-stakes testing, with the result of diminishing local control and reducing classes in history, science, art, music, and other non-tested subjects. Increasing numbers of families opted out of schooling altogether, reaching 1.5 million children in 2007. Some homeschooling parents objected to the rigid, traditional pedagogy of public schools, but the large majority objected to their secular orientation.[4] Degrees of regulation and oversight of homeschooling varied by state, raising concerns about the narrow sectarian character of much homeschooling, which was antithetical to the child's development of understanding and respect for religious and cultural diversity, the acquisition of accurate knowledge of the world, and reasonable habits of analysis and critique that are hallmarks of democratic citizenship.

By the early twenty-first century, the result of this revolution and counterrevolution was a new politics of American education, in which many Americans seriously questioned one or more of the fundamental propositions of the public school first developed in the nineteenth century: that they should be maintained locally and democratically, for the public good, with a common curriculum, and free of sectarian bias. Many people called for more choices and innovation while the standards movement reinforced long-standing curricular patterns and practices.

The conservative revolution in education reflected another profound change in America: the fracturing of American religion. For the first two-thirds of the twentieth century, American politics was driven by coalitions of religious groups, with the split between Catholics and Protestants, and among liberal "mainstream" and fundamentalist Protestant groups being the most prominent. These groups were defined by tradition and identity, including ethnic cohesion, community, and cultural practices. In diverse districts, the politics of religion in public schools played out as a negotiation among these traditional belief systems. "Schools were like a demilitarized zone," recalls a former New Jersey public school administrator. "You had to avoid offending any of the major groups."[5] By the 1980s, however, American religion was realigning politically into two sides: the orthodox, conservative, and traditionalist of all faiths on one side, and the modernist, liberal, and progressive of all faiths on the other. Some remained centrists (adhering to the old traditional model) or gave up their affiliation.[6]

Even the black church, the heart and soul of the civil rights movement, experienced change. Since the nineteenth century, the black church had served as the center of African American community life. Liberation theology inspired and consoled during the monumental struggle against American slavery and apartheid. In an inherently unjust and antidemocratic society, religion gave African Americans the strength to push white America to live up to its democratic ideals. But after moderate success and the rise of a small but significant black middle class, many African Americans by the 1990s embraced a "prosperity gospel" that focused on individual responsibility, not group solidarity, and economic rather than political solutions to poverty. And in truth, even during the 1960s, African Americans split on the question of banning Bible reading and prayer in public schools in the name of protecting religious minorities. The result has been a deep, divisive debate about the role of religion in civic life.[7]

The reconstruction of traditional American religions aside, the civil rights movement's dismantling of racist immigration quotas resulted, by the early twenty-first century, in the emergence of significant communities of non–Judeo-Christian Americans: Muslims, Hindus, Buddhists, and others. It also increased the numbers and diversity of Latino groups. These populations added a further challenge to traditionalists' attempts to conserve their vision for a European, Judeo-Christian America, while people within these groups experienced their own internal divides over the place of faith and tradition in civic identities. The terrorist attacks on 9/11 exacerbated these issues, leading to historically familiar cries for a re-Christianization of America.

The Supreme Court

The rights revolution and ensuing conservative backlash were reflected in the Supreme Court's decisions on religion and public schooling. Beginning with the Jehovah's Witnesses cases in the 1940s and continuing through the 1970s, the court developed a "separationist" approach to religion and public education, defending a high wall of separation between public institutions and religious groups, while generally defending the rights of religious minorities, including atheists, to free expression of their religious views. The court enjoyed the support of religious liberals, primarily mainstream Protestants and Jews, joined by secular groups, even as politically conservative groups pushed hard in the opposite direction.[8]

The court ruled on a string of cases, delineating the proper relationship between religion and public schooling in all manner of detail, including organizational questions of state support for religious education by nonpublic schools, and content-related questions about symbols, celebrations, and curriculum. Until the 1980s, these rulings tended to erect a high barrier against religious establishment, which is to say, preventing public schools from engaging in activities that promote a religious purpose. Religious organizations could not directly benefit from government financial support. School rulings ranged from the mundane to the epic. Two cases in particular fit the latter category. In *Engel v. Vitale* (1962), the court banned a New York State requirement that all public school teachers read a prayer at the start of the school day. The following year, *Abington Township School District v. Schempp* (1963) banned a Pennsylvania law requiring Bible reading and the recitation of the Lord's Prayer. In both cases, the court challenged states' abilities to regulate by law what had once been a common result of negotiation at the local level. And in both cases, the decisions touched off a firestorm of criticism and inspired decades of failed constitutional amendments.[9]

In 1960 firebrand atheist Madalyn O'Hair's fourteen-year-old son, William Murray, seemed to feel as strongly about his atheism as his mother. To protest the daily Bible readings and Lord's Prayer recitation that took place at his Baltimore school, William engaged in a strike that kept him out of school for eighteen days. William and his mother viewed the required religious exercises as an affront to freedom of conscience and a clear violation of the First Amendment of the Constitution. Their objections to the school policy generated a great deal of controversy. O'Hair and her children were vilified as communists, and they were the target of intimidating threats to such a degree that they required police protection. By 1962 the matter went to court and was eventually integrated into the 1963 Supreme Court case *Abington School District v. Schempp*, in which the court declared Bible readings orchestrated by public schools to be unconstitutional. Though enormously politically significant, O'Hair's victory may have been Pyrrhic from a personal point of view. Her notoriety was such that she described herself as "the most hated woman in America." William O'Hair would go on not only to repudiate his atheism and embrace Christianity but also to found the Religious Freedom Coalition, an organization devoted to, among other things, restoring prayer to school.

Engel and *Schempp* illustrated the way in which fair legislative procedures may not be sufficient to generate fully legitimate political outcomes. Negotiated compromises that are acceptable or even popular for most people can still be contested as unreasonable by small and unpopular minorities, if their fundamental rights are violated. For contemporary public-reason theorists, the idea that neither teachers nor students at public schools could be compelled to lead or participate in even minor religious exercises will seem rather obvious. After all, for the nonbeliever or the non-Christian, neither state-sanctioned devotional Bible readings nor prayer in school can be viewed as nonsectarian or innocuous. Nevertheless, the demands of political legitimacy are sometimes more evident to people who enjoy the benefits of historical hindsight.

The bans had a moderately strong effect. In a national survey conducted during the 1964–1965 school year, teachers reported that regular morning prayers had declined from 60 percent to 28 percent after *Engel*. The numbers for Bible reading pre- and post-*Schempp* were 48 percent and 22 percent. Not surprisingly, those places with the strongest commitment to public religion, and the weakest regard for the civil-rights-era Supreme Court, resisted the hardest. An estimated 60 percent of southern districts continued morning prayers in the late 1960s, for example.[10] Not until the twenty-first century did organized prayer and Bible reading become rare in all regions of the country. Other kinds of symbolic exercises—even ones explicitly banned by the court—have continued, however, with the highest levels of noncompliance tending to be in communities that are southern, rural, and less educated, with high concentrations of conservative Christians.[11]

But what should happen in cases where the very idea of public education, and not just symbolic exercises, seem to conflict with religious beliefs? The Supreme Court soon considered this question. Jonas Yoder did not want his daughter, Frieda, to attend school beyond grade 8, but Wisconsin state law required that children be enrolled in school until age sixteen. Jonas believed that his daughter had already received sufficient education to prepare her for life in the traditional Amish community to which she belonged. He feared, moreover, that further education would expose her to different ideas and values at odds with traditional Amish religious commitments. Yoder and other Amish parents claimed that attending high school was "contrary to the Amish religion and way of life and that they would endanger their own salvation and that of their children by complying with the law." Fifteen-year-old Frieda, who had little knowledge or experience of life outside her isolated rural community, seemed to agree. In the 1972 landmark case, *Wisconsin v. Yoder*, the high court revisited the question of compulsory school attendance, which it had first considered during the 1920s.[12] Frieda testified that she wanted to be raised in the Amish faith and that it would be against her religious beliefs to attend high school. Although it seems doubtful that Frieda was in a good position to make an informed and autonomous choice at the matter, the Supreme Court sided with the Yoders and exempted Amish children from compulsory school attendance beyond age fourteen. The ruling signaled the court's endorsement of the controversial idea that religious parents have enormous authority to try to secure their children's allegiance to a particular faith. Since the Amish are a relatively small group whose views about modernity have little broader uptake, however, the political and cultural outfall of the decision was relatively limited. Most Americans were not concerned about the accommodation of the wishes of small outlier religious groups, even if such accommodation denied some children feasible access to the modern world.

Indeed, while the Yoder decision might appear to have opened the door to any parent opting out of compulsory school laws on religious grounds, the court began its decision by affirming that "[t]here is no doubt as to the power of a State, having a high responsibility for education of its citizens, to impose reasonable regulations for the control and duration of basic education . . . Providing public schools ranks at the very apex of the function of a State." The crux of the majority opinion was that the state's educational responsibility to children living in separate Amish farming communities was adequately fulfilled by an eighth-grade education.

The court's opinion suggested that the Amish might be a unique case in this respect, citing the long history of the Amish as a distinct people who consistently rejected all aspects of modernity, including the forward march of human knowledge and public affairs, as a core article of faith that affected every aspect of their daily lives, or "mode of life." And it signaled that the decision was idiosyncratic enough to minimize its general applicability. "Their rejection of telephones, automobiles, radios, and television, their mode of dress, of speech, their habits of manual work do indeed set them apart from much of contemporary society," the court observed. "These customs are both symbolic and practical." The Amish had no intention to participate in the public and political life of American democracy, and offered a viable, cloistered community to its children.[13]

Notwithstanding the caveats about the limited scope of the *Yoder* decision, many contemporary political theorists think the court failed to adequately recognize the right of children to an autonomy-facilitating education. Although the court broached the important question of the degree to which a democratic education should permit children to meaningfully contemplate and pursue opportunities and values outside a traditional religious community, it fell short of acknowledging that education should facilitate critical deliberation about traditional religious commitments. If, as we have suggested, children are entitled to an autonomy-facilitating education that prepares them both for effective democratic citizenship and for informed reflection on spiritual matters, then the court's reasoning was problematic. It is highly doubtful that Frieda's limited education equipped her with reasoning skills and knowledge needed for that kind of deliberation.

The separationist court also heard cases on local and state efforts to use public tax money to support religious (usually Roman Catholic) educational institutions. In the most significant of these, *Lemon v. Kurtzman*, the court found that state laws in Pennsylvania and Rhode Island supplementing parochial school teachers' salaries violated the First Amendment. The ruling established the "*Lemon* test," which it hoped would guide local and state governments as they legislated on religious matters. To comport with the First Amendment, the *Lemon* decision ruled, the government's action must (1) have a secular legislative purpose, (2) have a *primary* effect that neither advances nor inhibits religion, and (3) must not result in excessive government entanglement with religion. For example, a local government could pay for the transportation costs of all children to go to any school they want because an educated citizenry is important, even though a secondary effect of such a decision (covering the cost of transport to nonpublic schools) would certainly be welcomed by some religious groups (*Everson v. Board of Education*, 1947). On the other hand, even though the Pennsylvania and Rhode Island statutes claimed on the face of things to have a secular purpose similar to the transportation example (paying teachers only for the part of their teaching that covered the public school curriculum), there was no feasible way to ensure that the laws actually conformed to a secular purpose. Any serious attempt to make these laws truly secular in purpose would require public officials to monitor what, when, and how the teachers taught while on the "public" part of their salary—just as it did with regular public school teachers. This, the court argued, was excessive entanglement.

Alarmed at the court's separationist agenda and the ever-diminishing role of local control in public schools, conservative activists worked to put religion-and-public-education issues front and center in national politics. Joined by white advocacy groups, evangelical Protestants adopted the language of the civil rights movement to claim that they were victims of discrimination. Conservative Republican presidential candidates adopted a tough-on-crime, anti-integration, antiabortion, anti-affirmative-action agenda, while Republican presidents nominated Supreme Court justices they thought were committed to rolling back the civil rights revolution in American jurisprudence. As a result of conservative appointments, the court focused more on accommodating organized religion (but remaining neutral among religions), and less on policing a high wall of separation and protecting individual and minority rights.[14]

On several issues, the accommodationist court seemed to abandon *Lemon*.[15] In a string of school-funding cases, the court ruled that states (and the federal government) could use public money to assist religious organizations in a number of ways, as long as it did not choose among religions. Thus in *Zelman v. Simmons-Harris* (2002), the court cleared the way for public-voucher programs to finance parochial schools, provided that parents, not the state, determined the selection of the school programs (though many state-level constitutional prohibitions against such programs remained). In other cases, the court erected a high wall of "standing," making it more difficult for religious minorities to bring constitutional challenges to court, while radically increasing the power of government to punish the free exercise of religion when that exercise violated the law.[16]

Despite its rightward shift, the court continued to apply the principles of *Lemon* in certain situations where public schools appeared to endorse or compel a particular religious belief. Whether it was a case of public school–sponsored prayers at graduation ceremonies or high school football games, or setting aside time for silent prayer or meditation, a divided court continued to forbid religious expressions that were sponsored or encouraged by school officials.[17] At the same time, lower courts joined the Supreme Court in favor of student religious speech, including voluntary prayer, and the right of religious groups to gain the same access to school facilities for after-school programs that was granted to other groups. Likewise, Bible study as a critical, scholarly endeavor was permissible, but Bible study as an uncritical devotional activity was not.[18] In what could have been the most symbolically significant decision in a generation, the court refused to hear a 2004 appeal on whether the phrase "under God," added by Congress to the Pledge of Allegiance fifty years earlier, violated the First Amendment. The court declined on the grounds that the plaintiff, a father suing on behalf of his noncustodial daughter, had no legal standing.[19]

The separationist court of the 1960s and 1970s had resolved the tension between religion and democracy more often by protecting minority rights against majorities, and keeping government money separate from religious education. The underlying theory of the accommodationist approach, on the other hand, was that local and state government should have much more authority when it came to determining the relationship between democracy, education, and religion, while religious traditions should be preserved even in cases where they may not be shared by all members of a community. More generally, accommodationists saw the encouragement and protection of religion, as a general matter, to be the business of government. Their decisions reflected the new politics of American religion, in which one's general orientation toward religion— authoritarian and traditionalist versus liberal and open to difference— mattered more than adherence to specific doctrines or sects. Nonetheless, the orientation to religion that the accommodationist court favored had a Judeo-Christian character, making its commitment to a religiously neutral political stance doubtful.[20]

Science and the Secular Curriculum

In 1957 the Soviet Union launched the first manmade object, Sputnik, into orbit, leading to a frenzy of hand-wringing and calls for reform in American science education. Over the next fifty years, evolution went from being a subject that was often ignored and sometimes outlawed to being the core of American science education, while biblical stories about the origins of life on Earth lost their place in the public school. Liberal religious groups and most scientists supported the move toward rigorous science education in public schools, while pro-creation advocates, on the defensive, evolved.

Initially the federal government played a leading role. President Eisenhower famously requested a billion dollars from Congress to further science education and research. The National Science Foundation funded the Biological Sciences Curriculum Study in 1959, which produced a series of revised high school textbooks that restored the theory of evolution to the center of the biology curriculum. These quickly captured half the textbook market.[21]

State-level anti-evolution statutes soon fell as well. In 1967 the Tennessee legislature repealed its Scopes-era law due to the legal challenge of a high school science teacher. The following year, the US Supreme Court favored Arkansas science teacher Susan Epperson, ruling that the state's anti-evolution law violated the First Amendment. In 1970 the final "monkey" law fell when the Mississippi supreme court struck down that state's anti-evolution law, citing the *Epperson* decision.[22] Mainstream media supported the resurgence of evolution in the curriculum, just as it had during the Scopes trial.[23]

In response to these victories for modern science, creationists changed their strategies.[24] They adopted a two-pronged attack: raise doubts about the theory of evolution's credibility, and insist on equal time for creationism as a valid alternative that is commensurate with scientific reasoning. Ironically, this strategy seemed to involve implicit acceptance of the idea that the curriculum should focus on public knowledge—knowledge claims that could be presented and assessed via common standards of reasoning and evidence. Religious reasons grounded in particular faith traditions could not be represented as ways of justifying the inclusion of traditional religious teachings in the curriculum. Some creationist parents seized on the *Schempp* decision to argue that their children's religious civil rights were being violated when public schools insisted that their children study information that contradicted their beliefs. They demanded equal time in the science classroom for Bible stories of the origins of life on Earth.[25] Other creationists pushed the equal-time argument by imagining a field called "creation science," which sought to use scientific evidence to support Old Testament claims about the origins of life. Evolution and creation science, they argued, were equally valid theories supported by equally valid evidence and deserved to be taught side by side in the interest of good science instruction. As they did during the Scopes era, these scientific creationists concocted curriculum materials to teach children the supposed "proofs" of the biblical accounts of geological and biological history, while making erroneous and misleading arguments about supposedly fatal flaws in the fields of geology, biology, physics, and astronomy. The theory of evolution was the greatest fallacy of all, some argued—quite literally the work of Satan implanted in wicked minds.[26] Though neither strategy, equal time or anti-science, was successful in the courts of law, several national surveys suggested that half of all Americans believed that Adam and Eve founded the human race, while a large majority, from all walks of life, supported teaching creationism in schools.[27]

Creationism made limited headway in some state legislatures. During the 1970s and early 1980s, several southern states passed laws permitting or mandating "equal time" for creationism. These did not survive long, however. An American Civil Liberties Union–led challenge to an Arkansas law led to victory in federal district court, in *McLean v. Arkansas Board of Education* (1982), with the presiding judge finding that creation science was not science at all, but an attempt to use public education to promote Christianity. Five years later, in 1987, a divided Supreme Court overturned an equal-time Louisiana law in *Edwards v. Aguillard*, based on the *Lemon* test: clearly, a majority of the justices wrote, the intent of requiring the teaching of creationism was to advance a particular religious viewpoint. The *McLean* and *Aguillard* cases cast a pall over existing equal-time laws and dampened efforts to pass new ones.[28]

The fundamentalist attack against the public school curriculum was not limited to booby-trapping science curricula and then playing defense in court. Unlike Jonas Yoder, Vicki Frost was very much a part of mainstream American Christian culture. In the early 1980s her children attended public schools in Tennessee, and she had no reservations about providing them with an education that would equip them to be participants in the modern economy. She cared passionately, however, about the threat to the spiritual well-being of her children that she thought was posed by textbooks used by the local public school. As she interpreted them, stories in the Holt Reading Series presented a direct assault on Christianity and patriotic American values. The readers contained stories and content that mentioned topics that Frost found objectionable to her religious beliefs—references to witchcraft and magic, relative (as opposed to absolute) moral values, disrespect of parents, prayer to idols, and evolution, among other things. Frost spent hundreds of hours studying the Holt textbooks that had been adopted by the Hawkins County school board as compulsory elements of the curriculum. She compiled a litany of objections to the supposedly offensive and corrupting content she claimed to detect in them. Frost became so incensed by the unwillingness of her daughter's school to provide alternative readings that she entered the school on numerous occasions to remove her daughter Sarah from class, so that she could learn to read using religiously appropriate materials. Her refusal to respect school rules led to her being charged with trespass.

Frost was perhaps the most vocal and dramatic opponent to the readers, but she was by no means alone in her battle against the school board. Some other local parents, including Bob Mozert, shared her concerns, as did prominent members of fundamentalist groups such as Concerned Women of America and the Moral Majority. With financial and legal assistance from Concerned Women of America, legal action was taken against the Hawkins County school board. Frost and her allies won an initial legal victory. By 1987, however, *Mozert v. Hawkins* reached its final destination, the US Court of Appeals for the Sixth Circuit. By this time, the children at the heart of the case had been transferred to private schools that employed curriculum materials more palatable to Christian fundamentalists.

In three separate but concurring opinions, the court decided unanimously against the plaintiffs. Chief Judge Lively and Judge Kennedy pointed to the difference between exposure to ideas and compulsion to believe them, finding that the state had a compelling interest in exposing students to controversial topics to encourage their civic skills. In this respect, the ruling represented an important advance on the view of parental authority in *Yoder*. Preparation for meaningful democratic citizenship might require exposure to and consideration of controversial ideas. In the context of a public education, parents could not insulate children from the pluralism of a democratic society. Arguably this represented a step toward recognition of the state's responsibility to help facilitate the development of children's autonomy. The court also shared the Supreme Court's concern in *Wisconsin v. Yoder* about setting the bar for free exercise objections too low. Judge Kennedy concluded, quoting Justice Jackson in the *McCollum* decision: "If we are to eliminate everything that is objectionable to any of these warring sects or inconsistent with any of their doctrines, we will leave public education in shreds."

In his contrarian concurrence, however, Judge Danny Boggs argued that the plaintiffs did indeed have a legitimate free exercise complaint against the curriculum, and that, in opposition to the *Yoder* decision, the bar should be as low as possible in deciding what content might infringe on professed religious beliefs. Anticipating the libertarian wing of the school-choice movement, Boggs insisted that public schools as they currently existed could, unfortunately, be sites for teaching all manner of offensive material as long as it did not promote religion or nonreligion. School choice, he implied, was the only way to protect a parent's alleged right to teach children any values or version of reality they chose. (On this view, a child's right to autonomy development was not important, nor was concern for public reason.) Incredibly, however, the judge concurred with his colleagues on originalist grounds. "The drafters of the Bill of Rights never contemplated a school system that would be the most pervasive benefit of citizenship for many, yet which would be very difficult to avoid," he wrote. And so the judge felt he could not apply free exercise to this case. Judge Boggs was wrong, of course. James Madison, Thomas Jefferson, and other founding fathers did indeed contemplate public school systems both pervasive and difficult to avoid, seeing the inculcation of public reason and virtue, as well as creating common identity, as critical to the success of the republic. Fortunately his error had no bearing on the court's ruling.[29] Nevertheless, if Frost ultimately lost the legal battle, it appears that she indirectly won a battle in the culture wars between liberal and conservative elements of American society. In 1986 a revised edition of the Holt Reading Series was issued, and many of the passages in the earlier edition to which Frost had objected were removed.

By the 1990s a broad movement to create state and national curriculum standards for public schools brought even more pressure to bear against creation stories in the science classroom—both from physical sciences and from biological ones. The National Academy of Science published recommended standards in 1996, placing the theory of evolution at the heart of scientific inquiry. Soon the No Child Left Behind Act tied federal funding for public schools to the adoption of state standards in reading and mathematics, routine testing regimes, and policy making rooted in scientific research (narrowly conceived). The act prompted states to create rigorous science standards for upper grades as well.

Abandoning the idea of creation science, prominent fundamentalist school reformers instead promoted the idea of "intelligent design," insisting that public schools teach students that a supreme being lay behind the scientifically supported processes that created the planet and life on it. By softening and broadening its claims, the intelligent-design movement hoped to enjoy wider support and better chances in court than with creation science. As with the creation-science strategy, however, intelligent design failed. In *Kitzmiller v. Dover* (2005) a federal district judge ruled that a 2004 Dover (Pennsylvania) Area School District policy requiring the teaching of intelligent design as an alternative theory to evolution was creationism by another name, and thus violated the First Amendment prohibition against establishing religion.[30]

During the early 2000s, public opinion showed growing acceptance of evolution. According to a 2006 survey sponsored by the Pew Foundation, 51 percent of Americans accepted the theory of evolution, while 62 percent acknowledged that scientists agreed on the theory among themselves.[31] On the other hand, the equal-time movement enjoyed popularity as well: a 2005 Pew poll found that 64 percent of Americans favored the teaching of creationism alongside evolution in public schools.[32] Later polls, however, showed signs of religion's declining significance in American life in general. A 2012 Pew poll found that the number of Americans who reported no religious affiliation had increased from 15 to 20 percent in just six years, and was expected to grow significantly as older, more religiously committed generations passed on.[33] Such demographic changes did not bode well for the movement to revive a Christian fundamentalist view of human origins in the public schools.

Blurring the Line between Church and State

While the public education curriculum became more narrowly secular after the 1960s, the boundaries between public and religious oversight of public education eroded. The causes can be traced to the new politics of education and religion following the civil rights movement. The resurgence of conservative reaction against public education, while born among white supremacists, eventually attracted a diverse coalition of supporters: right-wing free marketeers, left-wing advocates for the urban poor, and advocates of public funding for religious education, including the Roman Catholic Church (which had been seeking public tax dollars since the nineteenth century), evangelical Protestants, and other religious groups. Religion may have been only one among many issues at the heart of this movement, but from a legal standpoint, it was the most challenging.[34]

Initially, the late-twentieth-century effort to introduce free-market principles into public schooling, called the choice movement, rose and fell with the massive resistance to *Brown v. Board of Education*. While voucher advocates in the early 1960s could be found among a handful of right-wing thinkers—secularists like Milton Friedman, and Catholics like Virgil Blum of Wisconsin—it was conservative southern white supremacists who pushed the movement with the most vigor and success. Rather than desegregate their neighborhood public schools, southern states tried a variety of strategies to maintain white supremacy. Creating "freedom of choice" among schools became the most common strategy. In some cases parents could, ostensibly, choose among public schools. (In reality this was rarely a choice at all, and whites used violence, economic oppression, and other nefarious means to maintain segregation.) More radical plans simply ended public schools, or claimed to, and awarded tuition vouchers and tax credits to choose among private academies that were in essence the same segregated public schools as before. The Supreme Court struck down these and other policies in a string of 1968 decisions.[35] Importantly, these voucher plans avoided direct funding for religious schools; their primary purpose was to maintain Jim Crow education.[36] Conservatives like Blum and Friedman, adopting a see-no-evil stance toward the racists, simply ignored the role of voucher plans in reinforcing segregated schooling.[37]

By the early 1990s, however, the tide had turned. While protecting white privilege continued to fuel some of the conservative movement in the United States, the main arguments in favor of school choice came from religious sectarians who sought to soften the separation of church and state in education, and a diverse coalition of reformers who believed that using business principles of free markets would improve public schools (or simply enrich businesses eager to penetrate the public market). Dysfunctional urban schools, the advocates promised, would respond favorably to market forces because they would lose their "monopoly" of public management. Rather than view education as a public good, to be managed democratically (which big-city school districts often did not, really), promoters argued that a child's education was a private good, best managed by businesses or business-like entities, which included religious authorities. Critics of vouchers, on the other hand, saw them as a way to divert even more resources from struggling public schools into the hands of private entities that were neither regulated nor accountable, undermining the civic as well as academic mission of public schools.

States tried several approaches to privatizing public education—handing over struggling public school districts to private management companies, offering open enrollment programs allowing parents free choice among district public schools, providing tuition tax credits for private schools, issuing charters for specific groups to operate public schools with reduced public regulation, and, in the most radical departure from tradition, offering vouchers directly to parents, to be redeemed at any participating public or private school, including religious schools. Built on lofty rhetoric and promises of radical improvement, the school-choice movement enjoyed slow but steady growth, lubricated by favorable state policy and Supreme Court decisions.[38]

The most radical of school-choice plans, vouchers given directly to parents to spend at any participating school they chose, had the broadest implications for church-state relations. Under the guise of improving academic standards and student achievement, voucher plans provided a way of publicly supporting schools with expressly religious aims and thereby blurring the separation between church and state. Starting with Milwaukee in 1990 and Cleveland in 1995, diverse city and state coalitions of advocates created voucher programs whereby families could redeem a voucher at any participating school—public, secular private, or religious—as long as the education the school provided for that voucher was religiously neutral.[39] Both cities were ripe for such a radical change. Each had a long history of Catholic Church attempts (some successful) to win state assistance for its work with the poor, some of which was exemplary. Ohio governor George Voinovich, a former mayor of Cleveland, spoke for many when he expressed his view to the right-wing Catholic advocacy group, the Knights of Columbus, that "state legislators look upon Catholic education as a yardstick by which to measure other schools."[40] And both Milwaukee and Cleveland had endured decades of urban decay, thanks to the disappearance of economic opportunities for low-skill workers combined with middle-class flight to the suburbs and state-level neglect. Touted as the panacea to the problems of urban public schooling, vouchers appeared to many to be the only way out of a dire situation, short of addressing underlying economic inequalities.

The Supreme Court agreed. In 2002 the court ruled in favor of these types of programs in the landmark case *Zelman v. Simmons-Harris*. The 5–4 majority decision found voucher programs to be constitutionally permissible as long as they had a valid secular purpose; the aid went directly to parents, not schools; they targeted a broad class of beneficiaries; they were religiously neutral; and they offered adequate nonreligious options.[41]

Despite the favorable court ruling in *Zelman*, however, voucher programs did not spread as quickly as promoters had hoped. By 2013 only a handful of voucher programs existed in the United States, the largest by far being a statewide system for low- and middle-income students across the entire state of Indiana, including religious schools. Why did voucher plans fail to take off? Approximately thirty state constitutions contained language forbidding varying degrees of state support for religious schooling, both within public schools and through giving public tax dollars directly to religious groups.[42] Demographics played an important role as well. Pleased with their high-quality neighborhood schools, suburban Americans had little incentive to threaten the system that made such schools possible, while in rural areas, it was difficult to have choice among schools, just as it had been in the nineteenth century. Finally, the glue that held the diverse pro-voucher coalitions together—the promise of fixing urban education—may have lost its grip when decades of experience and dozens of studies showed that school vouchers failed to achieve their promised results.[43] Choice, it turned out, was not a panacea.

In the early 2000s, charter schools eclipsed vouchers as the educational policy of choice among school reformers, attracting attention from religious leaders and groups interested in breaking down the barriers between church and state in the delivery of public education. A charter school could be proposed by any group who designed a school to be governed by a charter, as long as that charter was approved by a state-approved agency. Begun as a way to encourage innovation among public schools by reducing regulation, charter schools suspended many of the ordinary rules of public education. By 2007, 2 percent of American school children were enrolled in charter schools.[44] By 2013, 4.6 percent of all American public schools were charter schools.[45] As with vouchers, however, charter schools on the whole did not significantly raise student achievement. Indeed, researchers found that while some charters outperformed typical public schools, a greater percentage of them actually did worse.[46]

While charter schools were, in theory, secular educational institutions, in reality a significant number were sponsored by religious organizations. The same constitutional prohibitions that applied to regular schools still applied to charters—they had to have a secular purpose and could not promote a particular religious view in the classroom or discriminate against teachers or students on account of faith. Nevertheless, charter schools presented a middle ground for religious groups to participate in public education. In 2010, for example, more than 20 percent of Texas charter schools were run by religious groups. Nationally, Islamic and Jewish groups joined Roman Catholic and evangelical Protestants to create networks of hundreds of religiously affiliated charter schools.[47]

The situation was not politically black and white. Some conservatives cheered Tarek ibn Ziyad Academy in Minneapolis, for example, which offered a curriculum and environment that celebrated Arabic language, as well as the cultures and history of Africa, Asia, and the Middle East, while claiming not to promote Islam per se. At this and other religious charter schools, children of any faith, or none at all, could in theory attend just as they would any public charter school. Those who chose to could remain after school for additional religious activities.[48] Nevertheless, an ACLU lawsuit charged that the school did conduct prayer during the school day, while teachers promoted Islam through bulletin-board postings, within Arabic-language instruction, and through its dress code. Indeed, even as some religious conservatives cherished the possibility that charters offered public support for their particular religions, however, other conservative activists railed against charters for unpopular Islamic schools like Tarek ibn Ziyad, because such schools promoted a religious viewpoint they feared.[49] Just as James Madison had once predicted, opening the door for one group meant opening it to all, igniting intergroup animosities.

Whether or not they improved academic instruction, charters reopened an old chapter in the relationship between church and state in education. On one hand, the deregulation of school administration led to widespread fraud, corruption, and abuse of the secular democratic purposes of public schooling—not a surprising result in a rapidly deregulated marketplace. On the other hand, charter schools provided a pathway for many alienated religious groups to engage the public sphere. Researchers found, for example, that parents and students enrolled in charter schools were happier with the education they were receiving, even if there was no measurable difference in the quality of teaching and learning.[50] As charter schools drew religious groups into the public sphere, the "strings attached" to charters required them to meet the broader democratic society halfway. This process, some scholars argued, was good for religious minorities and the majority alike, even if it made violations of individual civil rights more likely.[51] In this way, religious charter schools resembled arrangements like the Poughkeepsie plan of old.

What was new was the groups involved. While Muslims accounted for less than 1 percent of the American population in 2010, in the wake of the 9/11 terror attacks in particular, anti-Islam animus complicated the crusade for state support of religion. From 2000 to 2010, for example, over thirty state legislators introduced laws banning the consideration of "foreign or religious laws" in state courts—bills implicitly or explicitly targeting Islamic sharia.[52] Historically, religious laws and courts have always governed some forms of personal behavior in the United States (Jewish law regulating divorce, for example, or Roman Catholic canon law discouraging bishops from reporting child rape to the police). On their face, these anti-sharia laws sought to prevent courts from permitting unpopular cultural practices. While concern about the antidemocratic tendencies of some Islamic laws were intellectually valid (just as concerns about some Christian or Jewish laws would be), these efforts also represented deeper changes in the demographics of the United States—changes that inspired xenophobia and political opportunism.

Indeed, changing demographics and changing social norms in the early twenty-first century promised fresh complications in the relationship between democracy and religion in American public schools. The increasing acceptance, and legal status, of gay and lesbian youth and their families challenged the homophobic teachings of many traditionalist religions. The continued immigration of non-Europeans with religious and cultural practices outside of the Judeo-Christian family, and changing political balance among existing groups, has once again made old compromises over least-common-denominator religious practices untenable. Other shifts—the cultural diversification of suburbs, the decline of rural life, and the rise of online education, to name a few—all promised to change the curriculum, management, and very meaning of public schooling.

SIX

Finding Faith in Democracy: Three Cases

In the previous chapters, we have seen that the pursuit of democratic legitimacy in public education is an ongoing process that often involves heated disputes about what is politically reasonable and acceptable to all. Yet within the debates, legal wrangling, and hard-fought political compromises, we detect a concern to articulate and realize a vision of democratic education suitable for a religiously diverse citizenry. In many ways the historical challenges that Americans have faced in the educational domain have enriched the vocabulary of public reason and our understanding of democratic legitimacy. Challenges remain, and it is to some of these challenges that we now turn.

Today religion, democracy, and American public education are at a crossroad. While politicians and pundits are experiencing mass amnesia about the democratic purposes of public education, and while state and national standards are squeezing the remnants of citizenship education out of the school curriculum, scholars now have a more compelling understanding than ever about why we need to keep it in, and how to do it. This book argues that legitimate resolutions to controversies about the place of religion in public schools depend on the exercise of public reason. In this chapter, we want to offer some reflections about how public schools can be sites where public reason is cultivated and deployed.

Here is what we know: Democracy does not come to us naturally. It requires belief in procedures that delay our gratification and try our patience with results that may, at times, disappoint us. In our view, democracy requires reason giving and reason taking among citizens committed to finding mutually acceptable solutions to political problems. All this takes practice. The best way to learn to engage democracy is not to passively memorize lists of dead presidents, to read textbook entries about the three branches of government, or to wave around pocket copies of the Constitution like talismans (the kind of political theater currently popular in the US Congress). Certainly, accurate knowledge is vital to being an effective citizen, but knowledge that is dead lies still, forgotten more quickly than the test grade it earned. People learn best by understanding the facts they possess and putting that knowledge to use—the more frequently the better. Democratic citizens are best made in classrooms and schools where they not only learn the facts about their system of government, but also analyze and employ them in reasoned deliberations over points of controversy.

In this chapter we reframe current controversies over religion and public education, placing less attention on what courts determine is constitutionally permissible (which is often itself a contested measure) and instead focusing on what we see as optimal for democratic education. We examine three recent controversies that highlight the challenges that religion brings to public education in the early twenty-first century. In each case there is opportunity in the controversy—money on the floor, as the saying goes, if only public schools would pick it up.

The first area of controversy is *student voice*. Given the vital importance of student self-expression, how can we reasonably protect spaces in public education for students to develop their civic competence without sacrificing their religious identity? The question of student voice leads naturally to our second challenge: the rise of *inclusion* as a legal—as well as cultural—value in public schooling. What should we do when religious beliefs teach intolerance toward other students in the same school, never mind other citizens in the same nation? Do religious teachings of hatred and exclusion deserve special protections because they are religious? Finally, *market-based reform*, in the form of charter schools and voucher systems, is an issue that is likely to be with us for some time to come, bringing with it a whole new set of challenges. Can religious organizations be trusted to offer a democratic education despite their dogmatic opposition to democratic values? Can the individual choice to segregate by religious faith be a virtue?

In each instance, we try to bring our knowledge of history and philosophy to bear on the problem. At the very least, history helps us understand how things came to be, while philosophy helps us think deeply about how to evaluate the goodness of this state of affairs, to weigh policies, and to make choices. While historians and philosophers are poor predictors of the future, we see student voice, inclusion, and market-based reform as challenges that are unlikely to go away. In fact, in a healthy democracy, we would not *want* all challenges to go away: it is in the negotiation over what it means to be a public school that democratic citizens are made.

Our first stop is East Texas.

Cheerleading in Kountze

Kountze is a very small town. It sits in the heart of Hardin County, Texas, about fifty miles north of the Gulf Coast as the crow flies, and only thirty miles west of the Louisiana border. The demographics of the town's 2,100 people are what one might expect in the region: 70 percent white, 23 percent black, 5 percent Latino, and a handful of mixed races, Asians, Native Americans, and others. The people are generally working class or poor, with a 2013 median household income of $34,682 (compared to a statewide income of $51,704). A quarter of residents twenty-five years or older lack a high school diploma; only 12 percent graduated from a four-year college. In 2012, 83 percent of Hardin County voters went for Romney.[1]

When it comes to religion, Hardin County is much like a nineteenth-century American town—diverse in a homogeneous sort of way. According to county-wide data, about 59 percent of residents claim to be affiliated with a particular religious organization. Of those, a large majority, nearly 70 percent, are Southern Baptists, about 10 percent are Roman Catholic, another 10 percent Methodist. The rest are a mix of Protestant denominations, a handful of Mormons, and others.[2]

Sited just west of the town center, Kountze High School is small, too, and serves both Kountze and the neighboring unincorporated community of Honey Island, the ghost of a former lumber town that is home to some 400 residents. The high school serves approximately 400 students, graduates around 80 annually, and has a faculty (including administration and staff) of around 36 members. The school mascot is the lion (for boys) or the lionette (for girls).[3]

In 2012 Kountze High's cheerleaders became the center of a national controversy. Over the summer, members of the squad decided to write biblical passages on the large paper banners that the boys' football team runs through at the start of each game. The point, the girls explained later, was to focus on positive, inspirational messages. The first one read, "I can do all things through Christ which strengthens me."[4] Others followed.

In mid-September the school principal ordered the squad to stop, expressing concern that the Christian messages violated the establishment clause of the First Amendment. Fifteen of the girls then sued the district, claiming that the ban was a violation of their First Amendment rights to religious expression. The district court placed a temporary injunction on the ban, allowing the girls to continue their practice until it could formally decide on the case. Meanwhile the district formulated a policy that affirmed its right to regulate the students' speech on the banners, but also declared that the banners were only "fleeting expressions of community sentiment" that did not constitute government endorsement of religion. The following spring the Texas court did rule—in favor of the girls and the district's new policy, endorsing the "fleeting sentiment" argument. The banners, the judge found, were private religious expression, not government speech.[5]

Despite the pack of reporters in the courtroom and the heavily armed police officer on the roof, the hearing was a relatively anodyne affair. The girls claimed to be seeking positive messages to help their school. The principal who issued the ban claimed to be a Christian who was sympathetic to the girls and wanted only to do what was legal. The district's new policy endorsed the squad's banners without denying that the speech was, to some degree, formally regulated and sanctioned. Both the district and the girls expressed relief at the ruling. Perhaps, as the ACLU suggested, the district feared a potential federal court ruling on the banners. In any case the die was cast. State and national groups on both sides of the issue had taken interest, as had the media. An appeal followed quickly.[6]

There is not much new legal ground in the Kountze controversy. Since the early 1960s, the Supreme Court has consistently determined that traditional public schools may not advocate or endorse religion—whether that endorsement be teaching Christian mythology in biology class, posting holy scriptures on school walls, or sponsoring school prayer at the start of the school day or at an after-school football game. This prohibition is likely to stand. If a federal judge finds evidence of school oversight and endorsement of the Kountze banners (which the school district has already conceded), she will find them in violation. The "fleeting" aspect, too, has been settled by precedent (and is not especially persuasive, because the expressions are systematic and regular). On the other hand, federal courts have also defended the rights of individual students to religious expression, such as wearing religious garb or emblems, praying, or displaying religious writings. Courts largely concern themselves today with controversies like that at Kountze because they lie at the intersection of school authority (establishment) and student voice (free expression). It is in these controversies that we see one of the key ongoing struggles to define what it means to be a democratic citizen in a religiously pluralistic society. It is also in these controversies that we see the limitations of resolving educational problems solely through recourse to constitutional litigation.

Were the banners government speech or private religious expression? While the question is significant, it misses a more important one: Were the banners good for the kids at Kountze High School? If we define goodness not in strict constitutional terms (was the behavior lawful?) or in evangelical Christian terms (did the banners help save nonbelievers or invite the favor of God upon the Kountze Lions?), but in educational terms (did the banners advance students' civic capacity?), the answer is, well, *sort of.*

From the standpoint of democratic theory, there's a lot to like about the cheerleaders' decision to make the banners. According to their court testimony, the girls generated the banner ideas themselves, bringing their notions of goodness to bear on the collective problem of how to increase school spirit and inspire the athletes. Given the demographics of the town, it would be surprising if religion did *not* crop up in discussions of inspiration and hope. Breaking down the artificial barriers between the school and the broader society is an important aspect of authentic learning. Making the banners is a form of community civic engagement, building social and human capital. That young women in particular are voicing their beliefs and taking a leadership role in this sphere is all the better.

There's also a lot to like about the district superintendent's original decision to stop them. School officials originally signed off on the cheerleaders' decision to use Bible quotes (and even assisted them at times). When the district superintendent received a letter from the Freedom from Religion Foundation on behalf of a complainant who felt uncomfortable with the signs, however, he consulted the Texas Association of School Boards, which advised him that the banners were likely unconstitutional, since they were very similar to other instances that were violations of the First Amendment. He then ordered the Christian messaging to stop. If the superintendent worried about whether the messages made students feel pressured to conform to evangelical Christianity, offended their own religious beliefs, or worse, alienated them from the community, such worries would be healthy signs of democracy as well.

Even if the process of making the banners had been highly legitimate in a procedural sense, democracy also demands a substantive component: a respect for the basic rights of minorities to be full members of the broader public. Applying a standard of public reason, the superintendent could ask whether all students could reasonably accept any particular faith's beliefs being written on the banners (such as weekly Koran verses, or explicitly atheistic messages). Christian theology has a similar theory, though it is often negated by evangelical impulses: do unto others as you would have them do unto you. In a democracy, the golden rule is not merely about abiding by fair procedures of majoritarian rule no matter who the majority is, but also about addressing substantive concerns about individual rights of conscience. The question is not so much about individual versus government speech, but about democratic versus undemocratic practices.

In that sense, there is also much to dislike about the superintendent's decision. The creation of the new school policy, allowing banners to continue as "fleeting expressions of community sentiment," indicates little concern with either the procedural or substantive dimensions of endorsing religion on the banners, but merely a concern about not getting in trouble by violating the law. It seems to say that a little bit of the wrong thing is okay, rather than taking the objections to the practice seriously.

What's not to like about the banners? Many of the constitutional concerns overlap with democratic ones. In an amici curiae brief filed in the appeal of the Kountze case, the ACLU of Texas, joined by the Anti-Defamation League and several denominational and interdenominational groups, laid out several serious concerns about these supposed "fleeting expressions." Obviously, the cheerleading squad was the official squad of the school, serving as school representatives at special events, enjoying special privileges during school hours, and enjoying the support and sanction of the school administration. By putting explicit Christian messages on the run-through banner, these school representatives sent a not-so-subtle message that non-Christians were second-class citizens, and exerted pressure for students to support majoritarian religious views as a way to show school spirit. "'Community sentiment,' is merely a euphemism for the majority's religious beliefs," the brief explained, "and if the Establishment clause means anything, it means that the government may not be complicit in imposing the majority's religious doctrine on followers of minority faiths."[7] Imagine being a member of the football team, required to run, week after week, through the evangelical Christian banner, who was not a Christian, whose faith was historically persecuted by evangelical Christian teachings, or who was a Christian but who believed (as some do) that there should be a strong separation between church and state.

The real problem at Kountze High School was not the cheerleaders' decision or the principal's principled response per se (nor even the inevitable intrusion of lawyers and advocates for both sides at the local, state, and national level). Each group or individual was, apparently, acting in good faith. The problem in Kountze was a collective misunderstanding of the role of public education and the place of religion in it. Thus the best remedy is not simply to allow or to ban religious expression at the football game. The remedy is to rethink how Kountze High School educates democratic citizens, and how, within that mission, the cheerleading squad plays an important role as a laboratory of democracy. A run-through banner with scripture on it could work very well at Kountze High, if the context and purposes were different.

The failure of democratic education at Kountze High may be seen in a brief look at the formal curriculum. Where do Kountze High students learn how to be effective democratic citizens? Not in the formal curriculum. According to the district website, the high school offers a mix of traditional academic subjects—math, science, social studies, and so forth, as well as vocationally oriented courses. If there is a space for democratic education, it comes in social studies, taught by two full-time teachers for US history and world history. Both courses, according to Texas state standards, should include thematic strands of "government" and "citizenship."

By many measures the Texas standards for social studies are among the most politically biased in the country. Both textbook selection and statewide standards in history and social studies have long reflected the Republican Party's political domination, while controversial changes in the curriculum have tended to reflect a divide among fiscal and social conservatives within that party, rather than between more mainstream liberal and conservative camps. In 2010 Texas attracted international attention when social conservatives radically altered already conservative standards to scrub out nonwhite perspectives and critical analyses of capitalism, while injecting neo-Confederate ideology and a Christian-nation viewpoint.[8] Not surprisingly, major scholarly organizations condemned the standards. The American Historical Association expressed particular concern about the US history standards, which "may reduce or render invisible certain individuals and events, considered central to the story for the last fifteen years."[9]

Yet for a deeply red state, the standards ask students to learn precious little of substance about religion or democratic values. In world history they are required to learn a superficial overview of world religions. In US history they may catch fleeting references to televangelist Billy Graham, the 1972 Supreme Court decision in *Wisconsin v. Yoder*, and "how the contributions of people of various racial, ethnic, gender, and religious groups shape American culture." But there is no recognition of religion as a major, recurring historical force, never mind standards organizing a systematic analysis of the various religious sects in the United States or their theological, political, and scientific views. Likewise, the "civic education" strand devolves into learning facts about government and history and higher-order academic skills, but offers no guidelines for practicing how to resolve disputes, deliberate democratically, or weigh the competing values of majoritarianism versus protection of minority rights.[10] If Kountze High School social studies follows the Texas standards to any reasonable degree, students get very little preparation in the skills or knowledge necessary for effective democratic citizenship in a religiously diverse community.

Contrast Kountze High School's commitment to democratic education with its commitment to vocational education. The high school employs five teachers to teach vocational courses (compared to two for social studies). Course titles conform to Texas state standards and reflect areas that are, presumably, locally relevant to the kids of Hardin County, such as agricultural and horticultural sciences, meat processing, welding, information technology, and construction. Classes blend academic study with hands-on work to prepare students for the real world. Teachers attempt to meet student interests. In carpentry, for example, students learn to make deer blinds for hunting. Knowledge is relevant. In the end, students are evaluated not only on what they know, but on what they can do.

Extracurricular groups, which are elective (and thus do not reach all students), may be much more effective spaces for lessons in citizenship. Student government, for example, may be one such space. Sports teams may be another. And so might cheerleading. Yet given the manner in which the cheerleading squad came to define its role in the school—promoting one particular religious viewpoint on behalf of all students, which the administration eventually condoned—suggests that the lessons of democratic citizenship are not well learned there either.

If the banners are a problem not by virtue of their existence, but by virtue of the manner and context of their creation, what can we do about it? One remedy would be to overhaul social studies—treating preparation for democratic life as seriously as preparation for work life in a market economy. This would include bringing religion more fully into the curriculum as a topic of discussion and critical analysis. Students should have "religious literacy," including an awareness of the diversity of religions locally, nationally, and globally. They should also learn the habits of respectful inter- and intrafaith dialogue as a vital component of democratic life. Such study requires sensitivity to the moral and cognitive developmental stages of children, of course, and a recognition that such a goal takes scaffolded instructional practices and time.

A complementary remedy would be for Kountze High School to better organize the cheerleading squad as an educational opportunity for students of any faith to find ways to build community spirit as an inclusive, rather than exclusive, process. Instead of creating one-size-fits-all banners policed by school personnel, the cheerleading squad could invite people of different faiths—including no faith at all—to express their enthusiasm for the football team in ways that are important to them. The decision to make particular banners should be an open process whereby students find positive personal messages that celebrate their enthusiasm for the common good in ways that are meaningful. Indeed, given the small size of the community, the team would do best by attempting to reach out to and be considerate of faiths not represented within their ranks—making it the job of the cheerleading squad to become true community builders who mark Kountze High as an inclusive public space. Team members could celebrate each other's right to diverse messaging, even if they do not share each other's faith. The students could directly broach the ideal of mutual justification and reflect upon the reasons for and against different kinds of expression. In that context, the members of the cheerleading squad could build far more meaningful relationships to each other and to the town by giving voice to diverse identities in a common cause. Free speech on the official school cheerleading squad would be speech on behalf of freedom, and not merely a private right that is exercised like a consumer spending money.

Such a remedy would still require oversight from the cheerleading staff and the school administration. But this kind of leadership would not be a form of establishment—promoting or endorsing religion. Instead, it would be a form of democratic instruction. Rather than asking only whether each run-through banner is legally permissible (government speech or private expression), the superintendent should first be asking what the cheerleaders and football team members are learning about democratic living and how their activities effectively promote that goal. Second, school leaders should ask how and whether the cheerleaders' actions are strengthening the school community and broader communities of Kountze and Honey Island—which is, presumably, what cheer*leaders* are for. Within bounds of those goals, student free speech must include the right to try to persuade others—of Christianity, of atheism, or of any faith practice. Creating a space where students and the broader public learn to equally respect each person's religious beliefs (or lack thereof) as one important aspect of social diversity would provide students with vital apprenticeship in public reason—and would, it turns out, be legal as well.

Kountze Independent School District has the raw materials necessary for this kind of relationship between religion, democracy, and public schooling. Diversity is one component. Overall, Texas is surprisingly diverse. For example, more Muslims live in Texas than in any other state.

Even in rural areas, religious minorities can live and achieve prominence. In 1992 Kountze was the first town in the United States to elect a Muslim mayor. While Kountze's largest faith community by far is Southern Baptist, it also includes a significant Roman Catholic contingent, other denominations, and a large number of people who report no affiliation at all. The nearby city of Beaumont hosts a vibrant Jewish community. Another raw material is good faith, and Kountze Independent School District appears to have that, too, as evidenced by the initial decision by the school superintendent to suspend the cheerleaders' activities, knowing that the decision would be widely unpopular.

To be fair to the very small town of Kountze, the collective misunderstanding surrounding the high school cheerleading squad's banners is a ubiquitous feature of American public education. Due to their unique historical evolution, public schools have been controversial sites of democracy, where differences were usually settled locally either by finding the lowest common denominator among religious groups or, failing that, subtracting religion altogether. The result of this compromise through subtraction has been, from the very start of public education, the avoidance of critical study of religion. An alternative approach—well-informed, democratic deliberation—was both too complicated pedagogically and too unpalatable theologically, offending those religious groups who insisted that they simply could not abide the others, or who feared that their adherents would learn about alternative faiths or think critically about their own.

Democratic education requires public schools to walk a fine line between allowing students to freely express their religious views and avoiding practices that marginalize or threaten other students. Furthermore, schools themselves must remain neutral toward religion, but at the same time would be most effective if they taught students *about* religion as well as about challenges to religion. The First Amendment of the US Constitution captures part of this challenge: "Congress shall make no law respecting an establishment of religion" (the establishment clause) "or prohibiting the free exercise thereof" (the free exercise clause). But the constitution offers little guidance for resolving the problem of when allowing too much free exercise becomes a form of establishment—a problem that can be acute in public schools. And rulings by distant courts can also undermine the legitimacy of local public schools, a value that doesn't just indulge free exercise, but *depends* on it.

We are sympathetic with the duties of the court system to adjudicate conflicts when people's rights are at stake. Legislators concern themselves with politics of the moment; executives with leading effectively. Courts decide what is constitutional, which is as close as the American system comes to determining what is fair. We should not be surprised that questions over the procedural and substantive aspects of democracy have ended up there: that's partly what courts are for. But there is a price, and the remedies have often been shortsighted and ineffective.

Americans now live in a society where schools are radically secular and society is strongly religious, while most western Europeans have public schools that are explicitly religious in societies that are strongly secular. What is more, we as a people lack a common language or shared norms for how to resolve differences outside of courts. The specialized language of constitutional law has become our only proxy for democratic deliberation. Schools worry about what is legal, not what is most effective for making good citizens. And we are impoverished for it.

Incivility in the Classroom

"Islam is of the Devil." That is what the T-shirts said on the back. And that is why Alachua County, Florida, school district administrators asked the kids wearing them in class and at an after-school football game to cover up or go home. But it did not end there. While Muslim parents gathered at a school board meeting to thank the administrators for protecting their children from hate speech, the ACLU joined the T-shirt parents in a suit against the district for violating their children's First Amendment rights to freely express their religious beliefs.

The issue of student free speech within school, first engaged by the US Supreme Court in *Tinker v. Des Moines* (1969), raises important questions for religion and democratic education. Some of these questions cut to the heart of the Constitution: Are schools public forums where students, as citizens, may express their beliefs regardless of whether other people approve of them? Or are public schools government-sponsored learning sites where the rights of religious minorities to feel safe and welcomed must be protected? Are all forms of speech in the name of religion equally protected by the free exercise clause of the First Amendment, and is religious speech more protected than regular speech under the other part of the First Amendment?

Thinking about schools as sites of democratic education, and not battlegrounds for constitutional principles, requires us to ask a slightly different question: What ingredients are necessary for public schools to best achieve their mission of preparing children to become democratically capable adults? In his decision in favor of the school district and against the

ACLU, US district judge Stephan P. Mickle addressed the educational issue in two ways: "'Islam is of the Devil' presents a highly confrontational message. It is akin to saying that the religion of Islam is evil and that all of its followers will go to hell," he wrote. "The message is not conducive to civil discourse on religious issues; nor is it appropriate for school generally."[11]

While the ACLU contended that public school was a public forum for children to say virtually anything, the judge saw schools as special sites where some forms of speech that are protected in the general public cannot be permitted. Civil discourse must prevail. So too must the psychological safety of all students—particularly groups like Muslim Americans, who already face physical and emotional threats in the broader society. Traditionally, federal courts have held that positive expressions of personal religious faith are not only permissible, but healthy for civil discourse about religion. But negative or hostile speech is threatening, and cannot be protected at the expense of other students' right to feel safe.

The judge's reasoning squared with the democratic purposes of public schooling, but did not settle the issue. Outrageous expressions like that in Florida are uncommon. The children in question came from families belonging to the Dove World Outreach Center, a tiny, fringe fundamentalist Christian group who, like the better-known Westboro Baptists, engaged in provocative public theater to draw attention to their extreme views. Both have been designated as hate groups by the Southern Poverty Law Center, and by no means represent the mainstream of fundamentalist Christian thought.

But other forms of free student expression of religious views raise more difficult questions, and can create excellent opportunities for learning or lead to subtle forms of antidemocratic behavior—attacks on public reason or micro-aggression toward students whose religious views or sexual orientation are viewed as evil. There are no easy answers to these questions, because at heart, America is a religiously diverse, democratic society; nevertheless, the claims of particular groups can run counter to fundamental democratic values.

The need for public reason, for example, requires that citizens find ways to engage each other in recognition of neutrally ascertained facts and standards of argument making. As George Orwell's character Winston wrote desperately in his diary, "Freedom is the freedom to say that two plus two make four. If that is granted, all else follows."[12] Orwell worried about a world where despots had seized control of knowledge itself, so that two plus two equaled whatever the ruling party said it equaled. In a democracy, public reason depends on two plus two equaling four and not what one's cleric, or favorite news network, or state senator says it equals.

Democracy requires a shared discursive space where the truth will out—and this requires well-trained and well-informed citizens who have the tools to make informed choices about whom and what to believe.

Any meaningful public education requires right and wrong answers where such are called for, and strong and weak forms of reasoning, logic, and rules of evidence. Democracy does not include the right to have whatever you *want* to be true to *actually be* true. It is the job of the public school to train citizens with accurate information, habits of mind, and skills necessary for democratic life, even if this means that such information, habits of mind, and skills may challenge a student's misconceptions or inabilities.

Nevertheless, democratic theory suggests that it's beneficial to the individual and the community for students to voice their religiously based truth claims. In order for schools to be perceived as legitimate, students must experience them as inclusive spaces, where subjects important to them personally (race, religion, gender, etc.) enjoy equal status as forms of identity and topics of discussion. When teachers and administrators exclude certain forms of speech, it must be for good reason—protecting the psychological and physical safety of other students being an obvious example. What fair reason is there to exclude a student's positive and good-faith expressions of their religious identity in school? Moreover, how can a school effectively meet its goals of training engaged citizens if it does not provide them with exposure to diverse identities and worldviews?

Even in subjects such as science, education can be enhanced by allowing students to bring their religious ideas into the classroom. Student religious expression can make learning stronger. *How Students Learn*, a classic series sponsored by the National Research Council in 2005, drew on a large body of research to suggest that there are three vital dimensions to learning:

1. Students come to class with preconceptions about how the world works. If their initial understanding is not engaged, they will fail to grasp the new concepts and information, or they may learn them for the purposes of a test but revert to their preconceptions outside the classroom.
2. To develop competence in a field of inquiry, students must (a) have a deep foundation of factual knowledge, (b) understand facts and ideas in the context of a conceptual framework and (c) organize knowledge in ways that facilitate retrieval and application.
3. A "metacognitive" approach to instruction can help students learn to take control of their own learning by defining learning goals and monitoring their progress in achieving them.[13]

While *How Students Learn* does not engage religious issues, we argue that shutting out religious experience and perspective from the learning process can have detrimental effects, while finding an appropriate space for religious expression can bring great benefits. The point is neither to uncritically endorse the religious views of students nor to subject them to withering criticism, but rather to encourage a reflective stance toward one's own beliefs and the beliefs of others. For some faiths, scientific knowledge may seem to be in tension with important religious convictions. A democratic education cannot magically eliminate such a tension, but it can provide students with the opportunity to reflect on the tension and its relevance to a politics of mutual justification.

Preconceptions are critical to learning. Human beings learn best when they can relate new information and ideas to preexisting ones. Good teachers describe this phenomenon as "meeting the kids where they are." Children describe it as "being able to relate." Teachers who recognize where children are coming from and allow them to ask questions openly and integrate new information into their worldview not only enjoy happier, more productive classrooms; they also see children learn more and better. Students who cannot connect what they learn inside of school to what they learn outside of it are more likely to revert to the outside way once they leave the classroom. If the goal of public education is to prepare students for the world beyond the school, students must be encouraged to bring the world to class: their sense of vernacular history (their family and community perspective on the past), their worldviews on the present, and their theories for why things happen. To the extent that religion informs those things, students need to express themselves openly and safely. These ideas may well become deeper and better informed. They may also change.

Competence in fields of inquiry, whether they be scientific, historical, literary, or otherwise, requires students not only to gain factual knowledge, but also to develop appropriate conceptual frameworks, strategies, and concepts for rapid retrieval and application of knowledge. Each of these facets of inquiry is best acquired and retained through practice. Students need to be in classroom settings where they ask questions about accuracy, which in turn requires rich discussions of the nature of knowledge, expertise, and authority. The benefits of having children raise religious objections to truth claims, or bring religious perspectives to bear on their interpretive and analytic claims, can be of enormous benefit to them and their classmates. Religious objections to scientific claims force teachers and students to stay sharp and to scrutinize their assumptions. Ensuing conversations about the nature of theories, for example, can strengthen lessons on evolutionary biology rather than weaken them. Students who hold religious perspectives can, in turn, gain deeper understandings of their personal beliefs. In discussions of morality, philosophy, history, and social values, students' religious perspectives can greatly enrich all students' learning, and better prepare them for engaging citizens with differing views on moral and political questions when they reach adulthood.

Strategies for metacognition flow naturally from healthy home-to-school relationships, where students can see their personal goals as being served by their school experiences. In an age where the purposes of schooling are narrowly and cynically defined as getting ahead, students who can see the democratic enterprise of public schooling as consistent with their spiritual values are more likely to develop a deeper sense of efficacy, identifying goals that serve their sense of the good.

It's important to acknowledge that there are risks to encouraging students to bring their religious ideas into their public school learning. The first is that they could learn to question and think critically about their religious beliefs (or lack of beliefs) and assumptions. This "risk" is negative only from the perspective of those who view unthinking adherence to any particular belief as desirable. We do not. Indeed, unthinking adherence to dogma is indicative of authoritarianism. We seek to put such thinking at great risk indeed. In finding a space for religious expression within the tradition of democracy, we do not intend to erect our own temple to the cult of reason. But meaningful autonomy does involve the capacity to reflect on one's own commitments and the commitments of others. Just as exposure to and consideration of possible challenges to religion contributes to the autonomy of religious students, exposure to and consideration of religious perspectives contributes to the autonomy of students with more secular orientations. A student's desire to critique democracy and advocate other forms of government must be welcomed within the democratic space, or the space has no meaning. But there must be rules of engagement within the sphere of the public school that anticipate a healthy, deliberative, and reasoned democratic life after it. Whether or not students alter their religious beliefs (and we have no dog in that fight), they should, as autonomous citizens, be able to understand them, and know that they have the right to believe otherwise if they choose. Nel Noddings has referred to such a process as "educating for intelligent belief or unbelief."[14]

A second, more real risk is that aggressive religious (or antireligious) speech may marginalize, threaten, or dehumanize other children. It is in the nature of people to organize themselves in opposition to others, and religion has been the prime vehicle, historically, for providing ideological justifications for such divisions. All the major religious systems in the

United States, for example, have been implicated in antidemocratic teachings and dogmatic "othering." Earlier chapters have shown that schools have often been sites for inflicting religious wounds. In recent decades, Americans who are Muslim, in particular, have faced extraordinary discrimination by government officials in and outside of schools, as well as by other children. Any serious entry of religious belief in schools must be skillfully and honestly monitored by teachers and administrators to make sure that students engage in safe and civil discourse. Reason giving and taking of the sort integral to the practice of public reason is not advanced by permitting students to casually demean the faith of others by wearing T-shirts emblazoned with simplistic and inflammatory rhetoric.

Our concern about religious speech extends to teachers as well as students. As a curricular subject unto itself, religion is rarely taught in public schools, and this has been true for two centuries. One reason, quite simply, is that Americans have not been able to trust that teachers could simultaneously set aside their own religious prejudices and have adequate content knowledge of other religions to do the job justice. Despite this concern, Texas, Tennessee, Oklahoma, and Arizona enacted laws in the early years of the twenty-first century encouraging schools to offer electives in Bible study, while South Carolina awards school credit for Bible study off campus. These states offer little or no guidance on how to teach such courses, which, not surprisingly, are often thinly disguised evangelism with little academic rigor or merit. Whether or not its intent is academic, however, Bible study is not the same as a course in comparative religion, and does not serve democratic ends without being set in a broader study of religion generally.[15]

Take, for example, the two most popular Bible-study programs in the United States. *The Bible in History and Literature*, a deceptively titled Protestant fundamentalist curriculum, provides neither rigorous historical analysis of the documents in the Bible or the context in which they were created, nor a critical examination of biblical references in literature. The program uses the King James (Protestant) Version of the Bible as its textbook, uncritically marching students through Bible stories and asking them to memorize details and discuss positive moral lessons.[16] In 2008 the ACLU led a successful lawsuit against a Texas school board that had adopted the phony religious-studies course, on the grounds that it used the public schools to promote a particular religious viewpoint.

A more moderate and popular evangelical effort, *The Bible and Its Influence*, offers students a Bible-study curriculum that draws on multiple biblical texts and an ecumenical Judeo-Christian viewpoint. The textbook presents students with multiple ways of interpreting Bible stories, and invites students to use a Bible version of their own choosing. The textbook has won the praise of numerous scholars, including some mainstream university professors and religious bodies. Nevertheless, the textbook fails to look at the negative aspects of the Bible as a force in history, including how it has been used as a weapon against particular groups (Jews, queer folk, indigenous people, and African Americans, for example). It focuses only on positive and uncritical views. *"The Bible and Its Influence* builds character through daily exposure to Biblical narratives," boasts the publisher's website. "Upon completion of the course, 71 percent of students indicate that they will continue to read the Bible."[17] While such teaching might barely cross the constitutional threshold, such a course still curtails democratic education.

The Supreme Court has been clear and consistent in its encouragement of non-confessional study of religion (meaning without regard to belief or adherence) in public schools, and this opinion has been joined by a variety of legal and religious organizations of all political stripes and commitments.[18] There is nothing stopping state governments from developing standards for religious studies either to be integrated into existing social studies programs or as a stand-alone subject. Unlike weekday religious instruction programs of the 1950s, which were designed to encourage belief, balkanized learners, and alienated nonbelievers and religious minorities, a non-confessional religious education can accomplish democratic goals without promoting or denigrating belief.[19]

Such models are not only possible—they are happening. In a 2014 study, for example, Feinberg and Layton observed several high school comparative religion courses that were nestled within the humanistic traditions of detached inquiry, empathy and respect, and autonomy enhancement. Teachers not only organized a curriculum that examined major faiths, but also made inquiry into faith itself part of the course, and gave students legitimate spaces for personal religious expression—including disagreement with others. One teacher explained, "I don't think that if an evangelical Christian says that 'if you don't accept Christ then you're going to hell,' it is disrespectful. This is the academic environment. In the academic environment, you are allowed to come and express your views, and if somebody else's view is offensive to you, then you have a right to respond."[20] The teacher's statement might seem alarming to those who fear conflict in the classroom or a vocal majority of students hijacking the conversation to put down minorities. But that same teacher insists that students develop specific discursive conventions to foster dialogue across theological divides. Students responding to such a statement from an evangelical student, for example, are taught explicitly to avoid emotional escalation through personal attack or derogatory retort, such as "Go to hell yourself!" or "That's crazy!" Instead, the teacher explains, the students are trained to respond in an "academic" way: "I disagree with that concept because for you to say to me that I'm going to hell because I don't accept your view is both irrational to me and judgmental."[21] The evangelical student, in turn, might elaborate on why she sees her statement as an expression of caring about the fate of nonbelievers. Similarly, the evangelical student can be invited to grapple thoughtfully with how the problem of evil posed by the atheist student provides a reasonable basis for the atheist's conviction, or why the Conservative Jewish student believes that same-sex marriage is consistent with her faith.

A suitable course would also alert students to the democratic salience of perspectives on faith that are not represented in the classroom. The absence of Muslim students in a Midwest classroom does not justify inattention to Islamic doctrine and the diverse understandings of Islam embraced both by practicing Muslims and those whose Islamic identity is more a matter of cultural familiarity than adherence to specific religious doctrines. The purpose of the course, then, is not merely to learn a set of general facts about major religions, but to engage religion as a living concept and learn to apply reason and respect to opposing viewpoints while finding, or sharpening, one's own.

Wearing a T-shirt that attacks a specific religious group—"Islam is of the Devil"—remains inappropriate even in a context like that described above, because it is a provocative attack on a faith practice made with no academic purpose. Banning the shirt without following up as a learning community, however, is a lost opportunity. In the context of a school that offers effective religious instruction, students can learn a sophisticated set of skills and understandings for how to negotiate their own expression of faith (or lack of faith) in a pluralistic and democratic context.

We do not pretend that such classrooms are easy to replicate. Feinberg and Layton found that teachers' skills and attitudes played a crucial role in how they teach about religion in the classroom. They also found that appropriate curriculum materials are difficult to find at the high school level, putting even more burden on teachers. Moreover, such classrooms require the support of school administrators and local school boards.[22]

Of more concern, however, is doing nothing. In our polarized political climate, speaking across faiths has become imperative, and can be accomplished only if we become a nation of adults who are knowledgeable about, and comfortable with, our religious differences. Considering how people learn and what they value, this goal can best be accomplished by welcoming students to engage in positive expressions of religious opinion and belief. Unfortunately, school reformers in recent years have launched a crusade against religious compromise, fueled by an even more dysfunctional approach than doing nothing: paying for students to attend the sectarian school of their choosing.

School Choice

It was supposed to be a panacea—a cure-all for everything wrong with American education. A Superman swooping in to save the poor. A triumph of those conservative neoliberal principles that made America the greatest nation on earth. Inject free-market principles into public education by radically reducing rules and regulations for anyone who wants to start a school, and then let parents plunk down public dollars where they choose. Originally used to maintain racial segregation during the civil rights movement, school choice is now touted as the way to close the achievement gap between black and white children. While full-blown voucher programs have been slow to catch on, charter schools have spread like wildfire, growing from 0.7 percent to 4.6 percent of all public schools between 2000 and 2013, with state and federal authorities teaming with private businesses to fan the flames.[23] Most astonishingly, this policy push happened despite a lack of evidence that school choice makes any significant difference in student learning, and in spite of a large body of evidence that removing accountability leads to corruption, rights violations, and, of greatest concern here, antidemocratic practices.[24]

School choice comes in two basic forms. Charter schools are public schools with special charters. Any group, including a religious one, may operate a chartered public school as long as the curriculum and purposes of the school are wholly secular, and the school meets other requirements laid down by nondiscrimination laws. Charter schools may meet within religious buildings, such as mosques or temples. Even groups who are overtly hostile to the curriculum they are supposed to teach and to the democratic purposes of public education itself can run charter schools. Because the First Amendment has been interpreted to mean that the government may not make substantive choices among religious groups, when the door is open to one, it is open to all.

While the majority of charter schools are independent entities, a growing number are operated by nonprofit or for-profit management companies, called charter maintenance organizations (CMOs).[25] Large CMOs can operate dozens of schools in multiple states, with some of the largest networks being religious. Responsive Education Solutions (RES), an outfit catering to Christian fundamentalists, is centered in Texas but operates over sixty charter schools in three states, enrolling some 17,000 students as of 2014 on a budget of $90 million in taxpayer dollars.[26] The Gulen Islamic movement, a political group rooted in Turkey, has given rise to a nationwide network of well over a hundred Muslim charter schools in the United States, including Harmony Public Schools CMO, the name of a private company that operated over forty charter schools in Texas in 2013.[27]

The second, more extreme, form of choice is school vouchers, where students can take a payment voucher with them to any school that will have them, public or private, provided that the overall system of allocating vouchers meets very basic criteria. A variation of vouchers, called tuition tax credits, essentially does the same thing by allowing parents who send their children to private schools to receive a break on their income taxes. Scholars often refer to these tax breaks as neo-vouchers. The Supreme Court has ruled that voucher and neo-voucher programs are permissible as far as federal law goes, as long as they meet various criteria, such as being large enough to provide students with genuine choices and having a secular purpose and content.[28] Nevertheless, many state constitutions still prohibit voucher programs that give money to religious groups.

From the standpoint of democratic theory, the basic problem with school choice is this: Religious belief and affiliation can be a vital site of civic learning for many Americans. In their temples, mosques, and mega-churches, Americans learn to cooperate, organize, and identify and engage social problems. These skills help them develop the kind of bonding capital that forms the basis of a democracy; from that platform, citizens can develop the bridging capital that allows them to identify with and engage civil society as a whole. On the other hand, some religious groups preach beliefs and false information that are hostile to fellow citizens and dangerous to civil society. Any old bonding capital is not good enough. As John Dewey once observed, belonging to a gang may provide a member with opportunities for connection and growth toward the pursuit of destructive ends. The question of what to do with religion in school-choice programs is how, or whether, to keep the baby while ditching the bathwater.

School choice, whether in the form of vouchers or charters, is a procedural reform built on the supposition that one can separate who runs public schools from their content and purposes. CMOs replace geographically based, democratically run school district systems with private, ideologically based ones with very little public oversight. Distant state-level authorities evaluate schools by their compliance with minimal regulations. What we need schools to accomplish with democratic education, it is assumed, will just happen naturally—if, in fact, charter promoters even identify democratic education as a goal at all. States attempt to keep antidemocratic religion in check either by banning all religious groups from participating in such programs or by attaching strings to the programs, so that groups who want to participate must comply with minimal regulations.

In some ways, deregulating public education and transcending the geographic limitations of nineteenth-century districting laws can enhance democratic education. Giving families a stronger sense of control and making schools more culturally relevant can help make public schooling more legitimate, bringing groups of outsiders into the public fold. Stephen Macedo has argued that such strings can even encourage religious groups to modify their beliefs and practices.[29] Large public school districts can be highly impersonal and bureaucratic—indeed, a popular reform in the early twenty-first century was to create smaller schools, including schools within schools. High quality regulations and curriculum standards, robust oversight and accountability, and careful attention to school climate can potentially make charter schools excellent places to learn, and can make them attractive alternatives to traditional public schools where such things are insufficient. Likewise, as Kathleen Knight Abowitz has argued, themed charter schools have the potential to create "counterpublics" for members of oppressed groups where they can enjoy safety and build solidarity in cases when pluralistic public schools cannot offer them adequate protections.[30]

Unfortunately the reverse can also be true—individuals and groups can use school choice to promote their private interests in ways that undermine the common good. Rather than changing the views of antidemocratic groups, choice programs can provide them with publicly funded platforms for spreading their ideology, while strings are either loosened, twisted, or dropped by the secular authorities who have no interest in holding them. Private religious schools can convert to public ones with little substantive change in who they teach and to what ends. School leaders can wink at state and federal regulations, sneak religion into the curriculum, and in the most egregious (but predictable) examples, advance private agendas that clash with public values.

In the last decade, religious organizations have flocked to charter schools as a way to get public tax dollars to promote their private agendas. Sometimes religious schools simply close at the end of the school year and reopen in the fall as public charter schools, hiring many of the same teachers and taking on most of the same students. By law, these schools should be open and accepting of students of any background and be secular in purpose and in practice. Thematic language and cultural instruction are often the secular justifications for these institutions, although cultural preservation for one particular group of students is clearly the intention. A Greek Orthodox community opens a charter school in Brooklyn with a Greek language and culture theme, with a predominantly Greek staff and clientele; a Florida Jewish school reopens as a Hebrew-theme academy that focuses on Jewish history and culture and teaches the Hebrew language, explicitly serving "Jewish communal purposes."[31] A different kind of conversion, more typical of Roman Catholic parochial schools, reconstitutes a religious school that serves no particular cultural group or even religious one, but hews instead to a mission of Christian service and (usually) light evangelism. In Washington, DC, Roman Catholic schools serving primarily African American children have recently begun converting to charters.[32]

Historically speaking, these conversions are nothing new. During the nineteenth century, public schools developed in a context where district schools reflected local culture. There was much variation. Across the country, common schools were once conducted in German, Norwegian, Spanish, French, Cherokee, and other languages, celebrated culturally specific religious holidays, and served after school hours as community centers and meetinghouses for religious groups. It's hard to imagine that nineteenth-century Americans would have agreed to fund public schools had there not been some benefit to the community beyond mere academics. These practices diminished for several reasons—because districts became more diverse, because some languages became politically suspect to the Anglo majority (German instruction all but disappeared as a result of World War I), or because cultural assimilation became a more valued goal. In other late-nineteenth-century cases, such as the Poughkeepsie plan in New York or the Pittsburgh experiment in Pennsylvania, Catholic Church compromises with secular authorities pitted local religious leaders against their more separatist superiors, while the same was true of local versus state officials. At the same time, however, favoring a specific religion in a public school (known as sectarianism) was widely understood to be antidemocratic and antithetical to the purpose of public schooling—both because picking one over others seemed unfair and because many people were bothered by others' particular political and social visions.[33] Fudging the boundaries between local values and state law was always a challenge in public education.

Are charter school conversions good or bad for democratic education? It depends on what's in the fudge. Do the state charter laws enable or discourage antidemocratic behaviors that are held in check in traditional public schools? The answer depends on questions that courts are reluctant to ask: Which groups are running the schools and to what ends? Do the schools have a democratic purpose (and not merely a "legitimate secular" one)? Culturally specific schools can potentially serve the goal of strengthening democracy if they are truly geared to the common good—welcoming students of all backgrounds and promoting a positive social vision, while offering a thematic curriculum that could engage any students who choose to attend. Such schools can also retard the development of citizens by balkanizing our population, curtailing the free exchange of diverse ideas, limiting exposure to diversity, and creating ideological bubbles. Certainly, private schools already have wide latitude in this regard. But the question of whether the state should regulate private education (or homeschooling) is a different question than whether the state should encourage certain practices by investing public dollars to promote private agendas. The question of whether a public school can separate sectarian religion from a monocultural context is no less pressing in a Jewish school turned Hebrew charter school in Florida than it is in a traditional public school in East Texas.

Whether or not charter schools are former sectarian schools with a makeover, the lack of public accountability for charter school providers encourages fraud. The financial cases are many and disturbing, and reports of intellectually bogus curricula are common too, particularly as Christian fundamentalists make war on history and science. RES, the Texas-based CMO, is a powerful example of the perils of charter school curriculum, and the fallacy that "the marketplace" will police itself. RES was founded by Donald R. Howard, former owner of Accelerated Christian Education, and is currently headed by CEO Charles Cook, who was formerly in charge of marketing for Accelerated Christian Education as well. Accelerated Christian Education has published fundamentalist curriculum materials that teach, among other things, that separating people by race is desirable, that homosexuality is learned behavior, and that the Loch Ness monster is real and proves that the theory of evolution is wrong. This curriculum has actually been used in Texas and Louisiana schools funded through charter and voucher programs, as well as in the United Kingdom.[34]

Neither Nessie nor Bigfoot has been sighted yet in RES charter school curriculum materials, but false and misleading political propaganda and fundamentalist fairy tales about science certainly have. The biology text presents creationism and evolution as equally valid theories, with the latter being widely questioned and full of inconsistencies and contrary evidence (which is nonsense). Other examples of a desperately right-wing agenda include teaching that the feminist movement "created an entirely new class of females who lacked male financial support and who had to turn to the state as a surrogate husband," that Democrat John Kerry's war medals for bravery were "suspect at best," and that the decline in Christian values caused World War I. These and many other examples from the RES materials are not good-faith differences of opinion. The extreme and unsubstantiated claims advanced in these materials lie well outside the ambit of public knowledge. They are designed to obfuscate and distort deliberation rather than to inform debate. As such, they are direct attacks on public reason and democratic life. George Orwell could not have imagined it better.[35]

RES is not alone. Fundamentalist attacks on public reason have been an ongoing and evolving fact of life for American public education for nearly a century. In the Christian homeschooling and private-schooling marketplace, materials abound that deceive children about science and history. An important feature of American democracy is that private individuals and groups enjoy the freedom to publish such drivel, and even to pass it off to children as knowledge. Paying public money to schools that teach these things, however, does a great disservice to children and great damage to our democracy. A 2013 summary of state laws by *Slate* found that ten states funded creationist schools through voucher programs.[36]

It is important to note that not all religious groups make war on science. There are clear differences among faiths and within them. While it still retains miraculous elements in its rituals and doctrinal teachings, for example, the Roman Catholic Church has reconciled itself to modern science, including Darwin's theory of evolution. The (Mormon) Church of Jesus Christ of Latter-day Saints insists that "man is the child of God, formed in the divine image" but hedges on the nature of that formation and resolves to "leave geology, biology, archaeology, and anthropology, no one of which has to do with the salvation of the soul of mankind, to scientific research."[37] In faiths where authority is more diffuse—mainstream Protestantism, Islam, and Judaism, for example—the question of evolution invites a multitude of answers.

But on the question of diversity—that is, the acceptance of differences not only of faith, but of race, culture, sexual orientation, and others—many faiths clash with democratic values in ways that raise serious concerns about their fitness to be school providers in choice programs. The most obvious example is when groups target other groups: Muslims preaching anti-Semitism, Jews condemning Islam, Protestants and Catholics exchanging barbs with each other and everyone else. The tensions among religions are many and deep, and raise obvious questions about how safe children would be in a school run by a faith-based group that believes they are the enemy, or how much our society benefits from publicly funded schools that preach religious bigotry.

Even if we put those concerns aside, there are secular forms of inclusion that are necessary in the public sphere for which faith-based groups are ill equipped. Homophobia is one area of bigotry where many faiths find common cause, even as public schools across the country are building anti-bullying programs and safe spaces for LGBTQ youth. The Church of Jesus Christ of Latter-day Saints urges viewers of its website to "live the Law of Chastity," including to "avoid viewing pornography and engaging in homosexual relations," and has played an aggressive and leading role in fighting gay marriage.[38] As part of his effort to clean up the public image of the Roman Catholic Church, Pope Francis famously asked, "Who am I to judge [gay priests]?" a seeming reversal of his predecessor's statement that homosexuality is an "intrinsic moral evil." But doctrinally speaking, the former pope Benedict XVI was more honest about the church's doctrinal stance toward homosexuality. Despite Pope Francis's seemingly tolerant talk, fighting gay marriage and fighting the public acceptance of homosexuality are high priorities for Catholic Church leaders in America, even if their lay members tend to hold more tolerant views.[39] Among Jews, individual communities and congregations set their own standards, although among the orthodox and ultraorthodox communities, homosexuality is a scriptural sin, and homophobia can be a strong community value.[40] Islam is a vastly diverse and diffuse religion, with no uniform set of doctrinal claims or stance toward LGBTQ youth, and in many cases fundamentally different cultural understandings of the meaning of queer identity and practices.[41] Nevertheless, the Hadith and Seerah demand the death penalty for male sodomy, and homosexual behavior is not only a sin, but a crime in most of the Islamic world.[42] And so on.

We must ask whether appreciation of public reason of the sort integral to a democratic education can be cultivated in schools that encourage doctrines that flout it. We must also ask whether schools operated by these and other faith-based organizations are places where children who are homosexual or gender nonconforming can expect to participate in the same positive, safe learning environment that we would expect from any public school. In 2013 parents and students in Wilmington, North Carolina, asked just this question when Myrtle Grove Christian School decided to participate in a state voucher program for low-income students, but only if the students promised not to engage in or support a "gay lifestyle."

Facing criticism, the school did not modify its teachings or reverse the policy, but withdrew from the voucher program instead.[43]

It's not surprising that these abuses are happening. Public oversight of public education has historically operated in a way that sought to interweave local, state, and national levels of government in order to balance majority rule and minority rights. By assuming that private schools will promote the common good in general, and democratic values in particular, without incentives to do so, defies common sense. Moreover, laws that supposedly police the boundaries of choice programs are problematic. Research shows that state courts have been inconsistent in their interpretation of when and how choice programs are public and when and how they are private, with the civil rights protections of teachers and students being a casualty.[44]

From the standpoint of democratic education, the remedy for choice programs gone off the rails is not necessarily to eliminate all forms of school choice. Putting public education on a procrustean bed has its own perils, and the significant minority of charter schools that have achieved impressive academic results should call our attention to the importance of experimentation and flexibility within public education. Nevertheless, state legislators and courts must recognize the fallacy of the claim that a school is likely to provide democratic education without democratic oversight, that educational markets are self-regulating, and that all religious groups are equally committed to American democracy. They are not. Choice programs that maintain high levels of oversight and protection of the core democratic values of our society, however, may work well to achieve other important goals, such as academic achievement.

The questions are whether and how faith-based groups should participate in these programs. The answers depend on whether we can trust groups fervently committed to antidemocratic principles to set them aside to run a school. In practice, some groups take the funding and mask their beliefs, while the strings attached are ignored or evaded. Effective strings require strong attachments, and as the Supreme Court ruled in *Lemon v. Kurtzman*, significant government entanglement is required to fully monitor when and how religious groups comply with public intentions—particularly when religious groups have histories of opposition to those strings, and when (in states like Texas and Louisiana) state leaders officially endorse fundamentalist positions. Abandoning the layered network of democratic local and state control and constitutional protections of individual rights in favor of "the marketplace" is, at best, democratically naïve and fraught with dangers.

An alternative approach would be to focus less on procedure and more on substance. In this approach, the state could fund groups to run public schools based on their proven track record: What is their mission? What are their merits? Those religious groups who have a proven track record of embracing diversity, accepting reason, and pursuing the common good would be as welcome to run schools as other groups. Such a system would take a commonsense approach to the problem of reconciling who runs schools with what they teach and to what ends. While this system would not necessarily address the other concerns with choice systems, it would go a long way toward curbing antidemocratic religious practices.

Such a shift in focus would also require major changes in American politics and constitutional jurisprudence. Antidemocratic religions have a good deal of power in American society. Fundamentalism wins elections. In Kansas, Texas, Louisiana, and elsewhere, state-level officials routinely advocate teaching creationism in public schools. A second, even more significant, obstacle is the long history of state and federal jurisprudence interpreting the establishment clause as requiring the state to treat all religions equally, emphasizing procedural relationships between church and state and gutting substantive relationships. The government cannot like some religions more than others, even if some are clearly, from a democratic standpoint, much more likeable. Thus choice programs are really a Hobson's choice, which is to say, no choice at all: if any religious group gets to participate, they all do. The only "choice" we as citizens get in such a system is whether to include or exclude religious groups as an establishment matter.

Because we cannot choose among religious groups to run schools in a choice system, we are better off excluding them all. Separating who runs schools from what they teach and the ends they seek is a mistake. As much as it would be desirable to capitalize on the civic capacity that religious organizations can give to citizens, we are hamstrung by our constitutional framework. Instead, we should reconsider how better to rely on our current public system, drawing on its strengths to make more positive spaces for making citizens in a religiously diverse society. We should engage in the hard but rewarding democratic work of finding a place for religion (and its critics) in public schools.

Where Do We Go from Here?

What began as a locally rooted social movement in the nineteenth century, when diverse religious groups committed to a common education for all children, has grown into a national schooling system blending local, state, and federal governance and enrolling some fifty million children. The tensions that have emerged between religion, democracy, and that system of public education are deep and complex, and defy the heated and oversimple rhetoric that seems to be on offer for American citizens. Two hundred years of history and a good deal of philosophical discussion make it clear that we cannot separate what schools teach from who controls them and who and what we think they are for. Reformers who seek to alter one of these aspects of public education must account for all of them.

We are discouraged that the media and politicians are largely silent on the role of schools as places where children from all faiths, races, and walks of life learn to become smart, engaged democratic citizens. We are discouraged by the federal government's push to create national standards that focus narrowly on math and reading to the exclusion of the development of citizenship skills, including religious literacy. And we are discouraged, for similar reasons, by efforts to dismantle public education in the name of so-called market efficiency and consumer choice.

On the other hand, we see encouraging signs on the horizon. Mass-communications media now allow Americans to know about local school events on a national scale. Grossly undemocratic practices of religious or antireligious bias in traditional public schools are subject to greater scrutiny than ever before. Federal courts have ruled consistently and definitively that religion is not a form of science. If the essence of democracy is a balance between substantive and procedural legitimacy, public schools are places where the boundaries of what is reasonable for both are increasingly clear. Public schools where religious differences in the American political community are honestly addressed will become even more important as more Americans come to realize that the rhetoric that depicts America as a polity united under a common Christian God is increasingly a myth. As we noted in the introduction, religious belief outside of the Judeo-Christian faiths is on the rise. Nonreligiosity is on the rise, too, including the unprecedented finding by the Pew Research Center in 2012 that nearly one in five Americans claim no particular religious affiliation at all—a rate that rises to one in three Americans aged eighteen to twenty-nine, and that includes nearly eight million atheists (2.4 percent of the population).[45]

If public schools are to fulfill their mission of creating engaged, smart, capable democratic citizens, they must find new ways to engage America's religious diversity. Removing religion entirely from public education will not accomplish these goals. Neither will allowing local majorities to use the school as a bully pulpit for converting others, or using vouchers and charters to balkanize mass education through choice systems. All these approaches, from the political left and the political right, risk leaving our society at the mercy of demagogues who benefit from dividing us. Instead, schools must become sites of education for mutual and self-understanding. Such a move requires religious groups and public schools alike to encourage open, intelligent, and respectful discourse. American public schools have the necessary ingredients to offer a rich and productive democratic education that builds on our diverse beliefs. All we need is a little faith.

Notes

INTRODUCTION

1. Kate Taylor, "East Ramapo School Board Is Criticized by New
    York State Monitor," *New York Times*, November 17, 2014,
    http://www.nytimes.com/2014/11/18/nyregion/east-ramapo
    -school-board-is-criticized-by-new-york-city-monitor.html?_r
    =0; *This American Life*, episode 534, "A Not-So-Simple Major-
    ity," http://www.thisamericanlife.org/radio-archives/episode
    /534/transcript; Henry Greenberg, "East Ramapo: A School
    District in Crisis," New York State Education Department, No-
    vember 17, 2014, http://www.p12.nysed.gov/docs/east-ramapo
    -fiscal-monitor-presentation.pdf.
2. Greenberg, "East Ramapo"; "Letter: NAACP Leaders Support
    East Ramapo Oversight," *Lohud*, March 15, 2015, http://www
    .lohud.com/story/opinion/readers/2015/03/15/naacp-backs
    -east-ramapo-oversight/70261766/.
3. Pew Research Center, *America's Changing Religious Landscape*,
    May 12, 2015, http://www.pewforum.org/2015/05/12/chap
    .-1-the-changing-religious-composition-of-the-u-s/. The
    diversity within Christianity is reflected in the fact that the
    Pew Research Center identifies fifteen major denominations
    within Protestantism.

CHAPTER ONE

1. We give special emphasis to facets of John Rawls's highly
    influential conception of a pluralist liberal democracy: John
    Rawls, *Justice as Fairness: A Restatement* (Cambridge, MA:
    Harvard University Press, 2001); John Rawls, *Political Liberal-
    ism*, exp. ed. (New York: Columbia University Press, 2005).
    The conception of democratic education we advance is not

Rawls's, however, and we do not take a position on his overall theory of political liberalism or the special social contract argument that he develops to defend and articulate his theory of "justice as fairness." Our characterization of a democratic education is also influenced by the work of other theorists working in a broadly liberal framework, such as Eamonn Callan, *Creating Citizens: Political Education and Liberal Democracy* (Oxford: Oxford University Press, 1997); Amy Gutmann, *Democratic Education* (Princeton, NJ: Princeton University Press, 1987); Meira Levinson, *The Demands of a Liberal Education* (Oxford: Oxford University Press, 1999).

2.   Rawls, *Justice as Fairness*, 3.

3.   Although we focus on a conception of political legitimacy that is rooted in ideals drawn from contemporary political philosophy, it is worth noting that empirical psychological research indicates that the efficacy of political authority is highly dependent on power being exercised in a way that manifests officials' commitment to procedural and substantive fairness. Our account of legitimacy is consistent with these findings and thus does not face the objection that it is psychologically unrealistic or infeasible. For a helpful review of the psychological literature on legitimacy, see Tom R. Tyler, "Psychological Perspectives on Legitimacy and Legitimation," *Annual Review of Psychology* 57, no. 1 (2006): 375–400.

4.   Contemporary theories of deliberative democracy are "talk-centric": they involve the giving and taking of reasons in politics. They are often contrasted with "voting-centric" conceptions of democracy, in which legitimacy is wholly grounded in the aggregation of preferences in elections and referenda. As Simone Chambers notes, "Talk-centric democratic theory replaces voting-centric democratic theory. Voting-centric views see democracy as the arena in which fixed preferences and interests compete via fair mechanisms of aggregation. In contrast, deliberative democracy focuses on the communicative processes of opinion and will-formation that precede voting. Accountability replaces consent as the conceptual core of legitimacy." "Deliberative Democratic Theory," *Annual Review of Political Science* 6, no. 1 (2003): 308. Chambers's essay provides a valuable overview of recent work on deliberative democracy.

5.   To say that legitimacy requires that citizens can accept laws and basic political institutions does not mean that all citizens will always, as a matter of sociological fact, view laws they consider objectionable as nonetheless politically acceptable. The idea is that legitimate laws are ones that, all things considered, reasonable citizens *should* view as acceptable.

6.   Rawls's identification of the basic liberties that are assigned special constitutional protection includes "political liberty (the right to vote and to hold political office) and freedom of speech and assembly; liberty of conscience and freedom of thought; freedom of the person, which includes freedom from psychological oppression and physical assault and dismemberment (integrity of the person); the right to hold personal property and freedom

from arbitrary arrest and seizure as defined by the concept of the rule of law." *A Theory of Justice*, rev. ed. (Cambridge, MA: Harvard University Press, 1999), 53. Controversies turn not on the liberties listed per se but rather on how they are related to one another and what their determinate implications are for important and contested issues.

7. Rawls, *Justice as Fairness*, 27.

8. The phrase "free and equal persons" comes from Rawls, and this idea plays a central role in his political philosophy. Rawls provides his own detailed elaboration of this fundamental idea in *Justice as Fairness*, 18–23. Although our use of the idea is indebted to Rawls's work, we are not committed to the details of his articulation of it.

9. The ideal of toleration does not mean that citizens cannot publicly express their controversial views and try to persuade others to adopt them. Toleration here does not require citizens to refrain from judging the different (but politically reasonable) personal beliefs and practices of others. It only requires that such judgments should not be appealed to in the justification of state policies.

10. The atheist and Catholic in this example may both express concerns about school prayer based on different criteria, however, as we explain below.

11. Rawls, *Justice as Fairness*, 32–38.

12. Rawls, *Political Liberalism*, 454.

13. Some critics hold that public-reason theories unfairly exclude religious perspectives from public discourse; e.g., Christopher Eberle, *Religious Conviction in Liberal Politics* (New York: Cambridge University Press, 2002); Jeffrey Stout, *Democracy and Tradition* (Princeton, NJ: Princeton University Press, 2004).

14. This does not mean the views and preferences of children are irrelevant to determining the appropriate content of their education. As they mature, children may reasonably have a significant voice in shaping their own education. Teenagers may have a good deal of authority, independent of their parents, to make significant educational choices. For recent work on the importance of respect for the emerging agency of children, see David Archard, "Children, Adults, Autonomy and Well-Being," in *The Nature of Children's Well-Being: Theory and Practice*, ed. Alexander Bagattini and Colin Macleod (Dordrecht, The Netherlands: Springer, 2014), 3–14; Monika Betlzer, "Enhancing the Capacity for Autonomy," in Bagattini and Macleod, *Nature of Children's Well-Being*, 65–84; Paul Bou-Habib and Serean Olsaretti, "Autonomy and Children's Well-Being," in Bagattini and Macleod, *Nature of Children's Well-Being*, 15–34.

15. Callan, *Creating Citizens*, 154–55.

16. For further discussion of the nature and significance of autonomy facilitation, see Harry Brighouse, "Civic Education and Liberal Legitimacy," *Ethics* 108, no. 4 (1998): 719; Eamonn Callan, "Autonomy, Child-Rearing, and Good Lives," in *The Moral and Political Status of Children*, ed. David Archard and Colin Macleod (Oxford: Oxford University Press, 2002), 118; Matthew Clayton,

Justice and Legitimacy in Upbringing (Oxford: Oxford University Press, 2006); Joel Feinberg, "A Child's Right to an Open Future," in *Whose Child? Children's Rights, Parental Authority, and State Power*, ed. W. Aiken and H. LaFollette (Totowa, NJ: Littlefield, Adams, 1980), 124; Levinson, *Demands of a Liberal Education*; Colin Macleod, "Conceptions of Parental Autonomy," *Politics & Society* 25, no. 1 (1997): 117.

17. It's not clear that schools should encourage law-abidingness per se. From a democratic point of view, some state laws that fail to fulfill criteria of legitimacy do not merit respect. Thus civil rights protestors who engaged in civil disobedience and violated racist (and democratically illegitimate) laws arguably displayed a greater fidelity to core democratic values than those who believed that such laws merited respect simply on the grounds that they were laws.

18. Needless to say, the United States is not alone in its failure to give full expression to democratic ideals. The fact that so many immigrants sought refuge in America from religious oppression elsewhere is a good indication that even a deeply flawed American democracy was, for many, a great improvement on the political regimes elsewhere in the world.

19. We also realize that currently the state plays almost no role in regulating the democratic content of private schools. Moving in this direction would be a departure from the sharp partition between public and private schools that has traditionally existed in America. Yet just as other aspects of American political practice have been revised in light of developments in our understanding of the demands of democracy and justice, there may be reason to revisit and modify the tradition of lax public regulation of private religious schools. We do not pursue this theme in depth, but we think it deserves serious attention. For an extended discussion of religious education and children's rights, see James Dwyer, *Religious Schools v. Children's Rights* (Ithaca, NY: Cornell University Press, 1998).

20. Most obviously, slavery was expressly antidemocratic as was the denial of the franchise to women and indigenous peoples and other minorities. Of course, other political communities purporting to be democracies at the time also denied basic rights to many of their citizens.

CHAPTER TWO

1. John Adams, *A Dissertation on the Canon and the Feudal Law* (May–October 1765), in *The Works of John Adams, Second President of the United States: With a Life of the Author, Notes and Illustrations*, ed. Charles Francis Adams (Boston: Little, Brown, 1851), 3:447–64.

2. John Adams, "Novanglus Essays" and "Thoughts on Government," in *The Works of John Adams, Second President of the United States: With a Life of the Author, Notes and Illustrations*, ed. Charles Francis Adams (Boston: Little, Brown, 1856), 4:3–180.

3. Kathryn Kish Sklar, "The Schooling of Girls and Changing Community Values in Massachusetts Towns, 1750–1820," *History of Education Quarterly* 33 (1993): 511–42.

4. For an overview of colonial education patterns, see Jennings L. Wagoner and Wayne J. Urban, *American Education: A History* (New York: McGraw-Hill, 2009), chap. 2.

5. E. Jennifer Monaghan, *Learning to Read and Write in Colonial America* (Amherst: University of Massachusetts Press, 2007).

6. Noah Webster's unpublished memoir, Yale Manuscripts and Archives, Webster Family Papers, box 1, folder 10, p. 3.

7. David Tyack and Elisabeth Hansot, *Learning Together: A History of Coeducation in American Public Schools* (New Haven, CT: Yale University Press, 1990), chap. 2.

8. Jon Butler, Grant Wacker, and Randall Balmer, *Religion in American Life: A Short History*, 2nd ed. (New York: Oxford University Press, 2011), 142–60.

9. Ibid., 149, 154–55; Gordon Wood, *Empire of Liberty: A History of the Early Republic, 1789–1815* (Oxford: Oxford University Press, 2009), 580.

10. See generally Leonard Williams Levy, *The Establishment Clause: Religion and the First Amendment* (New York: Macmillan, 1986); Thomas J. Curry, *The First Freedoms: Church and State in America to the Passage of the First Amendment* (New York: Oxford University Press, 1986); Michael W. McConnell, "Establishment and Disestablishment at the Founding, Part I: Establishment of Religion," *William & Mary Law Review* 44 (2003): 2105.

11. John Locke, *Letter concerning Toleration*, in *The Works of John Locke in Nine Volumes*, 12th ed. (London: Rivington, 1824), vol. 5. For a general discussion, see Stephen Macedo, *Diversity and Distrust: Civic Education in a Multicultural Democracy* (Cambridge, MA: Harvard University Press, 2000), 28.

12. John Adams, "Literature and Morals," from John Adams to John Penn, March 27, 1776, Papers of John Adams, 4:78–84, in *The Adams Papers: Digital Editions*, Massachusetts State Historical Society website, https://www.masshist.org/publications/apde2/view?&id=PJA04dg2.

13. John Adams, *Notes on an Oration at Braintree* (Spring 1772), 59, in *Founding Families: Digital Editions of the Papers of the Winthrops and the Adamses*, ed. C. James Taylor (Boston: Massachusetts Historical Society, 2007), http://www.masshist.org/ff/.

14. See, e.g., ibid.; letters to Jefferson, June 25, 1813, and November 4, 1816, in *The Adam-Jefferson Letters: The Complete Correspondence between Thomas Jefferson and Abigail and John Adams*, ed. Lester J. Cappon (Chapel Hill: University of North Carolina Press, 1988), 334, 493–94; Massachusetts State Constitution (1780), chap. V, sec. 2.

15. Unlike Adams, Webster experienced a powerful religious conversion in the first decade of the 1800s, which led him to repudiate many of his earlier republican positions. Noah Webster the young, religiously skeptical patriot would have disagreed passionately with Noah Webster the elder, politically

conservative evangelical Protestant. See Richard M. Rollins, *The Long Journey of Noah Webster* (Philadelphia: University of Pennsylvania Press, 1980).

16. Noah Webster, "Education—Importance of Female Education, with a Brief Sketch of a Plan," *American Magazine*, May 1788, 367–74.

17. Noah Webster, *On the Education of Youth in America* (1788) in Noah Webster, *A Collection of Essays and Fugitiv Writings on Moral, Historical, Political and Literary Subjects* (Boston, 1790; repr., Delmar, NY: Scholars' Facsimiles & Reprints, 1977).

18. Rollins, *Long Journey*, 33–37.

19. Ibid., 109.

20. Noah Webster, "Education, Some Defects in the Mode," *American Magazine*, January 1788, 80–82. In 1801 he revised his *New England Primer* to include the original, Calvinistic rhymes. See Rollins, *Long Journey*, 118, 130–38, 140–41.

21. Benjamin Rush, "A Plan for the Establishment of Public Schools and the Diffusion of Knowledge in Pennsylvania; To Which Are Added Thoughts upon the Mode of Education, Proper in a Republic" (Philadelphia, 1786) and "To the Citizens of Philadelphia: A Plan for Free Schools" (Philadelphia, March 28, 1787), reprinted in *Letters of Benjamin Rush*, ed. L. H. Butterfield (Princeton, NJ: Princeton University Press, 1951), 2:412–15.

22. Alyn Brodsky, *Benjamin Rush, Patriot and Physician* (New York: St. Martin's, 2004), 283; Hyman Kuritz, "Benjamin Rush: His Theory of Public Education," *History of Education Quarterly* 7, no. 4 (Winter 1967): 432–51.

23. Benjamin Rush to Jeremy Belknap, Philadelphia, July 13, 1789, in *Letters of Benjamin Rush*, 1:520–21.

24. Benjamin Rush to James Hamilton, Philadelphia, June 27, 1810, in *Letters of Benjamin Rush*, 2:1053.

25. Thomas Jefferson, "Notes on the State of Virginia, Query XIV," in Thomas Jefferson, *Writings*, ed. Merrill D. Peterson (Washington, DC: Library of America, 1984), 273.

26. Thomas Jefferson, "Report of the President and Directors of the Literary Fund, October 7, 1822. From the Minutes of the Board of Visitors, University of Virginia, 1822–1825," in *Writings*, 478.

27. Jefferson, "Notes on the State of Virginia," 286. For a general overview, see Eugene R. Sheridan, "Liberty and Virtue: Religion and Republicanism in Jeffersonian Thought," in *Thomas Jefferson and the Education of a Citizen*, ed. James Gilreath (Honolulu: University of the Pacific Press, 2002), 242–63.

28. James Madison to William T. Barry, August 4, 1822, and to Edward Everett, March 19, 1823, in *James Madison: Writings*, ed. Jack Rakove (New York: Library of America, 1999), 790–798.

29. Seth Cotlar, "'Every Man Should Have Property': Robert Coram and the American Revolution's Legacy of Economic Populism," in *Revolutionary Founders: Rebels, Radicals, and Reformers in the Making of the Nation*, ed. Alfred Fabian Young, Gary B. Nash, and Ray Raphael (New York: Knopf, 2011), 337–54.

30. Benjamin Justice, "The Place of Religion in Early National School Plans," in *The Founding Fathers, Education, and "The Great Contest": The American Philosophical Society Essay Prize of 1797*, ed. Benjamin Justice (New York: Palgrave Macmillan, 2013), 155–74.

31. David B. Tyack, Thomas James, and Aaron Benavot, *Law and the Shaping of Public Education, 1785–1954* (Madison: University of Wisconsin Press, 1987), 43–76; Nancy Beadie, "'Encouraging Useful Knowledge' in the Early Republic: The Roles of State Governments and Voluntary Organizations," in *The Founding Fathers, Education, and "The Great Contest": The American Philosophical Society Essay Prize of 1797*, ed. Benjamin Justice (New York: Palgrave Macmillan, 2013), 85–102; Benjamin Justice, "The Originalist Case against Vouchers: The First Amendment, Religion, and American Public Schooling." *Stanford Law and Policy Review* 26, no. 2 (2015): 437–84.

CHAPTER THREE

1. As cited in Tyack, *Turning Points*, 171–72.

2. Ibid., 172.

3. Andy Green, *Education and State Formation: The Rise of Education Systems in England, France, and the USA* (Basingstoke, UK: Macmillan, 1990); Andy Green, *Education, Globalization, and the Nation State* (London: Macmillan, 1997).

4. US Bureau of the Census, *Historical Statistics of the United States, Colonial Times to 1970*, part 1, series H 412–432 (Washington, DC: Government Printing Office, 1975), 369.

5. David B. Tyack and Elisabeth Hansot, *Managers of Virtue: Public School Leadership in America, 1820–1980* (New York: Basic Books, 1982); David F. Labaree, *Someone Has to Fail: The Zero-Sum Game of Public Schooling* (Cambridge, MA: Harvard University Press, 2010); James D. Anderson, *The Education of Blacks in the South, 1860–1935* (Chapel Hill: University of North Carolina Press, 1988).

6. For an overview of the state-by-state changes in suffrage laws, see Alexander Keyssar, *The Right to Vote: The Contested History of Democracy in the United States* (New York: Basic Books, 2000).

7. Butler et al., *Religion in American Life*, 155, 182–212.

8. Don Harrison Doyle, *The Social Order of a Frontier Community: Jacksonville, Illinois, 1825–1870* (Urbana: University of Illinois Press, 1979).

9. The ability of free blacks to participate in the common schools varied by place and over time. The dynamics of the black experience with common schooling are detailed in Hilary Moss, *Schooling Citizens: The Struggle for African American Education in Antebellum America* (Chicago: University of Chicago Press, 2009).

10. Nancy Beadie, *Education and the Creation of Capital in the Early American Republic* (New York: Cambridge University Press, 2010).

11. Labaree, *Someone Has to Fail*.
12. As cited in David B. Tyack, ed., *Turning Points in American Educational History* (Toronto: Xerox College, 1967), 145.
13. Carl F. Kaestle, *Pillars of the Republic: Common Schools and American Society, 1780–1860* (New York: Hill and Wang, 1983), 13–25. Nancy Beadie has elaborated and theorized the district-to-common school process for an upstate New York community in *Education and the Formation of Capital*.
14. Tyack, *Turning Points*, 133.
15. Jonathan Messerli, *Horace Mann: A Biography* (New York: Knopf, 1972), 408–24.
16. Ruth Miller Elson, *Guardians of Tradition: American Schoolbooks of the Nineteenth Century* (Lincoln: University of Nebraska Press, 1972); David B. Tyack, "Monuments between Covers: The Politics of Textbooks," *American Behavioral Scientist* 42, no. 6 (March 1999): 922–932.
17. Benjamin Justice, *The War That Wasn't: Religious Conflict and Compromise in the Common Schools of New York, 1865–1900* (Albany: State University of New York Press, 2005), 38–43; R. Laurence Moore, "Bible Reading and Nonsectarian Schooling: The Failure of Religious Instruction in Nineteenth-Century Public Education," *Journal of American History* 86, no. 4 (March 2000): 1581–99.
18. Horace Mann, Twelfth Annual Report of the Secretary of the Board of Education (Boston: Dutton and Wentworth, 1849), 121.
19. David B. Tyack, "The Kingdom of God and the Common School: Protestant Ministers and the Educational Awakening in the West," *Harvard Educational Review* 36 (Fall 1966): 447–69; Timothy L. Smith, "Protestant Schooling and American Nationality, 1800–1850," *Journal of American History* 53, no. 4 (March 1967): 679–695.
20. John T. McGreevy, *Catholicism and American Freedom: A History* (New York: Norton, 2003), 12; Lloyd Jorgenson, *The State and the Non-public School, 1825–1925* (Columbia: University of Missouri Press, 1987), 72–111.
21. US Bureau of the Census, *Historical Statistics of the United States*, part 1, series A 57–72, p. 12.; David B. Tyack, "The Spread of Public Schooling in Victorian America: In Search of a Reinterpretation," *History of Education* 7, no. 3 (1978): 173–82.
22. James W. Fraser, *Between Church and State: Religion and Public Education in a Multicultural America* (New York: St. Martin's, 1999), 51–54; Carl F. Kaestle, *The Evolution of an Urban School System: New York City, 1750–1850* (Cambridge, MA: Harvard University Press, 1973).
23. Steven K. Green, *The Bible, the School, and the Constitution: The Clash That Shaped Modern Church-State Doctrine* (New York: Oxford University Press, 2012), 62–68.
24. Vincent P. Lannie and Bernard C. Diethorn, "For the Honor and Glory of God: The Philadelphia Bible Riots of 1840," *History of Education Quarterly* 8, no. 1 (Spring 1968): 47–48.
25. Ibid., 55–56.
26. Ibid.

27. Ibid., 44–106.
28. Ibid.
29. A fascinating exception was A. Bronson Alcott, *Conversations with Children on the Gospels* (Boston: James Munroe, 1836).
30. Actually sited on nearby Breed's Hill, where most of the fighting took place.
31. *Free Education in the United States. Petition of the Town of Medford, Middlesex County, Massachusetts,* [etc.], December 11, 1865, *House Miscellaneous Document no. 5*, 39th Congress, 1st session.
32. Ibid.
33. Maris A. Vinovskis, "Have Social Historians Lost the Civil War? Some Preliminary Demographic Speculations," in *Toward a Social History of the Civil War: Exploratory Essays*, ed. Maris A. Vinovskis (Cambridge: Cambridge University Press, 1990), 4–7.
34. George M. Fredrickson, "The Coming of the Lord: The Northern Protestant Clergy and the Civil War Crisis," in *Religion and the American Civil War*, ed. Randall Miller, Harry S. Stout, and Charles Reagan Wilson (New York: Oxford University Press, 1998), 110–30; Randall Miller, "Catholic Religion, Irish Identity, and the Civil War," in *American Jewry and the Civil War*, ed. Bertram W. Korn (New York: Atheneum, 1970), 15–56.
35. Ward M. McAfee, *Religion, Race, and Reconstruction: The Public School in the Politics of the 1870s* (Albany: State University of New York Press, 1998).
36. For a sympathetic account, see McGreevey, *Catholicism and American Freedom*, chaps. 4 and 5; Justice, *War That Wasn't*.
37. Anderson, *Education of Blacks in the South*; Heather Andrea Williams, *Self-Taught: African American Education in Slavery and Freedom* (Chapel Hill: University of North Carolina Press, 2007).
38. US Bureau of the Census, *Historical Statistics of the United States*, series H 412–432, p. 369.
39. Green, *Bible, the School, and the Constitution*.
40. For an overview, see William J. Reese, *America's Public Schools: From the Common School Era to No Child Left Behind* (Baltimore: Johns Hopkins University Press, 2011), chaps. 2 and 3.
41. Elson, *Guardians of Tradition*.
42. The study by Elizabeth Blanchard Cook, *The Nation's Book in the Nation's Schools* (Chicago: Chicago Women's Educational Union, 1898), is a difficult document to use definitively because it relied on surveys of school leaders and had a clear pro-Bible-reading agenda. Nevertheless, the report cited state school leaders directly in their claims, making it reasonable to make broad inferences.
43. Green, *Bible, the School, and the Constitution*, 36–44.
44. Emerson Keyes, *Laws of New York relating to Common Schools, with Comments and Instructions and a Digest of Decisions. Prepared under the Supervision of Neil Gilmour, Superintendent of Public Instruction* (Albany, NY: Weed, Parsons, 1879), 449–51.

45. Ibid., 135.
46. Justice, *War That Wasn't*; Tyack, "Schooling in Victorian America."
47. Patrick McSweeny, "Christian Public Schools," *Catholic World* 44, no. 264 (March 1887): 796; Justice, *War That Wasn't*, 197.
48. Benjamin Justice, "The Blaine Game: Are Public Schools Inherently Anti-Catholic?" *Teachers College Record* 109, no. 9 (November 2007): 2171–206.
49. Robert Gross, "A Marketplace of Schooling: Education and the American Regulatory State, 1870–1930" (PhD diss., University of Wisconsin, 2013).
50. Justice, *War That Wasn't*, 170.
51. Ronald E. Butchart, *Schooling the Freed People: Teaching, Learning, and the Struggle for Black Freedom, 1861–1876* (Chapel Hill: University of North Carolina Press, 2010), 9.
52. See generally Kim Warren, *The Quest for Citizenship: African American and Native American Education in Kansas, 1880–1935* (Chapel Hill: University of North Carolina Press, 2010); David Wallace Adams, *Education for Extinction* (Lawrence: University of Kansas Press, 1997).

CHAPTER FOUR

1. Walter Lippmann, *American Inquisitors: A Commentary on Dayton and Chicago* (New York: Macmillan, 1928), 21–22.
2. Ibid., 115, 85.
3. The idea that majorities cannot always be trusted to respect minorities and that courts have a crucial role to protect minority rights has become a central theme of many influential contemporary accounts of constitutional interpretation. See John Hart Ely, *Democracy and Distrust: A Theory of Judicial Review* (Cambridge, MA: Harvard University Press, 1980); Ronald Dworkin, *Taking Rights Seriously* (Cambridge, MA: Harvard University Press, 1977).
4. Nancy Maclean, *Behind the Mask of Chivalry: The Making of the Second Ku Klux Klan* (New York: Oxford University Press, 1994), 9–10.
5. Such as John Dewey, *The School and Society: Being Three Lectures* (Chicago: University of Chicago Press, 1900); John Dewey, *The Child and the Curriculum* (Chicago: University of Chicago Press, 1902); John Dewey, *Democracy and Education: An Introduction to the Philosophy of Education* (New York: Free Press, 1966).
6. US Bureau of the Census, *Historical Statistics of the United States Census*, series H 412–432, pp. 368–69.
7. David B. Tyack, *The One Best System: A History of American Urban Education* (Cambridge, MA: Harvard University Press, 1974).
8. On the involvement of the American Bar Association, see Tyack et al., *Law*, 170–71.
9. Jeffrey E. Mirel, *Patriotic Pluralism: Americanization Education and European Immigrants* (Cambridge, MA: Harvard University Press, 2010).
10. Richard J. Ellis, *To the Flag: The Unlikely History of the Pledge of Allegiance* (Lawrence: University of Kansas Press, 2005), 13–23.

11. Balch pledge from ibid., 18.
12. Ibid., 51–52.
13. Ibid., 79.
14. David R. Manwaring, *Render unto Caesar: The Flag Salute Controversy* (Chicago: University of Chicago Press, 1962).
15. Ellis, *To the Flag*, 86–89.
16. Manwaring, *Render unto Caesar*, 20.
17. Ibid., 24–28.
18. Vincent Blasi and Seana V. Shiffrin, "The Story of *West Virginia State Board of Education v. Barnette*: The Pledge of Allegiance and the Freedom of Thought," in *Constitutional Law Stories*, ed. Michael C. Dorf (New York: Foundation, 2004), 433–75; Sarah Barringer Gordon, *The Spirit of the Law: Religious Voices and the Constitution in Modern America* (Cambridge, MA: Harvard University Press, 2010), 3–4.
19. Manwaring, *Render unto Caesar*, 4–5.
20. For a vivid account, see Shawn Francis Peters, *Judging Jehovah's Witnesses: Religious Persecution and the Dawn of the Rights Revolution* (Lawrence: University of Kansas Press, 2000); Manwaring, *Render unto Caesar*, 163–67, 187–88.
21. Jackson, J., Opinion of the Court, *West Virginia State Board of Education v. Barnette*, 319 US 624 (1943), Legal Information Institute, Cornell University Law School, http://www.law.cornell.edu/supct/html/historics/USSC_CR_0319 _0624_ZO.html.
22. J. Ronald Oakley, *God's Country: America in the Fifties* (New York: Norton, 1986).
23. Manwaring, *Render unto Caesar*, 10.
24. Leo XIII, *Longinqua: Encyclical of Pope Leo XIII on Catholicism in the United States*, January 6, 1895, http://www.vatican.va/holy_father/leo_xiii /encyclicals/documents/hf_l-xiii_enc_06011895_longinqua_en.html; Leo XIII, *Testem Benevolentiae, concerning New Opinions concerning Virtue, Nature and Grace, with Regard to Americanism*, January 22, 1899, http://www .papalencyclicals.net/Leo13/l13teste.htm.
25. US Bureau of the Census, *Historical Statistics of the United States*, part 1, series H 535–544, p. 377.
26. Douglas J. Slawson, *The Department of Education Battle, 1918–1932: Public Schools, Catholic Schools, and the Social Order* (Notre Dame, IN: University of Notre Dame Press, 2005).
27. Tyack et al., *Law*, 177–83.
28. Ibid., 182–92.
29. *Gitlow v. New York*, decided one week after *Pierce*, specifically applied the incorporation doctrine to the First Amendment.
30. Adam Laats, *Fundamentalism and Education in the Scopes Era* (New York: Palgrave Macmillan, 2010), 3.
31. Jonathan Zimmerman, *Distilling Democracy: Alcohol Education in America's Public Schools, 1880–1925* (Lawrence: University Press of Kansas, 1999).

32. Tyack et al., *Law*, 165.
33. Laats, *Fundamentalism*, 139–56.
34. Jeffrey P. Moran, *American Genesis: The Antievolution Controversies from Scopes to Creation Science* (New York: Oxford University Press, 2012), 73.
35. The quotations come from Adam Laats's definitive study of the period, *Fundamentalism*, 4–5.
36. Edward J. Larson, *Summer for the Gods: The Scopes Trial and America's Continuing Debate over Science and Religion* (New York: Basic Books, 2006).
37. Dorothy Nelkin, "From Dayton to Little Rock: Creationism Evolves," in *Creationism, Science, and the Law: The Arkansas Case*, ed. Marcel C. LaFollette (Cambridge, MA: MIT Press, 1983), 75.
38. On fundamentalism and higher education in the 1920s, see Laats, *Fundamentalism*, 43–60, 121–38.
39. Gerald Skoog, "The Coverage of Human Evolution in High School Biology Textbooks in the 20th Century and in Current State Science Standards," *Science Education* 14 (2005): 395–422; Laats, *Fundamentalism*, 196–97.
40. Lippmann, *American Inquisitors*.
41. Benjamin Justice, "Released Time," in *The Encyclopedia of New York State*, ed. Peter Eisenstadt (Syracuse, NY: Syracuse University Press, 2005), 1291–92; Mary Dabney Davis, *Week-day Religious Instruction: Classes for Public-School Pupils Conducted on Released School Time*, US Department of the Interior, Bureau of Education, Bulletin 1941, No. 3 (Washington, DC: Government Printing Office, 1933), 1–5; Myron Settle, *The Weekday Church School: For the Guidance of Churches and Communities in the Organization and Administration of Weekday Schools of Religious Education*, Educational Bulletin No. 601 (Chicago: International Council of Religious Education, 1930).
42. Settle, *Weekday Church School*, 8–9, 47; Milton Shaver, *Weekday Church School* (New York: Pilgrim Press, 1956), 4
43. The best account of the released-time movement is Jonathan Zimmerman, *Whose America? Culture Wars in the Public Schools* (Cambridge, MA: Harvard University Press, 2002), 135–59.
44. International Council of Religious Education, *The Weekday Church School: A Guide for Churches and Communities in the Development of Curriculum, Organization and Administration of Weekday Church Schools*, New Educational Bulletin No. 601 (Chicago: International Council of Religious Education, 1940), 19–20.
45. Ibid., 22.
46. Davis, *Week-day Religious Instruction*.
47. Shaver, *Weekday Church School*, 45.
48. *Illinois ex rel. McCollum v. Board of Education of School District No. 71*, 333 US 203 (1948).
49. *Zorach v. Clauson*, 343 US 306 (1952).
50. Zimmerman, *Whose America*, 150–52; US Bureau of the Census, "School Enrollment No. 160: Public Elementary and Secondary Schools—Enrollment,

by Grade: 1940–1962," in *Statistical Abstract of the United States, 1963*, 84th annual edition (Washington, DC: Government Printing Office, 1963).

51. Zimmerman, *Whose America*, 161.

CHAPTER FIVE

1. Steven Mintz claims that the postwar era in the United States was seen by many to be a "child-centered era" in which there was greater attention in the economy and popular culture to the lives of children than in previous historical periods. There was, for instance, a massive increase in the sale of children's toys. See Steven Mintz, *Huck's Raft: A History of American Childhood* (Cambridge, MA: Belknap Press of Harvard University Press, 2004), 275–80. The period of postwar prosperity combined with attention to the extremely disturbing effects of racial segregation in education of the sort highlighted in *Brown v. Board of Education* (1954) may have provided a context in which there was greater receptivity to considering the idea of children's rights and rethinking the limits of parental authority over children.

2. Adam Fairclough, *A Class of Their Own: Black Teachers in the Segregated South* (Cambridge, MA: Harvard University Press, 2007), 394.

3. David B. Tyack and Larry Cuban, *Tinkering toward Utopia: A Century of Public School Reform* (Cambridge, MA: Harvard University Press, 1995).

4. Institute of Educational Sciences, National Center for Education Statistics, "1.5 Million Homeschooled Students in the United States in 2007," issue brief (Washington, DC: US Department of Education, 2008).

5. Conversation with Dr. John Admus, New Brunswick, NJ, February 3, 2012.

6. John C. Green, "Religious Diversity and American Democracy: A View from the Polls," in *Religion and Democracy in the United States: Danger or Opportunity?*, ed. Alan Wolfe and Ira Katznelson (Princeton, NJ: Princeton University Press, 2010), 46–88.

7. Frederick C. Harris, "Entering the Promised Land? The Rise of Prosperity Gospel and Post–Civil Rights Black Politics," in *Religion and Democracy in the United States: Danger or Opportunity?*, ed. Alan Wolfe and Ira Katznelson (Princeton, NJ: Princeton University Press, 2010), 255–78; Michael Dawson, *Black Visions: The Roots of Contemporary African-American Political Ideologies* (Chicago: University of Chicago Press, 2001).

8. Kenneth D. Wald and Allison Calhoun-Brown, *Religion and Politics in the United States*, 6th ed. (New York: Rowman and Littlefield, 2011), 86–104.

9. Among the many, many works on the subject, see Kenneth Dolbeare and Phillip E. Hammond, *The School Prayer Decisions: From Court Policy to Local Practice* (Chicago: University of Chicago Press, 1971).

10. Wald and Calhoun-Brown (*Religion and Politics*, 100) provide an excellent overview of the studies and statistics on the subject.

11. Kevin T. McGuire, "Public Schools, Religious Establishments, and the U.S.

Supreme Court: An Examination of Policy Compliance," *American Politics Research* 37, no. 1 (January 2009): 50–74.

12. See discussion of *Pierce v. Society of Sisters* in chap. 4.

13. *Wisconsin v. Yoder*, 406 U.S. 205 (1972), FindLaw, http://caselaw.lp.findlaw.com/scripts/getcase.pl?navby=CASE&court=US&vol=406&page=205.

14. Adam Laats, "Christian Day Schools and the Transformation of Conservative Protestant Educational Activism, 1962–1990," in *Inequity in Education: A Historical Perspective*, ed. Debra Meyers and Burke Miller (New York: Lexington Books of Rowman and Littlefield, 2009), 183–201; Robert Post and Reva Siegel, "Originalism as a Political Practice: The Right's Living Constitution," *Fordham Law Review* 75, no. 2 (2006): 545.

15. Wald and Calhoun-Brown, *Religion and Politics*, 86–101.

16. *Hein v. Freedom from Religion Foundation*, 551 US 587 (2007); *Employment Division v. Smith*, 494 US 872 (1990).

17. *Lee v. Weisman*, 505 US 577 (1992); *Santa Fe Independent School District v. Doe*, 503 US 290 (2000); *Wallace v. Jaffree*, 472 US 38 (1985).

18. For an overview of the landscape of early twenty-first-century jurisprudence on religion in public education, see Ira C. Lupu, David Masci, and Robert W. Tuttle, "Religion in the Public Schools," in Pew Forum on Religion and Public Life, *Religion and the Courts: The Pillars of Church-State Law* (May 2007), http://www.pewforum.org/uploadedfiles/Topics/Issues/Church-State_Law/religion-public-schools.pdf.

19. *Elk Grove Unified School District v. Newdow*, 542 US 1 (2004).

20. See *Salazar v. Buono*, 599 US 700 (2010), in which the five conservative (all Catholic) justices ruled that the cross is not a symbol promoting Christianity. Or contrast the court's ruling in *Burwell v. Hobby Lobby*, 573 US (2014), docket no. 13-354, with *Employment Division v. Smith*. The former upheld a corporation's refusal to comply with a legal requirement to provide reproductive health services (which violated their Christian beliefs), while the latter ruled that Native Americans could not violate antidrug laws in their religious ceremonies.

21. Edward Larson, *Trial and Error: The American Controversy over Creation and Evolution* (New York: Oxford University Press, 2003), 90–98. See generally John L. Rudolph, *Scientists in the Classroom: The Cold War Reconstruction of American Science Education* (New York: Palgrave, 2002).

22. Larson, *Trial and Error*, 104–8; Nelkin, "Creationism Evolves," 76.

23. Larson, *Trial and Error*, 120.

24. Adam Laats, *The Other School Reformers: Conservative Activism in American Education* (Cambridge, MA: Harvard University Press, 2015), 16.

25. Larson, *Trial and Error*, 96–97.

26. Laurie Godfrey, ed., *Scientists Confront Creationism* (New York: Norton, 1983).

27. See Larson, *Trial and Error*, 242, for an overview of surveys from the period.

28. Ibid., 165–66.

29. *Mozert v. Hawkins*, 827 F.2d 1058 (1987); Laats, *Other School Reformers*, 16. For a discussion of the founding fathers' ideas on education, see chap. 2.
30. *Kitzmiller v. Dover*, 400 F. Supp. 2d 707 (2005).
31. Pew Research Center for the People and the Press and Pew Forum on Religion and Public Life, *Many Americans Uneasy with Mix of Religion and Politics* (August 2006), http://www.pewforum.org/Politics-and-Elections/Many -Americans-Uneasy-with-Mix-of-Religion-and-Politics.aspx#3.
32. Pew Research Center for the People and the Press and Pew Forum on Religion and Public Life, *Public Divided on Origins of Life: Religion a Strength and Weakness for Both Parties* (August 2005), http://www.pewforum.org/Politics-and -Elections/Public-Divided-on-Origins-of-Life.aspx#3.
33. Pew Forum on Religion and Public Life, *"Nones" on the Rise: One-in-Five Adults Have No Religious Affiliation* (October 2012), http://www.pewforum.org/2012 /10/09/nones-on-the-rise/.
34. For an overview of public funding for private schools, see Jim Carl, *Freedom of Choice: Vouchers in American Education* (Santa Barbara, CA: Praeger, 2011).
35. *Raney v. Board of Education*, 391 US 443 (1968); *Green v. County School Board*, 391 US 430 (1968); *Monroe v. Board of Commissioners*, 391 US 450 (1968).
36. Carl, *Freedom of Choice*, chap. 2, offers an in-depth examination of the Louisiana voucher plan.
37. Ibid., Kindle edition, location 1376 of 3711.
38. For an overview of school choice, see Patricia Burch, *Hidden Markets: The New Education Privatization* (New York: Routledge, 2009). The most prominent voucher polemic was John Chubb and Terry Moe, *Politics, Markets, and America's Schools* (Washington, DC: Brookings Institution, 1990).
39. The Milwaukee plan was initially for secular private schools only, but it began including religious schools after a favorable state supreme court ruling in 1998.
40. George Voinovich, quoted in Carl, *Freedom of Choice*, location 2184 of 3711.
41. *Zelman v. Simmons-Harris*, 536 US 639 (2002).
42. Mark Edward DeForrest, "An Overview and Evaluation of State Blaine Amendments: Origins, Scope, and First Amendment Concerns," *Harvard Journal of Law and Public Policy* 26, no. 2 (Spring 2003): 551–626.
43. While several non-peer-reviewed studies by right-wing think tanks claimed that vouchers were a success, high-quality studies varied in their findings. Some found modest improvements in student achievement while others saw nothing significant. No study found the effects that had been promised. For examples, see Cecilia Rouse, "Private School Vouchers and Student Achievement: Evidence from the Milwaukee Choice Program," *Quarterly Journal of Economics* 113, no. 2 (1998): 553–602; Rajashri Chakrabarti, "Can Increasing Private School Participation and Monetary Loss in a Voucher Program Affect Public School Performance?" *Journal of Public Economics* 92, nos. 5–6 (June 2008): 1371–93; Carlos Lamarche, "Private School Vouchers and Student

Achievement: A Fixed Effects Quantile Regression Evaluation," *Labour Economics* 15, no. 4 (August 2008): 575–90; Lisa Barrow and Cecilia Rouse, "School Vouchers: Recent Findings and Unanswered Questions," *Economic Perspectives* 32, no. 3 (2008): 2–16.

44. Institute of Educational Sciences, National Center for Education Statistics, *Trends in the Use of School Choice, 1993–2007* (Washington, DC: US Department of Education, 2010).

45. National Center for Education Statistics, "Charter School Enrollment" (April 2015), website of the National Center for Education Statics, Institute of Education Sciences, US Department of Education, http://nces.ed.gov/programs /coe/indicator_cgb.asp.

46. Institute of Educational Sciences, National Center for Educational Evaluation and Regional Assistance, *The Evaluation of Charter School Impacts: Final Report* (Washington, DC: US Department of Education, 2010).

47. Jessica Meyers, "Charter Schools with Ties to Religious Groups Raise Fears about State Funds' Use," *Dallas Morning News*, November 22, 2010; Lawrence D. Weinberg, *Religious Charter Schools: Legalities and Practicalities* (New York: Information Age, 2007); Janet Mulvey, Bruce Cooper, and Arthur Maloney, *Blurring the Lines: Charter, Public, Private, and Religious Schools Coming Together* (New York: Information Age, 2010).

48. Weinberg, *Religious Charter Schools*, xx; Mulvey et al., *Blurring the Lines*.

49. Sarah Lemagie, "ACLU Settles with State, School Sponsor," *Star Tribune*, February 7, 2011, http://www.startribune.com/local/south/115533274.html ?refer=y; Andy Birkey, "Education Department Findings on Tarek ibn Ziyad Academy Contradict Published Reports," *Minnesota Monitor*, May 20, 2008, http://www.tcdailyplanet.net/article/2008/05/20/education-department -findings-tarek-ibn-ziyad-academy-contradict-published-report.

50. See, e.g., Judy Jackson May, "The Charter School Allure: Can Traditional Schools Measure Up?," *Education and Urban Society* 39, no. 1 (November 2006): 19–45.

51. Benjamin Siracusa Hillman, "Is There a Place for Religious Charter Schools?," *Yale Law School Journal* 118, no. 3 (December 2008): 554–99; Stephen Macedo, "Constituting Civil Society: School Vouchers, Religious Nonprofit Organizations, and Liberal Public Values," *Chicago-Kent Law Review* 75 (1999–2000): 417.

52. Pew Forum on Religion and Public Life, *Applying God's Law: Religious Courts and Mediation in the United States* (April 2013), http://www.pewforum.org /Church-State-Law/Applying-Gods-Law-Religious-Courts-and-Mediation-in -the-US.aspx.

CHAPTER SIX

1. The 2013 demographic data and 2012 election data from City-Data.com, http://www.city-data.com/city/Kountze-Texas.html.

2. Ibid.
3. Texas State Historical Association, "Honey Island, Texas," Texas State Histori-cal Association website, accessed January 3, 2014, http://www.tshaonline .org/handbook/online/articles/hlh53; "High School Graduates Longitudinal Data by District," Texas PK-16 Public Education Information Resource, Texas Education Agency, accessed January 3, 2014, http://www.texaseducationinfo .org/tea.tpeir.web/ViewReport.aspx; Kountze Independent School District website, accessed January 3, 2014; entry on Kountze High School, accessed January 3, 2014, http://www.kountzeisd.org/.
4. Manny Fernandez, "Cheerleaders with Bible Verses Set Off Debate," *New York Times*, October 4, 2012.
5. *Coti Matthews et al. v. Kountze Independent School District*, cause no. 53526, 356th Judicial District, Hardin County, TX, Summary Judgement Order May 8, 2013.
6. Brief of Amici Curiae ACLU, ACLU of Texas, et al., No. 09-13-00251-CV, Court of Appeals for the Ninth District, Beaumont, TX, *Kountze Independent School District v. Coti Matthews, on Behalf of Her Minor Child, Macy Matthews, Appellees*, September 4, 2013.
7. Ibid., 9.
8. Keith A. Erekson, ed., *Politics and the History Curriculum: The Struggle over Stan-dards in Texas and the Nation* (New York: Palgrave Macmillan, 2012).
9. American Historical Association, "AHA's Statement on Texas State Amend-ments to TEKS for Social Studies," *Perspectives on History* (September 2010), https://www.historians.org/publications-and-directories/perspectives-on -history/september-2010/ahas-statement-on-texas-state-amendments-to -teks-for-social-studies.
10. Texas Administrative Code, title 19, part 2, chap. 113, Texas Essential Knowl-edge and Skills for Social Studies, Texas Education Agency website, accessed January 17, 2014, http://ritter.tea.state.tx.us/rules/tac/chap.113/index.html.
11. As quoted in Cindy Swirko, "Judge Backs Schools in Suit over 'Islam is of the Devil' Shirts," *Gainesville Sun*, September 30, 2011, http://www.gainesville .com/article/20110930/ARTICLES/110939946.
12. George Orwell, *Nineteen Eighty-Four* (New York: Harcourt, Brace and World, 1949), 81.
13. M. Suzanne Donovan and John D. Blansford, eds., *How Students Learn: His-tory, Mathematics, and Science in the Classroom* (Washington, DC: National Academies Press, 2005), 1–2.
14. Nel Noddings, *Educating for Intelligent Belief or Unbelief* (New York: Teachers College Press, 1993).
15. Mark Chancey, *Reading, Writing, and Religion II: Texas Public School Bible Courses in 2011–2012*, Report from the Texas Freedom Network Education Fund, Texas Freedom Network website, http://www.tfn.org/site/DocServer /TFNEF_ReadingWritingReligionII.pdf?docID=3481.
16. See ACLU website, https://www.aclu.org/bible-public-schools; see also the

National Council on Bible Curriculum in Public Schools website, http://bibleinschools.net/The-Curriculum.php.

17. See Bible Literacy Project website, http://www.bibleliteracy.org/; for a critique of the textbook series, see Joseph Conn, "The Bible Literacy Project: Chuck Stetson's Trojan Horse?" (January 2006), Americans United for the Separation of Church and State website, https://www.au.org/church-state/january-2006-church-state/books-ideas/the-bible-literacy-project. For a fine-grained analysis of popular Bible-study programs, see Walter Feinberg and Richard A. Layton, *For the Civic Good: The Liberal Case for Teaching Religion in Public Schools* (Ann Arbor: University of Michigan Press, 2014).

18. See Religion in the Public Schools: A Joint Statement of Current Law, April 12, 1995, ACLU website, https://www.aclu.org/religion-belief/joint-statement-current-law-religion-public-schools. See also various publications by the First Amendment Center, http://www.firstamendmentcenter.org.

19. For an interesting discussion, see Ryan Bevan, "The Question of Consciousness and Religious Engagement in Public Schools," *Studies in Philosophy of Education* 30, no. 3 (2011): 257–69; Michael Hand, *Is Religious Education Possible?* (London: Continuum, 2006); Noddings, *Educating for Intelligent Belief or Unbelief.*

20. As quoted in Feinberg and Layton, *For the Civic Good*, 124.

21. Ibid., 124.

22. Ibid.

23. National Center for Education Statistics, "Charter School Enrollment."

24. For example, see Maria Paino, Linda A. Renzulli, Rebecca L. Boylan, and Christen L. Bradley, "For Grades or Money? Charter School Failure in North Carolina," *Educational Administration Quarterly* 50, no. 3 (August 2014): 500–526; Institute of Educational Sciences, National Center for Education Statistics, *Trends in the Use of School Choice, 1993–2007* (Washington, DC: US Department of Education, 2010), http://nces.ed.gov/pubs2010/2010004.pdf; Institute of Educational Sciences, *Evaluation of Charter School Impacts.* On rights abuses see Preston C. Green III, Bruce D. Baker, and Joseph O. Oluwole, "Having It Both Ways: How Charter Schools Try to Obtain Funding of Public Schools and the Autonomy of Private Schools," *Emory Law Journal* 63 (2013): 101–35.

25. National Study of Charter School Management Organization Effectiveness, *Charter-School Management Organizations: Diverse Strategies and Diverse Student Impacts* (Mathematica Policy Research, November 1, 2011), Education Week website, http://www.edweek.org/media/(cmo_final%20_report%2011%2002%2011.pdf.

26. Responsive Education Solutions, 2013 Annual Report, Responsive Education Solutions website, http://responsiveed.com/wp-content/uploads/2013/08/2013_RES_Annual_Report.pdf.

27. Stephanie Saul, "Charter Schools Tied to Turkey Grow in Texas," *New York Times*, June 6, 2011, http://www.nytimes.com/2011/06/07/education

/07charter.html?pagewanted=all; Harmony Public Schools website, http://
harmonytx.org/default.aspx; Valarie Strauss, "Islamic Cleric Linked to U.S.
Charter Schools Involved in Turkey's Political Drama," *Washington Post*, December 26, 2013, http://www.washingtonpost.com/blogs/answer-sheet/wp
/2013/12/26/islamic-cleric-linked-to-u-s-charter-schools-involved-in-turkeys
-political-drama/.

28. *Zelman v. Simmons-Harris*, 536 US 639 (2002).

29. Macedo, "Constituting Civil Society."

30. Kathleen Knight Abowitz, "Charter Schooling and Social Justice," *Educational Theory* 51, no. 2 (2001): 151–70.

31. Edgar Walters, "Trying to Keep Religion out of the Charter School Classroom," *New York Times*, October 17, 2013, http://www.nytimes.com/2013/10
/18/us/trying-to-keep-religion-out-of-the-charter-school-classroom.html?_r
=0; National Center for Science Education, "Creationism in Texas Charter
Schools" (January 21, 2014), http://ncse.com/news/2014/01/creationism
-texas-charter-schools-0015318.

32. Michel Martin and Claudio Sanchez, "Religion a Big Part of the Charter
School Debate," National Public Radio, June 16, 2009, http://www.npr.org
/templates/story/story.php?storyId=105461721.

33. Justice, *War That Wasn't*; Macedo, *Diversity and Distrust*.

34. Johnny Scaramanga, "Darwin Inspired Hitler: Lies They Teach in Texas,"
Salon, October 25, 2013, http://www.salon.com/2013/10/25/christian
_textbooks_darwin_inspired_hitler/.

35. Zack Kopplin, "Texas Public Schools Are Teaching Creationism: An Investigation into Charter Schools' Dishonest and Unconstitutional Science, History
and 'Values' Lessons," *Slate*, January 16, 2014, http://www.slate.com/articles
/health_and_science/science/2014/01/creationism_in_texas_public_schools
_undermining_the_charter_movement.html. This article was picked up by
a number of media outlets and led to formal challenges to RES by the Texas
Freedom Network.

36. Chris Kirk, "Map: Publicly Funded Schools That Are Allowed to Teach Creationism," *Slate*, January 16, 2014, http://www.slate.com/articles/health_and
_science/science/2014/01/creationism_in_public_schools_mapped_where
_tax_money_supports_alternatives.html.

37. The biology department in the College of Life Sciences at Brigham Young
University publishes several official statements by the Church of Jesus
Christ of Latter-day Saints on the subject of evolution. This site was ac-
cessed November 14, 2014, http://biology.byu.edu/DepartmentInfo
/EvolutionandtheOriginofMan.aspx.

38. Jesse McKinley and Kirk Johnson, "Mormons Tipped Scale in Ban on Gay
Marriage," *New York Times*, November 14, 2008, http://www.nytimes.com
/2008/11/15/us/politics/15marriage.html?pagewanted=all; the official website of the Church of Jesus Christ of Latter-day Saints, accessed November 14,
2014, http://www.mormon.org/beliefs/commandments.

39. Rachel Donadio, "On Gay Priests, Pope Francis Asks, "Who Am I to Judge?,"
    New York Times, July 19, 2013, http://www.nytimes.com/2013/07/30/world
    /europe/pope-francis-gay-priests.html?pagewanted=all; Catholic News
    Service, "Bishops Urge Constitutional Amendment to Protect Marriage,"
    Americancatholic.org website, accessed November 14, 2014, http://www
    .americancatholic.org/News/Homosexuality/; Michael O'Loughlan, "The
    Catholic Church Isn't Anti-gay, but Are Its Bishops?" *Huffington Post*, Decem-
    ber 12, 2013, http://www.huffingtonpost.com/michael-oloughlin/anti-gay
    -bishops_b_4414016.html.
40. For example, see Jayson Littman, "Wanted: Orthodox Rabbis to Sign
    Anti-gay Declaration," *Huffington Post*, November 28, 2011, http://www
    .huffingtonpost.com/jayson-littman/orthodox-rabbis-homosexuality
    -declaration_b_1114090.html.
41. J. Mark Halstead and Katarzyna Lewicka, "Should Homosexuality Be Taught
    as an Acceptable Alternative Lifestyle? A Muslim Perspective," *Cambridge
    Journal of Education* 28, no. 1 (March 1998): 49.
42. On high prevalence and severity of antigay policy in Islamic states, see Lucas
    Paoli Itaborahy and Jingshu Zhu, *State-Sponsored Homophobia: A World Survey
    of Laws: Criminalisation, Protection and Recognition of Same-Sex Love* (Interna-
    tional Lesbian Gay Bisexual Trans and Intersex Association, 2014), http://old
    .ilga.org/Statehomophobia/ILGA_SSHR_2014_Eng.pdf.
43. Pressley Baird, "North Carolina's Myrtle Grove Christian School to Refuse
    State Money over Anti-Gay Policy," *Star-News*, Wilmington, NC, Decem-
    ber 7, 2013, reposted by *Huffington Post* on February 7, 2014, http://www
    .huffingtonpost.com/2013/12/08/north-carolina-school-gay-policy-_n
    _4403722.html.
44. Preston C. Green III et al., "Having It Both Ways," 101–35.
45. Pew Forum, *"Nones" on the Rise.*

Bibliography

Abowitz, Kathleen Knight. "Charter Schooling and Social Justice." *Educational Theory* 51, no. 2 (2001): 151–70. doi:10.1111/j.1741-5446.2001.00151.x.

Adams, David Wallace. *Education for Extinction*. Lawrence: University of Kansas Press, 1997.

Adams, John. *A Dissertation on the Canon and the Feudal Law*. May–October 1765. In *The Works of John Adams, Second President of the United States: With a Life of the Author, Notes and Illustrations*, edited by Charles Francis Adams, 3:447–64. Boston: Little, Brown, 1851.

———. "Novanglus Essays." In *The Works of John Adams, Second President of the United States: With a Life of the Author, Notes and Illustrations*, edited by Charles Francis Adams, 4:3–180. Boston: Little, Brown, 1851.

———. "Thoughts on Government." In *The Works of John Adams, Second President of the United States: With a Life of the Author, Notes and Illustrations*, edited by Charles Francis Adams, 4:189–200. Boston: Little, Brown, 1851.

Alcott, A. Bronson. *Conversations with Children on the Gospels*. Boston: James Munroe, 1836.

Anderson, James D. *The Education of Blacks in the South, 1860–1935*. Chapel Hill: University of North Carolina Press, 1988.

Archard, David. "Children, Adults, Autonomy and Well-Being." In *The Nature of Children's Well-Being: Theory and Practice*, edited by Alexander Bagattini and Colin Macleod, 3–14. Dordrecht, The Netherlands: Springer, 2014.

Barrow, Lisa, and Cecilia Rouse. "School Vouchers: Recent Findings and Unanswered Questions." *Economic Perspectives* 32, no. 3 (2008): 2–16.

Beadie, Nancy. *Education and the Creation of Capital in the Early American Republic*. New York: Cambridge University Press, 2010.

———. "'Encouraging Useful Knowledge' in the Early Republic: The Roles of State Governments and Voluntary Organizations." In *The Founding Fathers, Education, and "The Great Contest": The American Philosophical Society Essay Contest of 1797,* edited by Benjamin Justice, 85–102. New York: Palgrave Macmillan, 2013.

Betlzer, Monika. "Enhancing the Capacity for Autonomy." In *The Nature of Children's Well-Being: Theory and Practice,* edited by Alexander Bagattini and Colin Macleod, 65–84. Dordrecht, The Netherlands: Springer, 2014.

Bevan, Ryan. "The Question of Consciousness and Religious Engagement in Public Schools." *Studies in Philosophy of Education* 30, no. 3 (2011): 257–69.

Blasi, Vincent, and Seana V. Shiffrin. "The Story of *West Virginia State Board of Education v. Barnette*: The Pledge of Allegiance and the Freedom of Thought." In *Constitutional Law Stories,* edited by Michael C. Dorf, 433–75. New York: Foundation, 2004.

Bou-Habib, Paul, and Serean Olsaretti. "Autonomy and Children's Well-Being." In *The Nature of Children's Well-Being: Theory and Practice,* edited by Alexander Bagattini and Colin Macleod, 15–34. Dordrecht, The Netherlands: Springer, 2014.

Brighouse, Harry. "Civic Education and Liberal Legitimacy." *Ethics* 108, no. 4 (1998): 719–45.

Brodsky, Alyn. *Benjamin Rush, Patriot, and Physician.* New York: St. Martin's, 2004.

Burch, Patricia. *Hidden Markets: The New Education Privatization.* New York: Routledge, 2009.

Butchart, Ronald E. *Schooling the Freed People: Teaching, Learning, and the Struggle for Black Freedom, 1861–1876.* Chapel Hill: University of North Carolina Press, 2010.

Butler, Jon, Grant Wacker, and Randall Balmer. *Religion in American Life: A Short History.* 2nd edition. New York: Oxford University Press, 2011.

Callan, Eamonn. "Autonomy, Child-Rearing, and Good Lives." In *The Moral and Political Status of Children,* edited by David Archard and Colin Macleod. Oxford: Oxford University Press, 2002.

———. *Creating Citizens: Political Education and Liberal Democracy.* Oxford: Oxford University Press, 1997.

Cappon, Lester J., ed. *The Adam-Jefferson Letters: The Complete Correspondence between Thomas Jefferson and Abigail and John Adams* (Chapel Hill: University of North Carolina Press, 1988).

Carl, Jim. *Freedom of Choice: Vouchers in American Education.* Santa Barbara, CA: Praeger, 2011.

Chakrabarti, Rajashri. "Can Increasing Private School Participation and Monetary Loss in a Voucher Program Affect Public School Performance?" *Journal of Public Economics* 92, nos. 5–6 (June 2008): 1371–93.

Chambers, Simone. "Deliberative Democratic Theory." *Annual Review of Political Science* 6, no. 1 (2003): 307–8.

Chancey, Mark. *Reading, Writing, and Religion II: Texas Public School Bible Courses in 2011–2012.* Report from the Texas Freedom Network Education Fund. http://

www.tfn.org/site/DocServer/TFNEF_ReadingWritingReligionII.pdf?docID=
3481.

Chubb, John, and Terry Moe. *Politics, Markets, and America's Schools*. Washington, DC: Brookings Institution, 1990.

Clayton, Matthew. *Justice and Legitimacy in Upbringing*. Oxford: Oxford University Press, 2006.

Cook, Elizabeth Blanchard. *The Nation's Book in the Nation's Schools*. Chicago: Chicago Women's Educational Union, 1898.

Cotlar, Seth. "'Every Man Should Have Property': Robert Coram and the American Revolution's Legacy of Economic Populism." In *Revolutionary Founders: Rebels, Radicals, and Reformers in the Making of the Nation*, edited by Alfred Fabian Young, Gary B. Nash, and Ray Raphael, 337–54. New York: Knopf, 2011.

Curry, Thomas J. *The First Freedoms: Church and State in America to the Passage of the First Amendment*. New York: Oxford University Press, 1986.

Davis, Mary Dabney. *Week-day Religious Instruction: Classes for Public-School Pupils Conducted on Released School Time*. US Department of the Interior, Bureau of Education, Bulletin 1941, No. 3. Washington, DC: Government Printing Office, 1933.

Dawson, Michael. *Black Visions: The Roots of Contemporary African-American Political Ideologies*. Chicago: University of Chicago Press, 2001.

DeForrest, Mark Edward. "An Overview and Evaluation of State Blaine Amendments: Origins, Scope, and First Amendment Concerns." *Harvard Journal of Law and Public Policy* 26, no. 2 (Spring 2003): 551–626.

Dewey, John. *The Child and the Curriculum*. Chicago: University of Chicago Press, 1902.

———. *Democracy and Education: An Introduction to the Philosophy of Education*. New York: Free Press, 1966.

———. *The School and Society: Being Three Lectures*. Chicago: University of Chicago Press, 1900.

Dolbeare, Kenneth, and Phillip E. Hammond. *The School Prayer Decisions: From Court Policy to Local Practice*. Chicago: University of Chicago Press, 1971.

Donovan, M. Suzanne, and John D. Blansford, eds. *How Students Learn: History, Mathematics, and Science in the Classroom*. Washington, DC: National Academies Press, 2005.

Doyle, Don Harrison. *The Social Order of a Frontier Community: Jacksonville, Illinois, 1825–1870*. Urbana: University of Illinois Press, 1979.

Dworkin, Ronald. *Taking Rights Seriously*. Cambridge, MA: Harvard University Press, 1977.

Dwyer, James. *Religious Schools v. Children's Rights*. Ithaca, NY: Cornell University Press, 1998.

Eberle, Christopher. *Religious Conviction in Liberal Policies*. New York: Cambridge University Press, 2002.

Ellis, Richard J. *To the Flag: The Unlikely History of the Pledge of Allegiance*. Lawrence: University of Kansas Press, 2005.

Elson, Ruth Miller. *Guardians of Tradition: American Schoolbooks of the Nineteenth Century*. Lincoln: University of Nebraska Press, 1972.

Ely, John Hart. *Democracy and Distrust: A Theory of Judicial Review*. Cambridge, MA: Harvard University Press, 1980.

Erekson, Keith A., ed. *Politics and the History Curriculum: The Struggle over Standards in Texas and the Nation*. New York: Palgrave Macmillan, 2012.

Fairclough, Adam. *A Class of Their Own: Black Teachers in the Segregated South*. Cambridge, MA: Harvard University Press, 2007.

Feinberg, Joel. "A Child's Right to an Open Future." In *Whose Child? Children's Rights, Parental Authority, and State Power*, edited by W. Aiken and H. LaFollette, 124–53. Totowa, NJ: Littlefield, Adams, 1980.

Feinberg, Walter, and Richard A. Layton. *For the Civic Good: The Liberal Case for Teaching Religion in Public Schools*. Ann Arbor: University of Michigan Press, 2014.

Fraser, James W. *Between Church and State: Religion and Public Education in a Multicultural America*. New York: St. Martin's, 1999.

Fredrickson, George M. "The Coming of the Lord: The Northern Protestant Clergy and the Civil War Crisis." In *Religion and the American Civil War*, edited by Randall Miller, Harry S. Stout, and Charles Reagan Wilson, 110–30. New York: Oxford University Press, 1998.

Godfrey, Laurie, ed. *Scientists Confront Creationism*. New York: Norton, 1983.

Gordon, Sarah Barringer. *The Spirit of the Law: Religious Voices and the Constitution in Modern America*. Cambridge, MA: Harvard University Press, 2010.

Green, Andy. *Education and State Formation: The Rise of Education Systems in England, France, and the USA*. Basingstoke, UK: Macmillan, 1990.

———. *Education, Globalization, and the Nation State*. London: Macmillan, 1997.

Green, John C. "Religious Diversity and American Democracy: A View from the Polls." In *Religion and Democracy in the United States: Danger or Opportunity?*, edited by Alan Wolfe and Ira Katznelson, 46–88. Princeton, NJ: Princeton University Press, 2010.

Green, Preston C. III, Bruce D. Baker, and Joseph O. Oluwole. "Having It Both Ways: How Charter Schools Try to Obtain Funding of Public Schools and the Autonomy of Private Schools." *Emory Law Journal* 63 (2013): 101–35.

Green, Steven K. *The Bible, the School, and the Constitution: The Clash That Shaped Modern Church-State Doctrine*. New York: Oxford University Press, 2012.

Gross, Robert. "A Marketplace of Schooling: Education and the American Regulatory State, 1870–1930." PhD diss., University of Wisconsin, 2013.

Gutmann, Amy. *Democratic Education*. Princeton, NJ: Princeton University Press, 1987.

Halstead, J. Mark, and Katarzyna Lewicka. "Should Homosexuality Be Taught as an Acceptable Alternative Lifestyle? A Muslim Perspective." *Cambridge Journal of Education* 28, no. 1 (March 1998): 49–64.

Hand, Michael. *Is Religious Education Possible?* London: Continuum, 2006.

Harris, Frederick C. "Entering the Promised Land? The Rise of Prosperity Gospel and Post–Civil Rights Black Politics." In *Religion and Democracy in the United*

States: Danger or Opportunity?, edited by Alan Wolfe and Ira Katznelson, 255–78. Princeton, NJ: Princeton University Press, 2010.

Hillman, Benjamin Siracusa. "Is There a Place for Religious Charter Schools?" *Yale Law School Journal* 118, no. 3 (December 2008): 554–99.

Institute of Educational Sciences, National Center for Educational Evaluation and Regional Assistance. *The Evaluation of Charter School Impacts: Final Report.* Washington, DC: US Department of Education, 2010. http://ies.ed.gov/ncee/pubs/20104029/pdf/20104029.pdf.

Institute of Educational Sciences, National Center for Education Statistics. "1.5 Million Homeschooled Students in the United States in 2007." Issue brief. Washington, DC: US Department of Education, 2008.

——. *Trends in the Use of School Choice, 1993–2007.* Washington, DC: US Department of Education, 2010. http://nces.ed.gov/pubs2010/2010004.pdf.

International Council of Religious Education. *The Weekday Church School: A Guide for Churches and Communities in the Development of Curriculum, Organization and Administration of Weekday Church Schools.* New Educational Bulletin No. 601. Chicago: International Council of Religious Education, 1940.

Jefferson, Thomas. "Notes on the State of Virginia, Query XIV." In *Writings: Thomas Jefferson*, edited by Merrill D. Peterson, 123–325. Washington, DC: Library of America, 1984.

——. "Report of the President and Directors of the Literary Fund. October 7, 1822. From the Minutes of the Board of Visitors, University of Virginia, 1822–1825." In *Writings: Thomas Jefferson*, edited by Merrill D. Peterson, 477–81. Washington, DC: Library of America, 1984.

Jorgenson, Lloyd. *The State and the Non-public School, 1825–1925.* Columbia: University of Missouri Press, 1987.

Justice, Benjamin. "The Blaine Game: Are Public Schools Inherently Anti-Catholic?" *Teachers College Record* 109, no. 9 (November 2007): 2171–206.

——. "The Originalist Case against Vouchers: The First Amendment, Religion, and American Public Schooling." *Stanford Law and Policy Review* 26, no. 2 (2015): 437–84.

——. "The Place of the Religion in Early National School Plans." In *The Founding Fathers, Education, and "The Great Contest": The American Philosophical Society Essay Contest of 1797*, ed. Benjamin Justice, 155–74. New York: Palgrave Macmillan, 2013.

——. "Released Time." In *The Encyclopedia of New York State*, edited by Peter Eisenstadt, 1291–92. Syracuse, NY: Syracuse University Press, 2005.

——. *The War That Wasn't: Religious Conflict and Compromise in the Common Schools of New York, 1865–1900.* Albany: State University of New York Press, 2005.

Kaestle, Carl F. *The Evolution of an Urban School System: New York City, 1750–1850.* Cambridge, MA: Harvard University Press, 1973.

——. *Pillars of the Republic: Common Schools and American Society, 1780–1860.* New York: Hill and Wang, 1983.

Keyes, Emerson. *Laws of New York relating to Common Schools, with Comments and Instructions and a Digest of Decisions.* Prepared under the supervision of Neil Gilmour, Superintendent of Public Instruction. Albany, NY: Weed, Parsons, 1879.

Keyssar, Alexander. *The Right to Vote: The Contested History of Democracy in the United States.* New York: Basic Books, 2000.

Kuritz, Hyman. "Benjamin Rush: His Theory of Public Education." *History of Education Quarterly* 7, no. 4 (Winter 1967): 432–51.

Laats, Adam. "Christian Day Schools and the Transformation of Conservative Protestant Educational Activism, 1962–1990." In *Inequity in Education: A Historical Perspective,* ed. Debra Meyers and Burke Miller, 183–201. New York: Lexington Books of Rowman and Littlefield, 2009.

——. *Fundamentalism and Education in the Scopes Era.* New York: Palgrave Macmillan, 2010.

——. *The Other School Reformers: Conservative Activism in American Education.* Cambridge, MA: Harvard University Press, 2015.

Labaree, David F. *Someone Has to Fail: The Zero-Sum Game of Public Schooling.* Cambridge, MA: Harvard University Press, 2010.

Lamarche, Carlos. "Private School Vouchers and Student Achievement: A Fixed Effects Quantile Regression Evaluation." *Labour Economics* 15, no. 4 (August 2008): 575–90.

Lannie, Vincent P., and Bernard C. Diethorn. "For the Honor and Glory of God: The Philadelphia Bible Riots of 1840." *History of Education Quarterly* 8, no. 1 (Spring 1968): 44–106.

Larson, Edward J. *Summer for the Gods: The Scopes Trial and America's Continuing Debate over Science and Religion.* New York: Basic Books, 2006.

——. *Trial and Error: The American Controversy over Creation and Evolution.* New York: Oxford University Press, 2003.

Leo XIII. *Longinqua: Encyclical of Pope Leo XIII on Catholicism in the United States.* January 6, 1895. Vatican website, http://www.vatican.va/holy_father/leo_xiii/encyclicals/documents/hf_l-xiii_enc_06011895_longinqua_en.html.

——. *Testem Benevolentiae, concerning New Opinions concerning Virtue, Nature and Grace, with Regard to Americanism.* January 22, 1899. Vatican website, http://www.papalencyclicals.net/Leo13/l13teste.htm.

Levinson, Meira. *The Demands of a Liberal Education.* Oxford: Oxford University Press, 1999.

Levy, Leonard Williams. *The Establishment Clause: Religion and the First Amendment.* New York: Macmillan, 1986.

Lippmann, Walter. *American Inquisitors: A Commentary on Dayton and Chicago.* New York: Macmillan, 1928.

Locke, John. "Letter concerning Toleration." In *The Works of John Locke in Nine Volumes,* 12th edition, 5:5–58. London: Rivington, 1824.

Lupu, Ira C., David Masci, and Robert W. Tuttle. "Religion in the Public Schools." In Pew Forum on Religion and Public Life, *Religion and the Courts: The Pillars*

of Church-State Law. May 2007. http://www.pewforum.org/uploadedfiles
/Topics/Issues/Church-State_Law/religion-public-schools.pdf.

Macedo, Stephen. "Constituting Civil Society: School Vouchers, Religious Non-profit Organizations, and Liberal Public Values." *Chicago-Kent Law Review* 75, no. 2 (1999–2000): 417–51.

———. *Diversity and Distrust: Civic Education in a Multicultural Democracy.* Cambridge, MA: Harvard University Press, 2000.

Maclean, Nancy. *Behind the Mask of Chivalry: The Making of the Second Ku Klux Klan.* New York: Oxford University Press, 1994.

Macleod, Colin. "Conceptions of Parental Autonomy." *Politics & Society* 25, no. 1 (1997): 117–40.

Madison, James. "Letter to William T. Barry, August 4, 1822," and "Letter to Edward Everett, March 19, 1823." In *James Madison: Writings,* edited by Jack Rakove, 790–98. New York: Library of America, 1999.

Manwaring, David R. *Render unto Caesar: The Flag Salute Controversy.* Chicago: University of Chicago Press, 1962.

May, Judy Jackson. "The Charter School Allure: Can Traditional Schools Measure Up?" *Education and Urban Society* 39, no. 1 (November 2006): 19–45.

McAfee, Ward M. *Religion, Race, and Reconstruction: The Public School in the Politics of the 1870s.* Albany: State University of New York Press, 1998.

McConnell, Michael W. "Establishment and Disestablishment at the Founding, Part 1: Establishment of Religion." *William & Mary Law Review* 44 (2003): 2105–208.

McGreevy, John T. *Catholicism and American Freedom: A History.* New York: Norton, 2003.

McGuire, Kevin T. "Public Schools, Religious Establishments, and the U.S. Supreme Court: An Examination of Policy Compliance." *American Politics Research* 37, no. 1 (January 2009): 50–74.

McSweeny, Patrick. "Christian Public Schools." *Catholic World* 44 (March 1887): 796.

Messerli, Jonathan. *Horace Mann: A Biography.* New York: Knopf, 1972.

Miller, Randall. "Catholic Religion, Irish Identity, and the Civil War." In *American Jewry and the Civil War,* edited by Bertram W. Korn, 15–56. New York: Atheneum, 1970.

Mintz, Steven. *Huck's Raft: A History of American Childhood.* Cambridge, MA: Belknap Press of Harvard University Press, 2004.

Mirel, Jeffrey E. *Patriotic Pluralism: Americanization Education and European Immigrants.* Cambridge, MA: Harvard University Press, 2010.

Monaghan, E. Jennifer. *Learning to Read and Write in Colonial America.* Amherst: University of Massachusetts Press, 2007.

Moore, R. Laurence. "Bible Reading and Nonsectarian Schooling: The Failure of Religious Instruction in Nineteenth-Century Public Education." *Journal of American History* 86, no. 4 (March 2000): 1581–99.

Moran, Jeffrey P. *American Genesis: The Antievolution Controversies from Scopes to Creation Science.* New York: Oxford University Press, 2012.

Moss, Hilary. *Schooling Citizens: The Struggle for African American Education in Antebellum America*. Chicago: University of Chicago Press, 2009.

Mulvey, Janet, Bruce Cooper, and Arthur Maloney. *Blurring the Lines: Charter, Public, Private, and Religious Schools Coming Together*. New York: Information Age, 2010.

National Center for Education Statistics. "Charter School Enrollment." April 2015. Website of the National Center for Education Statics, Institute of Education Sciences, US Department of Education, http://nces.ed.gov/programs/coe /indicator_cgb.asp.

Nelkin, Dorothy. "From Dayton to Little Rock: Creationism Evolves." In *Creationism, Science, and the Law: The Arkansas Case*, ed. Marcel C. LaFollette, 74–85. Cambridge, MA: MIT Press, 1983.

Noddings, Nel. *Educating for Intelligent Belief or Unbelief*. New York: Teachers College Press, 1993.

Oakley, J. Ronald. *God's Country: America in the Fifties*. New York: Norton, 1986.

Orwell, George. *Nineteen Eighty-Four*. New York: Harcourt, Brace and World, 1949.

Paino, Maria, Linda A. Renzulli, Rebecca L. Boylan, and Christen L. Bradley. "For Grades or Money? Charter School Failure in North Carolina." *Educational Administration Quarterly* 50, no. 3 (August 2014): 500–526.

Peters, Shawn Francis. Judging Jehovah's Witnesses: Religious Persecution and the Dawn of the Rights Revolution. Lawrence: University of Kansas Press, 2000.

Pew Forum on Religion and Public Life. *Applying God's Law: Religious Courts and Mediation in the United States*. April 2013. http://www.pewforum.org/Church -State-Law/Applying-Gods-Law-Religious-Courts-and-Mediation-in-the-US .aspx.

———. *"Nones" on the Rise: One-in-Five Adults Have No Religious Affiliation*. October 2012. http://www.pewforum.org/2012/10/09/nones-on-the-rise/.

Pew Research Center for the People and the Press and Pew Forum on Religion and Public Life. *Many Americans Uneasy with Mix of Religion and Politics*. August 2006. http://www.pewforum.org/Politics-and-Elections/Many-Americans -Uneasy-with-Mix-of-Religion-and-Politics.aspx#3.

———. *Public Divided on Origins of Life: Religion a Strength and Weakness for Both Parties*. August 2005. http://www.pewforum.org/Politics-and-Elections /Public-Divided-on-Origins-of-Life.aspx#3.

Post, Robert, and Reva Siegel. "Originalism as a Political Practice: The Right's Living Constitution." *Fordham Law Review* 75, no. 2 (2006): 545–74.

Rawls, John. *Justice as Fairness: A Restatement*. Edited by Erin Kelly. Cambridge MA: Harvard University Press, 2001.

———. *Political Liberalism*. Expanded edition. New York: Columbia University Press, 2005.

———. *A Theory of Justice*. Revised edition. Cambridge, MA: Harvard University Press, 1999.

Reese, William J. *America's Public Schools: From the Common School Era to No Child Left Behind*. Baltimore: Johns Hopkins University Press, 2011.

Rollins, Richard M. *The Long Journey of Noah Webster*. Philadelphia: University of Pennsylvania Press, 1980.

Rouse, Cecilia. "Private School Vouchers and Student Achievement: Evidence from the Milwaukee Choice Program." *Quarterly Journal of Economics* 113, no. 2 (1998): 553–602.

Rudolph, John L. *Scientists in the Classroom: The Cold War Reconstruction of American Science Education*. New York: Palgrave, 2002.

Rush, Benjamin. *Letters of Benjamin Rush*. Vol. 2. Edited by L. H. Butterfield. Princeton, NJ: Princeton University Press, 1951.

Settle, Myron. *The Weekday Church School: For the Guidance of Churches and Communities in the Organization and Administration of Weekday Schools of Religious Education*. Educational Bulletin No. 601. Chicago: International Council of Religious Education, 1930.

Shaver, Milton. *Weekday Church School*. New York: Pilgrim Press, 1956.

Sheridan, Eugene R. "Liberty and Virtue: Religion and Republicanism in Jeffersonian Thought." In *Thomas Jefferson and the Education of a Citizen*, edited by James Gilreath, 242–63. Honolulu, HI: University of the Pacific Press, 2002.

Sklar, Kathryn Kish. "The Schooling of Girls and Changing Community Values in Massachusetts Towns, 1750–1820." *History of Education Quarterly* 33 (1993): 511–42.

Skoog, Gerald. "The Coverage of Human Evolution in High School Biology Textbooks in the 20th Century and in Current State Science Standards." *Science Education* 14 (2005): 395–422.

Slawson, Douglas J. *The Department of Education Battle, 1918–1932: Public Schools, Catholic Schools, and the Social Order*. Notre Dame, IN: University of Notre Dame Press, 2005.

Smith, Timothy L. "Protestant Schooling and American Nationality, 1800–1850." *Journal of American History* 53, no. 4 (March 1967): 679–95.

Stout, Jeffrey. *Democracy and Tradition*. Princeton, NJ: Princeton University Press, 2004.

Tyack, David B. "The Kingdom of God and the Common School: Protestant Ministers and the Educational Awakening in the West." *Harvard Educational Review* 36 (Fall 1966): 447–69.

———. "Monuments between Covers: The Politics of Textbooks." *American Behavioral Scientist* 42, no. 6 (March 1999): 922–32.

———. *The One Best System: A History of American Urban Education*. Cambridge, MA: Harvard University Press, 1974.

———. "The Spread of Public Schooling in Victorian America: In Search of a Reinterpretation." *History of Education* 7, no. 3 (1978): 173–82.

———, ed. *Turning Points in American Educational History*. Toronto: Xerox College, 1967.

Tyack, David B., and Larry Cuban. *Tinkering toward Utopia: A Century of Public School Reform*. Cambridge, MA: Harvard University Press, 1995.

Tyack, David B., and Elisabeth Hansot. *Managers of Virtue: Public School Leadership in America, 1820–1980*. New York: Basic Books, 1982.

———. *Learning Together: A History of Coeducation in American Public Schools*. New Haven, CT: Yale University Press, 1990.

Tyack, David B., Thomas James, and Aaron Benavot. *Law and the Shaping of Public Education, 1785–1954*. Madison: University of Wisconsin Press, 1987.

Tyler, Tom R. "Psychological Perspectives on Legitimacy and Legitimation." *Annual Review of Psychology* 57, no. 1 (2006): 375–400.

US Bureau of the Census. *Historical Statistics of the United States, Colonial Times to 1970*. Washington, DC: Government Printing Office, 1975.

Vinovskis, Maris A. "Have Social Historians Lost the Civil War? Some Preliminary Demographic Speculations." In *Toward a Social History of the Civil War: Exploratory Essays*, edited by Maris A. Vinovskis, 1–30. Cambridge: Cambridge University Press, 1990.

Wagoner, Jennings L., and Wayne J. Urban. *American Education: A History*. New York: McGraw-Hill, 2009.

Wald, Kenneth D., and Allison Calhoun-Brown. *Religion and Politics in the United States*. 6th edition. New York: Rowman and Littlefield, 2011.

Warren, Kim. *The Quest for Citizenship: African American and Native American Education in Kansas, 1880–1935*. Chapel Hill: University of North Carolina Press, 2010.

Webster, Noah. "Education—Importance of Female Education, with a Brief Sketch of a Plan." *American Magazine*, May 1788, 367–74.

———. "Education, Some Defects in the Mode." *American Magazine*, January 1788, 80–82.

———. "On the Education of Youth in America" (1788). In Noah Webster, *A Collection of Essays and Fugitiv Writings on Moral, Historical, Political and Literary Subjects*. Boston, 1790. Reprint, Delmar, NY: Scholars' Facsimiles & Reprints, 1977.

———. "Webster's Unpublished Memoir." Webster Family Papers. Box 1, folder 10, p. 3. Yale Manuscripts and Archives, New Haven, CT.

Weinberg, Lawrence D. *Religious Charter Schools: Legalities and Practicalities*. New York: Information Age, 2007.

Williams, Heather Andrea. *Self-Taught: African American Education in Slavery and Freedom*. Chapel Hill: University of North Carolina Press, 2007.

Wood, Gordon. *Empire of Liberty: A History of the Early Republic, 1789–1815*. Oxford: Oxford University Press, 2009.

Zimmerman, Jonathan. *Distilling Democracy: Alcohol Education in America's Public Schools, 1880–1925*. Lawrence: University Press of Kansas, 1999.

———. *Whose America? Culture Wars in the Public Schools*. Cambridge, MA: Harvard University Press, 2002.

Index